6.⁰⁰

$6.00

SCH∞L

*pass at your
own risk*

ARTHUR DAIGON

RICHARD A. DEMPSEY

both of the University of Connecticut

PRENTICE-HALL, Inc., Englewood Cliffs, New Jersey

Library of Congress Cataloging in Publication Data

Daigon, Arthur, comp.
    School: pass at your own risk.

    1. Education—United States—Addresses, essays,
lectures. I. Dempsey, Richard A.,
joint comp. II. Title.
LA217.D34 1974 370'.973 73-13935
ISBN 0-13-793885-3
ISBN 0-13-793877-2 (pbk.)

Prentice-Hall International, Inc., *London*
Prentice-Hall of Australia, Pty. Ltd., *Sydney*
Prentice-Hall of Canada, Ltd., *Toronto*
Prentice-Hall of India Private Limited, *New Delhi*
Prentice-Hall of Japan, Inc., *Tokyo*

*We wish to express our thanks and appreciation to those
who have allowed us to use their material; individual
acknowledgments are listed beginning on page 279.*

CONTENTS

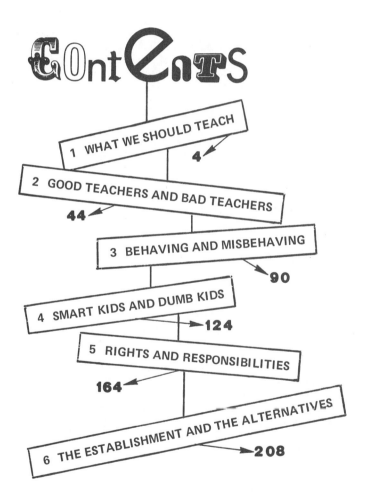

TITLES & AUTHORS

A NOTE TO THE READERS

You are holding the world's first documentary textbook — or, if you prefer, the first textbook *verité,* a melange of articles, letters, poems, pieces of novels, television dramas, interviews, photos, cartoons, polls, advertisements — produced by students, teachers, professors, school-board members, and citizens. Some of the material is profound, some is prosaic, but all of it is striking evidence of what is (and isn't) going on in American schools.

Each item is an artifact or document (deliberately brief) that sheds light — lyrically, bitterly, comically, or prophetically — on some important issue raging in or around the school scene. All are carefully arranged to stress both visual and intellectual interplay and to generate in the reader some of the drama, irony, frustration, and exaltation that teaching in the schools is all about.

By juxtaposing contrary philosophic and operational positions, we expect to engage

prospective teachers in a consideration of those pivotal ideas and concerns they soon will be asked to act upon in public school classrooms.

Each artifact or document may be viewed as a "piece of evidence," as an incentive to intellectual action, evidence to be weighed against the evidence of opposing positions. When the evidence is taken together, a picture emerges of "how it is" in schools today.

The authors take no position themselves. All they ask is for the reader — the prospective teacher — to begin the process of putting together his own working philosophy of what it means to be a teacher. *School: Pass At Your Own Risk* helps those interested in teaching to do just that by pressing them into face-to-face confrontation with those issues soon to demand their professional attention: what schools are for; dealing with increasingly hostile students; testing, grading, intelligence, and race; identifying good and bad teaching; delineating the rights and responsibilities of teachers and students; and finally, considering the alternatives to what we have now.

WHAT WE

1

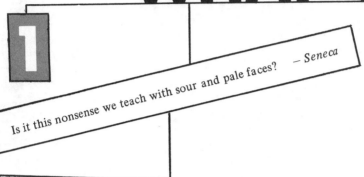

Is it this nonsense we teach with sour and pale faces? — *Seneca*

Our American professors like their literature clear, cold, pure, and very dead.

— *Sinclair Lewis*

"I only took the regular course," said the Mock Turtle. "What was that?" inquired Alice. "Reeling and Writhing, of course, to begin with," the Mock Turtle replied; "and then the different branches of Arithmetic — Ambition, Distraction, Uglification, and Derision."

— *Lewis Carroll*

Observations more than books, experience rather than persons, are the prime educators.

— *A.B. Alcott*

SHOULD TEACH

Let our teaching be full of ideas. Hitherto it has been stuffed only with facts.

— *Anatole France*

The only real education comes from what goes counter to you. — *Andre Gide*

. . . it is well to remember from time to time that nothing worth knowing can be taught.

— *Oscar Wilde*

In education we are striving not to teach youth to make a living, but to make a life.

— *William Allen White*

I think there's nothing more tragic to education than turning out students who understand all about their culture but nothing about making a living.

— *K. L. Ewigleben, Pres., Ferns State College*

5

IS YOUR HIGH SCHOOL OBSOLETE?

alvin toffler

No one has to tell you that something is wrong with America's high schools. And most thinking people of all ages are ready to agree that those institutions are suffering from some gut-deep disease. But there's little agreement about what is wrong. I'd like to suggest that the disease is obsolescence: most of our high schools are as outdated as the stone ax.

Routinely you are told that you must finish high school because it will help equip you to lead a better life "in the future." But how many teachers, principals or parents have any clear notions about the future for which they are supposed to be preparing you?

Most adults view the future as a straight-line continuation of the present. Yet we are living through a period of the most rapid change in history. Breakthroughs explode like tracer shells in biology, medicine, space and other scientific disciplines. In the relationship between the sexes, in global politics, in the arts, music, fashion, in life styles, nothing stays put. Everything changes. Not all these changes are necessarily good. Some (particularly a number of upcoming scientific astonishments) are dangerous. But good or bad, they are creating a future drastically different from the present.

This means that much of our education — premised on the indefinite continuation of the present — is inappropriate. It prepares us for jobs and roles that may, in fact, no longer exist when the time comes for us to fill them. It stuffs our skulls with facts and trains us for skills that may not be needed, while omitting information and skills upon which happiness and even survival may depend.

Of course, not all schools are obsolete, and not everything they do is anachronistic. Most are run with the best of intentions and a good deal of dedication on the part of at least some teachers and administrators. But they are trapped, for the most part, in a webwork of rules and regulations, approved syllabuses, state-determined requirements, budgetary constraints and bureaucratic routines that make it difficult to bring about even the most desperately overdue changes.

When we apply the idea of obsolescence to high schools, it's possible to come up with a checklist — a test that can tell us whether any particular school is obsolete — or whether it has begun to adapt itself responsibly and selectively to change. If I were judging a school, these are some of the questions I would ask:

1. Is its curriculum oriented toward the future?

Hundreds of schools are now introducing fascinating courses dealing with the future. They are not simply courses about computers and space, but courses in which future life styles, careers, crises and opportunities are discussed. Courses in which students have a chance to probe their own values with respect to change, and to help clarify one another's ideas about what futures (public and personal) might be preferable to the ones toward which we seem to be racing blindly.

The future can also be a component in existing courses. Traditionally, courses in social studies, art, music, science, English and other subjects have all told students about the way things were. Why can't they also move into (and beyond) the present and discuss the way things are and might be in the future? Even history, which by definition faces backward, can be taught in ways that make it pertinent to today and revealing about tomorrow. Students have a right to ask any teacher: "What does this have to do with my tomorrows?" Indeed, the *absence* of the future in the curriculum is itself a good clue to whether the school is obsolete or not.

2. Does it offer action-learning opportunities?

Not all learning takes place in the classroom. In recognition of that fact, some schools now make it possible for students to work at jobs, or to perform volunteer service in the community, and to get educational credit for it. Programs for care of the aged, for pollution control, traffic control or noise control, full or part-time jobs in fields like photography, journalism, construction, even routine clerical work or driving a delivery truck can, if the school cooperates, be turned into extremely valuable learning. Any school that does not recognize this, and reward it, still faces yesterday.

3. How diverse are the courses it offers?

Are students saddled with too many requirements? Or are they able to choose from many alternatives? Most of us do recognize a need for certain basic requirements. We need the ability to read, write and converse with others. We need certain shared knowledge. But all of us are different, and the society we are moving toward is going to be fragmented into tens of thousands of jobs, roles and life-ways. It's going to need more varied skills than the schools now teach. Does the school allow a student to work out an independent study program? Can he or she take a course at a nearby school or college, for credit? If not, why not?

4. Is the school run from the top down?

Today most businesses and government organizations are set up as rigid hierarchies, with orders coming down a chain of command, very much like the army. Tomorrow's corporations and government agencies are likely to be less top-down in character, with more decision-making done at the bottom.

Today violence is common in many high schools. Conflicts between students and teachers, between racial groups, between age groups, is barely suppressed. Schools are filled with tension. Much of this arises from the absence of real vehicles for change.

Can students at the school *really* influence schedules, dress codes, curriculum? Or is the school still autocratic? Certainly, students should not have full control of curriculum or administrative matters. But that's not the issue. Most student demands for participation have been rather modest. The fact is that in most schools students haven't a trace of real influence. Even the formal machinery — student councils, for example — tend to be Mickey Mouse. They may be permitted to decide how many dances to hold in a semester, but they are not allowed to deal with significant educational issues. Is the student government free to be critical of school policies? What about the student newspaper? Or are they simply a puppet government and a public relations mouthpiece? Is there a Council of the Future in which students, educators and parents can jointly discuss not merely the methods but the *goals* of the curriculum in terms of its relevance to the students' future lives?

5. Is the work largely routine?

Some routines are necessary in life. Eating and sleeping are biologically required routines. But obsolete schools are so busy training us to use routines that they often drill the adaptability out of us. In the past schools emphasized repetitive work because adult life was routine and repetitive. Most adults today are still trapped in monotonous jobs and household roles. But the world of work is beginning to change. Fewer blue-collar jobs remain and more jobs are cropping up that require judgment, even creativity.

At the same time, as change in all fields makes us confront *new* problems and first-time situations in our personal lives, old habits, programmed behavior and routine responses become less and less helpful. Faced by something new, we have to invent a response (something the schools don't teach us to do) rather than reach for a routine (something the schools do teach us to do). Thus, obsolete schools tend to make students considerably *less* adaptive to a changing world, rather than more resourceful.

6. Does it offer alternatives to the lecture?

Since time immemorial, school has meant a classroom in which an older person pumped knowledge into the heads of a large number of younger people. Educators debate whether it's better to have one teacher for twenty-five students, or whether one to ten is a better ratio. An educator friend of mine once tried to trace back the notion that one to twenty-five is the best teacher-student ratio. He found that it went back to the Talmud, the law books of the ancient Hebrews.

In tomorrow's fast-changing world all of us will probably be moving around a good bit changing jobs, working with temporary teammates and dealing with many different kinds of groups — not just the standard classroom model with one boss or teacher up front and everyone else subordinate. We may work with a group in which leadership rotates, or in which top-down hierarchy is replaced by participatory control. Chances are, few of us will get a job in one company and stay there the rest of our lives.

Obsolete schools give only one kind of organizational experience — the standard lecture type in which one person dominates the group. Innovative schools are trying to give students experience with a variety of forms: student-initiated and student-led seminars; faculty-student interdisciplinary problem-solving teams; "open," seemingly unstructured classes or projects; all in addition to the lecture system. This not only makes learning more interesting, it provides a taste of the organizational diversity we'll face in the future.

7. Is it still age-segregated?

Most high schools segregate one age group from another, creating a kind of age-based apartheid. Fifteen-year-olds mingle only with other fifteen-year-olds and have little opportunity to learn from older students or help younger ones.

Moreover, apart from parents, most teens seldom have the opportunity to converse naturally with any adult other than those *paid* to talk to them — teachers, counselors, ministers, probation officers and the like. This unnatural compartmentalization is typical of the obsolete school. It's possible to break the age-barrier by creating programs in which seniors work with juniors, juniors with sophomores, etc., giving each other the benefit of their experience.

At the same time, schools should invite adults of all ages — including retired people from the nearby community — into the classrooms and the work teams, so that the generation gap is bridged. People from the community have a lot to teach — about specific skills such as carpentry, accounting, physics or music, as well as just plain life experience. Similarly, older folks have a lot to learn from young people and can benefit from contact with the freshness of youth. One idea: Finding a "community mentor" for each student — an older person who is actually making use of some of what students are being taught, so that the student has a chance to see that knowledge being put to practical use and has a chance to talk about it with someone other than his teacher.

8. To what extent is racism (conscious or unconscious) part of the school atmosphere?

We are moving into a world in which peoples of diverse backgrounds — racial, religious, national, as well as economic and educational — will be brought into first-hand contact with one another. The student who grows up dealing only with his or her "own kind" is ill-prepared for the new realities. Racism is not just a matter of classroom segregation or nasty epithets. It is also, more basically, a question of psychological attitudes and hidden stereotypes.

We live at a moment when all our racial and ethnic groups are belatedly rediscovering their own rights and virtues. For a long time many blacks (not to mention Jews, Italians, Ukrainians, Catholics and others) were secretly ashamed of not looking like Doris Day or not being white Anglo-Saxon and Protestant. The big push to make all Americans alike (the old melting-pot idea) emphasized conformity to a single middle-class ideal called the American Way of Life. Survival in the decades ahead will be based on a recognition of the need for social diversity rather than uniformity, and schools that still try to machine all students, regardless of background, into the same mold are anachronisms.

9. Is the school itself an ecological menace?

Each school is part of the ecological network of the society. The school that pollutes or contributes to environmental breakdown is, by its very existence, teaching a lesson that damages the students' chances for survival.

Environmental Action (1346 Connecticut Avenue, Washington, D.C. 20036), one of the nation's most effective eco-activist groups, points out that schools can do a lot to clean up their own behavior. Whoever is responsible for purchasing or requisitioning should be pressured by students to use recycled paper; to use only safe pesticides and herbicides; to use only equipment with adequate antipollution devices, etc. Schools produce plenty of waste — sewage, smoke, chemical refuse and the like. Some schoolyards are filled with students' and teachers' cars, but provide no bike racks. Some schools, even in what they teach with respect to environment, are out of date and, indeed, irresponsible. How is the question of population and birth control handled? What is the school's attitude toward contraceptive information?

In short, schools teach both through the formal program in the classroom and by the way they are conducted in relation to the community. A school that is ecologically irresponsible is not only a menace, it is a bad teacher, since its purpose presumably is to help students live better in the future — or even just live.

10. Do values get short shrift?

The faster the world changes and the more complicated it grows, the harder it becomes for all of us as individuals, and as groups, to make sensible decisions. It's impossible to make good decisions about our own future unless we have some "fix" on our own values. Yet most schools pretend that they are "value-free." Their attitude is that they are only there to convey facts, not attitudes toward those facts. Anyone who thinks seriously about it for a moment will recognize that it is impossible for schools to avoid dealing with values. As soon as a teacher gets up in front of a classroom and students assume the subordinate role of students, nonverbal values are being transmitted.

Schools that *avoid* discussion of the hard questions (such as "What would I be willing to die for — if anything?" "What are my responsibilities to society and the people close to me?" "What things are more important than others?") fail to develop the student's ability to cope with rapid change and complex choice. It's necessary for seminars and classroom activity, as well as student bull sessions and private conversations, to raise value issues to the level of conscious discussion. "Teaching values" does not mean *imposing* a single set of officially approved values on the whole student body. It means continually discussing the ethical implications of the choices that face us. And that, in the end, is what education must be about, if students are to be able to face tomorrow.

This, then, is *my* test for academic obsolescence. High schools that flunk this test — and the vast majority of them will — are already relics of yesterday. It's up to students, along with change-oriented educators and community people, to help bring the schools into the present so that they can help prepare all of us — young and old alike — for the future.

fundamental
differences
do
exist

Mortimer Smith

The advocate of basic education maintains that education as carried on in schools must deal primarily with intellectual training, with making young people literate in the essential fields of human knowledge, with transmitting the heritage and culture of the race. He acknowledges that formal education also plays a role in the social adjustment of the individual child, that it contributes to his physical welfare, the development of his personality, and his vocational competence; he is even ready to agree that the school on occasion must be a combined social-service and baby-sitting agency, even sometimes an amateur psychiatric clinic. He acknowledges that the teacher and the administrator have many important things to do besides cultivate the youthful intellect. At the same time, however, he would insist that schools must have some priorities, must decide what is primary and what is secondary. The school, he insists, cannot be responsible for our total education, for the sum of experiences, information, and skills we acquire as we go through life.

In contrast to this viewpoint, an all-inclusive view of the purpose of education and schools has gained momentum during the last thirty or forty years. This viewpoint has been

11

summed up by a professor of education who says: "The chief goal of education is the development of physical health, mental and emotional stability, fine personality, and effective citizenship." The department of education in Connecticut has suggested that this total goal for schools be translated into an actual high school program that would include, in addition to the traditional subjects, the following: socio-economic problems, home care of the sick, driver education, personal grooming, hospitality, housing, boy and girl problems, and an understanding of reproduction (no stated relation between the last two items).

Another state department of education (California), in a list containing over fifty items, suggests that the school must help youth to "enjoy a rich, sincere, and varied social life," "observe the amenities of social behavior," "be skilled in homemaking," "become an informed and skillful buyer," "develop a sense of humor."

Schoolmen will recognize these catchall programs as a commonplace, similar to those advocated for many years by state departments, schools of education, and national educational organizations.

On this matter of priorities in education, the picture seems clear: One group believes that the school must maintain its historic role as the chief institution in charge of intellectual training; another group — and perhaps the dominant one in public education — maintains that intellectual training is only a part of the school's total program, and not necessarily the most important part.

A second ground for conflict is a natural corollary of the difference in viewpoint just described. If you believe that intellectual training is the primary function of schools you will naturally believe that education must have a particular content, that there is a hierarchy of subjects, that the important studies in the curriculum are English, history, the sciences, mathematics, foreign languages. On the other hand, if you think the school is required to teach everything, it is only a short step to thinking that nothing in the school program is any better than anything else, or even that the traditional subjects are slightly stuffy and probably unnecessary for many students.

??? ? ???

"why do we have to learn this??"

The meanings behind some stock answers interpreted by Dean Lobaugh.

The fifth grade teacher (or the high school English teachers, or the professors at the university) will expect you to know this. Listen, son, what I am saying is that, if I had my way, I wouldn't teach you this stuff at all. I just work here, you see, and I have to get along with the rest of the folks on the payroll. I can't have the fifth grade teacher yelling that the kids don't learn anything in my room, so I am going to teach you what she thinks ought to be taught.

Educated people are supposed to know this. Frankly, I don't think this will ever do you the least bit of good, but some people set great store by it, and if you want the social and financial advantages which may come to you through association with so-called educated persons, then you'd better have a speaking acquaintance with these things.

It will do you good when you grow up. I know this doesn't mean anything to you now, and I don't blame you for wiggling in your seats. But you want to be "big folks" some day, don't you? Well, then, you learn about the square on the hypotenuse and store it away in your mind, and some day, bingo! It will pop into your mind just when you need it. (Frankly, son, I have serious doubts about it, but that's what they always taught me, and I've got to motivate this lesson somehow.

This is good training for your mind. Frankly, I know you probably will never use this piece of knowledge, in either the immediate or the remote future. But here are some pretty good mental gymnastics, and if you can master them, you probably will be able to master something else which will make more sense to you. I really don't know why we don't work on the other things instead, but we've got to keep ourselves academically respectable.

Your parents expect you to learn this. Don't ask me why you have to learn this. Your folks want you to take algebra, even though most of them haven't done an algebra problem since they left school, and I am hired to teach it to you. If I want to keep the paychecks coming, I am going to have to teach what the papas and mamas in this community want taught.

It's the state law (or the course of study). Listen, kids, we really are in this together. I don't like to teach this any more than you like to study it. If any of the Big Shots come in while we are working on this, try to show an intelligent interest. We want them to think we're doing what we're supposed to do, don't we? Somebody handed us this, and we might as well make the best of it.

This will be in the examination on Friday. Listen now, we all understand the rules of this old school game. It isn't what you know that counts toward getting an education but what goes down in my little book, so I'm being a good sport and letting you know just what it is going to take to get the kind of marks you want in the little book. Furthermore, I know you kids well enough to realize that you won't waste your time on anything you think I might not check on, so let's understand each other right now. You're darned tootin' this is going to be in the examination Friday.

Unless you get this work in, I simply won't sign a slip for you to attend the game at Hillville Friday. Or you can't play basketball or you can't be in the junior play or you can't get out to decorate for the prom. Listen, son, I've got you where I want you. I know that you haven't the slightest interest in turning in a paper on "What 'Il Penseroso' Means to Me," but I think it is important or I wouldn't have assigned it. They tell me in the office that you have to have my signature to be excused for this trip. You know what the price of that signature is. Now get out of here and whip up a paper. I know it won't be any good, but you'll have gone through the motions.

? ? ?

"A little BOX"

... /or, the tale's the thing./by Joey Windham

A classroom is

a little box — and in

this box we put kids —

and label them students

and they wander

Purposelessly

a r o u n d

from topic

to topic

from

fact

to fact

within a classroom

that is a little box-and in this
box we put kids-and
label them students

students that do not

belong in a classroom

that is a little box —

and in this box we put kids —

and label them students — and

play an authoritarian and oppressive song — and

call this EDUCA TION

When a classroom is a little box

and in this box we put kids

and label them students

and close the lid on the box . . .

they are called problem

becoming good parrots or

and they learn to obey

Now if we ask what discipline the school is best equipped to impart, the answer is: intellectual discipline. In the realm of mind, things are true and false, right and wrong, orderly and confused, before and after, relevant and irrelevant, enlightening or obfuscating, inspiriting or dull. To learn these qualities and let them form one's judgment is a by-product of the fundamental act of learning. For my present purpose learning is simply the removal of ignorance. If you are a philosophical skeptic and say that man never truly knows anything, then I say that learning is the replacing of native ignorance by a superior and more complicated kind of ignorance, such as geometry or the contents of the Bill of Rights. The innocent child does not know that there is such a thing as a right-angle triangle. When he has learned of its existence, he is as far as before from ultimate wisdom, but he has replaced primary ignorance with that delightful secondary kind we call knowledge.

— Jacques Barzun

THE SABER-TOOTH CURRICULUM
J. Abner Peddiwell

The first great educational theorist and practitioner of whom my imagination has any record (began Dr. Peddiwell in his best professorial tone) was a man of Chellean times whose full name was *New-Fist-Hammer-Maker* but whom, for convenience, I shall hereafter call *New-Fist.*

New-Fist was a doer, in spite of the fact that there was little in his environment with which to do anything very complex. You have undoubtedly heard of the pear-shaped, chipped-stone tool which archeologists call the *coup-de-poing* or fist hammer. New-Fist gained his name and a considerable local prestige by producing one of these artifacts in a less rough and more useful form than any previously known to his tribe. His hunting clubs were generally superior weapons, moreover, and his fire-using techniques were patterns of simplicity and precision. He knew how to do things his community needed to have done, and he had the energy and will to go ahead and do them. By virtue of these characteristics he was an educated man.

New-Fist was also a thinker. Then, as now, there were few lengths to which men would not go to avoid the labor and pain of thought. More readily than his fellows, New-Fist pushed himself beyond those lengths to the point where cerebration was inevitable. The same quality of intelligence which led him into the socially approved activity of producing a superior artifact also led him to engage in the socially disapproved practice of thinking. When other men gorged themselves on the proceeds of a successful hunt and vegetated in dull stupor for many hours thereafter, New-Fist ate a little less heartily, slept a little less stupidly, and arose a little earlier than his comrades to sit by the fire and think. He would stare moodily at the flickering flames and wonder about various parts of his environment until he finally got to the point where he became strongly dissatisfied with the accustomed ways of his tribe. He began to catch glimpses of ways in which life might be made better for himself, his family, and his group. By virtue of this development, he became a dangerous man.

This was the background that made this doer and thinker hit upon the concept of conscious, systematic education. The immediate stimulus which put him directly into the practice of education came from watching his children at play. He saw these children at the cave entrance before the fire engaged in activity with bones and sticks and brightly colored pebbles. He noted that they seemed to have no purpose in their play beyond immediate pleasure in the activity itself. He compared their activity with that of the grown-up members of the tribe. The children played for fun; the adults worked for security and enrichment of their lives. The children dealt with bones, sticks, and pebbles; the adults dealt with food, shelter, and clothing. The children protected themselves from boredom; the adults protected themselves from danger.

"If I could only get these children to do the things that will give more and better food, shelter, clothing, and security," thought New-Fist, "I would be helping this tribe to have a better life. When the children became grown, they would have more meat to eat, more skins to keep them warm, better caves in which to sleep, and less danger from the striped death with the curving teeth that walks these trails by night."

Having set up an educational goal, New-Fist proceeded to construct a curriculum for reaching that goal. "What things must we tribesmen know how to do in order to live with full bellies, warm backs, and minds free from fear?" he asked himself.

To answer this question, he ran various activities over in his mind. "We have to catch fish with our bare hands in the pool far up the creek beyond that big bend," he said to himself. "We have to catch them in the same way in the pool just this side of the bend. And so we catch them in the next pool and the next and the next. Always we catch them with our bare hands."

Thus New-Fist discovered the first subject of the first curriculum — fish-grabbing-with-the-bare-hands.

"Also we club the little woolly horses," he continued with his analysis. "We club them along the bank of the creek where they come down to drink. We club them in the thickets where they lie down to sleep. We club them in the upland meadow where they graze. Wherever we find them we club them."

So woolly-horse-clubbing was seen to be the second main subject in the curriculum.

"And finally, we drive away the saber-tooth tigers with fire," New-Fist went on in his thinking. "We drive them from the mouth of our caves with fire. We drive them from our trail with burning branches. We wave firebrands to drive them from our drinking hole. Always we have to drive them away, and always we drive them with fire."

Thus was discovered the third subject — saber-tooth-tiger-scaring-with-fire.

Having developed a curriculum, New-Fist took his children with him as he went about his activities. He gave them an opportunity to practice these three subjects. The children liked to learn. It was more fun for them to engage in these purposeful activities than to play with colored stones just for the fun of it. They learned the new activities well, and so the educational system was a success.

As New-Fist's children grew older, it was plain to see that they had an advantage in good and safe living over other children who had never been educated systematically. Some of the more intelligent members of the tribe began to do as New-Fist had done, and the teaching of fish-grabbing, horse-clubbing, and tiger-scaring came more and more to be accepted as the heart of real education.

For a long time, however, there were certain more conservative members of the tribe who resisted the new, formal educational system on religious grounds. "The Great Mystery who speaks in thunder and moves in lightning," they announced impressively, "the Great Mystery who gives men life and takes it from them as he wills — if that Great Mystery had wanted children to practice fish-grabbing, horse-clubbing, and tiger-scaring before they were grown up, he would have taught them these activities himself by implanting in their natures instincts for fish-grabbing, horse-clubbing, and tiger-scaring. New-Fist is not only impious to attempt something the Great Mystery never intended to have done; he is also a damned fool for trying to change human nature."

Whereupon approximately half of these critics took up the solemn chant, "If you oppose the will of the Great Mystery, you must die," and the remainder sang derisively in unison, "You can't change human nature."

Being an educational statesman as well as an educational administrator and theorist, New-Fist replied politely to both arguments. To the more theologically minded, he said that, as a matter of fact, the Great Mystery had ordered this new work done, that he even did the work

17

himself by causing children to want to learn, that children could not learn by themselves without divine aid, that they could not learn at all except through the power of the Great Mystery, and that nobody could really understand the will of the Great Mystery concerning fish, horses, and saber-tooth tigers unless he had been well grounded in the three fundamental subjects of the New-Fist school. To the human-nature-cannot-be-changed shouters, New-Fist pointed out the fact that paleolithic culture had attained its high level by changes in human nature and that it seemed almost unpatriotic to deny the very process which had made the community great.

"I know you, my fellow tribesmen," the pioneer educator ended his argument gravely, "I know you as humble and devoted servants of the Great Mystery. I know that you would not for one moment consciously oppose yourselves to his will. I know you as intelligent and loyal citizens of this great cave-realm, and I know that your pure and noble patriotism will not permit you to do anything which will block the development of that most cave-realmish of all our institutions — the paleolithic educational system. Now that you understand the true nature and purpose of this institution, I am serenely confident that there are no reasonable lengths to which you will not go in its defense and its support."

By this appeal the forces of conservatism were won over to the side of the new school, and in due time everybody who was anybody in the community knew that the heart of good education lay in the three subjects of fish-grabbing, horse-clubbing, and tiger-scaring. New-Fist and his contemporaries grew old and were gathered by the Great Mystery to the Land of the Sunset far down the creek. Other men followed their educational ways more and more, until at last all the children of the tribe were practiced systematically in the three fundamentals. Thus the tribe prospered and was happy in the possession of adequate meat, skins, and security.

It is to be supposed that all would have gone well forever with this good educational system if conditions of life in that community had remained forever the same. But conditions changed, and life which had once been so safe and happy in the cave-realm valley became insecure and disturbing.

A new ice age was approaching in that part of the world. A great glacier came down from the neighboring mountain range to the north. Year after year it crept closer and closer to the head-waters of the creek which ran through the tribe's valley, until at length it reached the stream and began to melt into the water. Dirt and gravel which the glacier had collected on its long journey were dropped into the creek. The water grew muddy. What had once been a crystal-clear stream in which one could see easily to the bottom was now a milky stream into which one could not see at all.

At once the life of the community was changed in one very important respect. It was no longer possible to catch fish with the bare hands. The fish could not be seen in the muddy water. For some years, moreover, the fish in this creek had been getting more timid, agile, and intelligent. The stupid, clumsy, brave fish, of which originally there had been a great many, had been caught with the bare hands for fish generation after fish generation, until only fish of superior intelligence and agility were left. These smart fish, hiding in the muddy water under the newly deposited glacial boulders, eluded the hands of the most expertly trained fish-grabbers. Those tribesmen who had studied advanced fish-grabbing in the secondary school could do no better than their less well-educated fellows who had taken only an elementary course in the subject, and even the university graduates with majors in icthyology were baffled by the problem. No matter how good a man's fish-grabbing education had been, he could not grab fish when he could not find fish to grab.

The melting waters of the approaching ice sheet also made the country wetter. The ground became marshy far back from the banks of the creek. The stupid woolly horses, standing only five or six hands high and running on four-toed front feet and three-toed hind feet, although admirable objects for clubbing, had one dangerous characteristic. They were ambitious. They all wanted to learn to run on their middle toes. They all had visions of becoming powerful and aggressive animals instead of little and timid ones. They dreamed of a far-distant day when some of their descendants would be sixteen hands high, weigh more than half a ton, and be able to pitch their would-be riders into the dirt. They knew they could never attain these goals in a wet, marshy country, so they all went east to the dry, open plains, far from the paleolithic hunting grounds. Their places were taken by little antelopes who came down with the ice sheet and were so shy and speedy and had so keen a scent for danger that no one could approach them closely enough to club them.

The best trained horse-clubbers of the tribe went out day after day and employed the most efficient techniques taught in the schools, but day after day they returned empty-handed. A horse-clubbing education of the highest type could get no results when there were no horses to club.

Finally, to complete the disruption of paleolithic life and education, the new dampness in the air gave the saber-tooth tigers pneumonia, a disease to which these animals were peculiarly susceptible and to which most of them succumbed. A few moth-eaten specimens crept south to the desert, it is true, but they were pitifully few and weak representatives of a once numerous and powerful race.

So there were no more tigers to scare in the paleolithic community, and the best tiger-scaring techniques became only academic exercises, good in themselves, perhaps, but not necessary for tribal security. Yet this danger to the people was lost only to be replaced by another and even greater danger, for with the advancing ice sheet came ferocious glacial bears which were not afraid of fire, which walked the trails by day as well as by night, and which could not be driven away by the most advanced methods developed in the tiger-scaring courses of the schools.

The community was now in a very difficult situation. There was no fish or meat for food, no hides for clothing, and no security from the hairy death that walked the trails day and night. Adjustment to this difficulty had to be made at once if the tribe was not to become extinct.

Fortunately for the tribe, however, there were men in it of the old New-Fist breed, men who had the ability to do and the daring to think. One of them stood by the muddy stream, his stomach contracting with hunger pains, longing for some way to get a fish to eat. Again and again he had tried the old fish-grabbing technique that day, hoping desperately that at last it might work, but now in black despair he finally rejected all that he had learned in the schools and looked about him for some new way to get fish from that stream. There were stout but slender vines hanging from trees along the bank. He pulled them down and began to fasten them together more or less aimlessly. As he worked, the vision of what he might do to satisfy his hunger and that of his crying children back in the cave grew clearer. His black despair lightened a little. He worked more rapidly and intelligently. At last he had it — a net, a crude seine. He called a companion and explained the device. The two men took the net into the water, into pool after pool, and in one hour they caught more fish — intelligent fish in muddy water — than the whole tribe could have caught in a day under the best fish-grabbing conditions.

Another intelligent member of the tribe

wandered hungrily through the woods where once the stupid little horses had abounded but where now only the elusive antelope could be seen. He had tried the horse-clubbing technique on the antelope until he was fully convinced of its futility. He knew that one would starve who relied on school learning to get him meat in those woods. Thus it was that he too, like the fish-net inventor, was finally impelled by hunger to new ways. He bent a strong, springy young tree over an antelope trail, hung a noosed vine therefrom, and fastened the whole device in so ingenious a fashion that the passing animal would release a trigger and be snared neatly when the tree jerked upright. By setting a line of these snares, he was able in one night to secure more meat and skins than a dozen horse-clubbers in the old days had secured in a week.

A third tribesman, determined to meet the problem of the ferocious bears, also forgot what he had been taught in school and began to think in direct and radical fashion. Finally, as a result of this thinking, he dug a deep pit in a bear trail, covered it with branches in such a way that a bear would walk out on it unsuspectingly, fall through to the bottom, and remain trapped until the tribesmen could come up and despatch him with sticks and stones at their leisure. The inventor showed his friends how to dig and camouflage other pits until all the trails around the community were furnished with them. Thus the tribe had even more security than before and in addition had the great additional store of meat and skins which they secured from the captured bears.

As the knowledge of these new inventions spread, all the members of the tribe were engaged in familiarizing themselves with the new ways of living. Men worked hard at making fish nets, setting antelope snares, and digging bear pits. The tribe was busy and prosperous.

There were a few thoughtful men who asked questions as they worked. Some of them even criticized the schools.

"These new activities of net-making and operating, snare-setting, and pit-digging are indispensable to modern existence," they said. "Why can't they be taught in school?"

The safe and sober majority had a quick reply to this naive question. "School!" they snorted derisively. "You aren't in school now. You are out here in the dirt working to preserve the life and happiness of the tribe. What have these practical activities got to do with schools? You're not saying lessons now. You'd better forget your lessons and your academic ideals of fish-grabbing, horse-clubbing, and tiger-scaring if you want to eat, keep warm, and have some measure of security from sudden death."

The radicals persisted a little in their questioning. "Fishnet-making and using, antelope-snare construction and operation, and bear-catching and killing," they pointed out, "require intelligence and skills – things we claim to develop in schools. They are also activities we need to know. Why can't the schools teach them?"

But most of the tribe, and particularly the wise old men who controlled the school, smiled indulgently at this suggestion. "That wouldn't be *education*," they said gently.

"But why wouldn't it be?" asked the radicals.

"Because it would be mere training," explained the old men patiently. "With all the intricate details of fish-grabbing, horse-clubbing, and tiger-scaring – the standard cultural subjects – the school curriculum is too crowded now. We can't add these fads and frills of net-making, antelope-snaring, and – of all things – bear-killing. Why, at the very thought, the body of the great New-Fist, founder of our paleolithic educational system, would turn over in its burial cairn. What we need to do is to give our young people a more thorough grounding in the fundamentals. Even the graduates of the secondary schools don't know the art of fish-grabbing in any complete sense nowadays, they swing their horse clubs awkwardly too, and as for the old science of tiger-scaring — well, even the teachers seem to lack the real flair for the subject which we oldsters got in our teens and never forgot."

"But, damn it," exploded one of the radicals, "how can any person with good sense be interested in such useless activities? What is the point of trying to catch fish with the bare hands when it just can't be done any more. How can a boy learn to club horses when there are no horses left to club? And why in hell should children try to scare tigers with fire when the tigers are dead and gone?"

"Don't be foolish," said the wise old men, smiling most kindly smiles. "We don't teach fish-grabbing to grab fish; we teach it to develop a generalized agility which can never be developed by mere training. We don't teach horse-clubbing to club horses; we teach it to develop a generalized strength in the learner which he can never get from so prosaic and specialized a thing as antelope-snare-setting. We don't teach tiger-scaring to scare tigers; we teach it for the purpose of giving that noble courage which carries over into all the affairs of life and which can never come from so base an activity as bear-killing."

All the radicals were silenced by this statement, all except the one who was most radical of all. He felt abashed, it is true, but he was so radical that he made one last protest.

"But — but anyway," he suggested, "you will have to admit that times have changed. Couldn't you please *try* these other more up-to-date activities? Maybe they have *some* educational value after all?"

Even the man's fellow radicals felt that this was going a little too far.

The wise old men were indignant. Their kindly smiles faded. "If you had any education yourself," they said severely, "you would know that the essence of true education is timeless- ness. It is something that endures through changing conditions like a solid rock standing squarely and firmly in the middle of a raging torrent. You must know that there are some eternal verities, and the saber-tooth curriculum is one of them!"

a

vote
for

the beatles

Sir / Hurray for Ronald S. Berman, head of the Endowment for the Humanities [Sept. 4], who wants to revive Shakespeare and ignore the Beatles!

If Elizabeth I had commissioned him to promote cultural achievements during her reign, he would have tried to revive Virgil and ignore Shakespeare.

P. DAVID PRICE
Assistant Professor of Anthropology
Hamilton College
Clinton, N.Y.

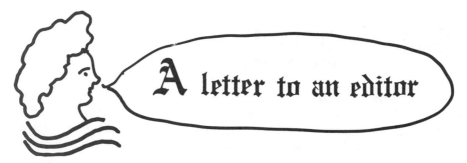

A letter to an editor

To THE EDITOR:

If Irving Kristol were actively engaged in teaching, he should have been able to answer most of the questions he poses. For example, he alludes to the number of students with high I.Q.'s who turn from academics to revolution. Has he ever wondered why gifted students would seek to destroy the only structure that offers them a temporary solace from a society that loathes the exceptional? In speaking with a number of such students, I have noted a frighteningly consistent educational pattern.

They are, for the most part, brilliant but undisciplined—highly articulate on matters they consider "relevant" (Vietnam, civil rights, sex), but the passion with which they speak dissipates on paper into tortured fragments conveying all the elegance of a telegram. In sociology and political science they excel; in languages and literature prior to 1960 they exhibit a Neanderthal apathy. And why?

In grammar school, many of them were never taught the parts of speech formally, but rather were exposed immediately to block paragraphs with the idea that they would learn the grammar "inductively." Consequently, they cannot distinguish adverbs from adjectives or "there" from "their" (the relative pronoun is *terra incognita* to most). They learned foreign languages from overhead projectors, transparencies, and the aural-oral method which taught them to say, "I want to go to the bathroom" in French and Spanish but never to translate the first sentence of "Les Misérables" or "Don Quixote."

In high school, they were given teachers who discreetly skirted a curriculum that required ancient history and moved as rapidly as possible to contemporary problems, with the genuine conviction that "the student is more interested in the present than the past." "Wuthering Heights" and "Pride and Prejudice" were bypassed in an effort to get to "Lord of the Flies" and "The Fall." The high-school student identifies the teacher with his material; if the teacher requires "Another Country" and uses Beatles records to explain prosody, he is a swinger, not a square. But what these students never realize is that they have been used by their teachers, who have relied on the oldest device in the profession to gain a class's acceptance—catering to adolescent immaturity by being immature themselves.

Thus, young people nurtured on the present come to a college that requires written expression, memorization and a foundation in the past. Of course their frustration grows when they are confronted with works like "The Republic" and "Utopia" which must be read slowly and digested; anyone would resent studying the grammar of a foreign language when he does not even know his own, although he presumably studied it for two years. But then for 12 years he was also told that understanding is far superior to the baser faculty of memory. Compared to Golding, Dickens is irrelevant and Homer passé.

Academic revolution stems from frustration and resentment. Who would not want a continuation of a high-school curriculum that pandered to every conceivable student urge — relevance, contemporaneity and the burial of the past? And who would not want to destroy the institution that destroys the dream?

BERNARD F. DICK, Chairman,

Classics Department,
Iona College.
New Rochelle, N. Y.

a talk to teachers
JAMES BALDWIN

I began by saying that one of the paradoxes of education was that precisely at the point when you begin to develop a conscience, you must find yourself at war with your society. It is your responsibility to change society if you think of yourself as an educated person. And on the basis of the evidence — one is compelled to say that this is a backward society.

Now if I were a teacher in this school, or any Negro school, and I was dealing with Negro children, who were in my care only a few hours of every day and would then return to their homes and to the streets, children who have an apprehension of their future which with every hour grows grimmer and darker, I would try to teach them — I would try to make them know that those streets, those houses, those dangers, those agonies by which they are surrounded, are criminal. I would try to make each child know that these things are the results of a criminal conspiracy to destroy him. I would teach him that if he intends to get to be a man, he must at once decide that he is stronger than this conspiracy and that he must never make his peace with it. And that one of his weapons for refusing to make his peace with it and for destroying it depends on what he decides he is worth. I would teach him that there are currently very few standards in this country which are worth a man's respect. That it is up to him to begin to change these standards for the sake of the life and the health of the country. I would suggest to him that the popular culture — as represented, for example, on television and in comic books and in movies — is based on fantasies created by very ill people, and he must be aware that these are fantasies that have nothing to do with reality. I would teach him that the press he reads is not as free as it says it is — and that he can do something about that, too. I would try to make him know that just as American history is longer, larger, more various, more beautiful, and more terrible than anything anyone has ever said about it, so is the world larger, more daring, more beautiful and more terrible, but principally larger — and that it belongs to him. I would teach him that he doesn't have to be bound by the expediencies of any given Administration, any given policy, any given time — that he has the right and the necessity to examine everything. I would try to show him that one has not learned anything about Castro when one says, "He is a Communist." This is a way of not learning something about Castro, something about Cuba, something, in fact, about the world. I would suggest to him that he is living, at the moment, in an enormous province.

America is not the world and if America is going to become a nation, she must find a way — and this child must help her to find a way — to use the tremendous potential and tremendous energy which this child represents. If this country does not find a way to use that energy, it will be destroyed by that energy.

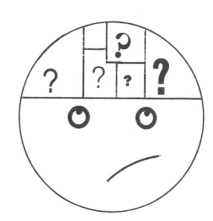

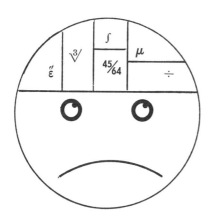

Certain intellectual disciplines are fundamental in the public-school curriculum because they are fundamental in modern life. Reading, writing, and arithmetic are indispensable studies in the elementary school because no intellectual life worthy of the name is possible or conceivable without these particular skills. Science, mathematics, history, English, and foreign languages are essentials of the secondary-school curriculum because contemporary intellectual life has been built upon a foundation of these particular disciplines. Some, but by no means all, of these studies can be described as "traditional." This fact, however, has next to nothing to do with the case. It is not tradition, but a realistic appraisal of the modern world, that points out these disciplines as fundamental.

– Arthur E. Bestor

I have taught in high school for ten years. During that time I have given assignments, among others, to a murderer, an evangelist, a pugilist, a thief, and an imbecile.

The murderer was a quiet little boy who sat on the front seat and regarded me with pale blue eyes; the evangelist, easily the most popular boy in the school, had the lead in the junior play; the pugilist lounged by the window and let loose at intervals a raucous laugh that startled even the geraniums; the thief was a gay-hearted Lothario with a song on his lips, and the imbecile, a soft-eyed little animal seeking the shadows.

The murderer awaits death in the state penitentiary; the evangelist has lain a year now in the village churchyard; the pugilist lost an eye in a brawl in Hong Kong; the thief, by standing on tiptoe, can see the windows of my room from the county jail, and the once gentle-eyed little moron beats his head against a padded wall in the state asylum.

All of these pupils once sat in my room, sat and looked at me gravely across worn brown desks. I must have been a great help to those pupils – I taught them the rhyming scheme of the Elizabethan sonnet and how to diagram a complex sentence.

– "I Taught Them All"
by N. J. W., *The Clearing House*

WHAT ARE SCHOOLS FOR?

Robert L. Ebel

Classics | Tradition | Moral Fiber | Knowledge | Heritage | Intellectual Rigor | Obeying Authority | Facts | Competition

1. Public education in America today is in trouble.

2. Though many conditions contribute to our present difficulties, the fundamental cause is our own confusions concerning the central purpose of our activities.

3. Schools have been far too willing to accept responsibility for solving all of the problems of young people, for meeting all of their immediate needs. That schools have failed to discharge these obligations successfully is clearly evident.

4. Schools are for learning. They should bend most of their efforts to the facilitation of learning.

5. The kind of learning on which schools should concentrate most of their efforts is cognitive competence, the command of useful knowledge.

6. Knowledge is a structure of relationships among concepts. It must be built by the learner himself as he seeks understanding of the information he has received.

7. Affective dispositions are important by-products of all human experience, but they seldom are or should be the principal targets of our educational efforts. We should be much more concerned with moral education than with affective education.

8. Intellectual skills are more often praised as educational goals than defined clearly enough to be taught effectively. Broadly general intellectual skills are mainly hypothetical constructs which are hard to demonstrate in real life. Highly specific intellectual skills are simply aspects of knowledge.

9. Wisdom depends primarily on knowledge, secondarily on experience.

10. Schools should not accept responsibility for the success of every pupil in learning, since that success depends so much on the pupils' own efforts.

11. Learning is a personal activity which each student must carry on for himself.

12. Individual learning is greatly facilitated by group instruction.

13. Schools should be held accountable for providing a good learning environment, which consists of a) capable, enthusiastic teachers, b) abundant and appropriate instructional materials, c) formal recognition and reward of achievement, and d) a class of willing learners.

14. Since learning cannot be made compulsory, school attendance ought not to be compulsory either.

"There are *no* facts which *everyone* needs to know — not even facts of the first historiographical magnitude. What real difference can knowledge of the fact of the fall of Babylon or Byzantium make in the daily life of anyone except a professional historian? Facts, discrete facts will not in themselves make a man happy or wealthy or wise. They will not help him to deal intelligently with any modern problem which he faces, as man or citizen. Facts of this sort, taught in this way, are merely empty emblems of erudition which certify that certain formal pedagogical requirements have been duly met. If this method is mistaken for the marrow of education, serious damage can result."

— David Hackett Fischer

College Graduate Complains Today's Education Inadequate

DEAR ANN LANDERS: I have been sitting here reflecting on my education — having just graduated from college — and I must say it was sadly inadequate. For example, neither in my standard high school biology course nor in my 12 hours of college biology was I ever taught the difference between a king snake and a copperhead. However, in the tenth grade I had to memorize verbatim the 17 steps to the conjugation of the Paramecium.

Never once in a classroom or a text, either in high school or college, was I told what I might expect in the way of job application blanks or interviews. I never knew what a split infinitive was until last week when a friend informed me I had used one. Although I took a course in typing I was never taught how to change a typewriter ribbon. The list goes on and on. And yet we are told that our education is "high quality."

The absence of classroom relevancy is a traumatic shock to one emerging from school and entering the real world. What gives? Don't the educators see this? Or do I have my glasses on crooked?

EDUCATION GAPPED

DEAR ED: You've struck a raw nerve. This has been one of my favorite beefs for the last 20 years. If you think education is irrelevant now you should have been around in the '30s and '40s.

I hope those responsible for planning curriculum at every level, from kindergarten up through medical school, will read your letter twice, and then read it a third time. You've hit America in a highly vulnerable spot.

pursuing relevance

from – TEACHING AS A
SUBVERSIVE
ACTIVITY
Neil Postman and
Charles Weingartner

PICTURE THIS SCENE: Dr. Gillupsie has grouped around him several of the young resident surgeons at Blear General Hospital. They are about to begin their weekly analysis of the various operations they have performed in the preceding four days. Gillupsie nods in the direction of Jim Kildear, indicating that Kildear's cases will be discussed first:

Gillupsie Well, Jim, what have you been up to this week?

Kildear Only one operation. I removed the gall bladder of the patient in Room 421.

Gillupsie What was his trouble?

Kildear Trouble? No trouble. I believe it's just inherently good to remove gall bladders.

Gillupsie Inherently good?

Kildear I mean good in itself. I'm talking about removing gall bladders *qua* removing gall bladders.

Gillupsie Oh; you mean removing gall bladders *per se*.

Kildear Precisely, Chief. Removing his gall bladder had intrinsic merit. It was, as we say, good for its own sake.

Gillupsie Splendid, Jim. If there's one thing I won't tolerate at Blear, it's a surgeon who is merely practical. What's in store next week?

Kildear Two frontal lobotomies.

Gillupsie Frontal lobotomies *qua* frontal lobotomies, I hope?

Kildear What else?

Gillupsie How about you, young Dr. Fuddy? What have you done this week?

Fuddy Busy. Performed four pilonidal-cyst excisions.

Gillupsie Didn't know we had that many cases.

Fuddy We didn't, but you know how fond I am of pilonidal-cyst excisions. That was my major in medical school, you know.

Gillupsie Of course, I'd forgotten. As I remember it now, the prospect of doing pilonidal-cyst excisions brought you into medicine, didn't it?

Fuddy That's right, Chief. I was always interested in that. Frankly, I never cared much for appendectomies.

Gillupsie Appendectomies?

Fuddy Well, that seemed to be the trouble with the patient in 397.

Gillupsie But you stayed with the old pilonidal-cyst excision, eh?

Fuddy Right, Chief.

Gillupsie Good work, Fuddy. I know just how you feel. When I was a young man, I was keenly fond of hysterectomies.

Fuddy [*giggling*] Little tough on the men, eh, Chief?

Gillupsie Well, yes [*snickering*]. But you'd be surprised at how much a resourceful surgeon can do. [*Then, solemnly.*] Well, Carstairs, how have things been going?

Carstairs I'm afraid I've had some bad luck,

Dr. Gillupsie. No operations this week, but three of my patients died.

Gillupsie   Well, we'll have to do something about this, won't we? What did they die of?

Carstairs   I'm not sure, Dr. Gillupsie, but I did give each one of them plenty of penicillin.

Gillupsie   Ah! The traditional "good for its own sake" approach, eh, Carstairs?

Carstairs   Well, not exactly, Chief. I just thought that penicillin would help them get better.

Gillupsie   What were you treating them for?

Carstairs   Well, each one was awful sick, Chief, and I know that penicillin helps sick people get better.

Gillupsie   It certainly does, Carstairs. I think you acted wisely.

Carstairs   And the deaths, Chief?

Gillupsie   Bad patients, son, bad patients. There's nothing a good doctor can do about bad patients. And there's nothing a good medicine can do for bad patients, either.

Carstairs   But still, I have a nagging feeling that perhaps they didn't *need* penicillin, that they might have needed something else.

Gillupsie   Nonsense! Penicillin never fails to work on good patients. We all know that. I wouldn't worry too much about it, Carstairs.

Perhaps our playlet needs no further elaboration, but we want to underscore some of its points. First, had we continued the conversation between Dr. Gillupsie and his young surgeons we could easily have included a half dozen other "reasons" for inflicting upon children the kinds of irrelevant curricula that comprise most of conventional schooling. For example, we could have had one doctor still practicing "bleeding" his patients because he had not yet discovered that such practices do no good. Another doctor could have insisted that he has "cured" his patients in spite of the fact that they have all died. ("Oh, I taught

them that, but they didn't learn it.") Still another doctor might have defended some practice by reasoning that, although his operation didn't do much for the patient now, in later life the patient might have need for exactly this operation, and if he did, *voila!*, it will already have been done.

The second point we would like to make is that we have not "made up" these "reasons." Our playlet is a parody only in the sense that it is inconceivable for doctors to have such conversations. Had we, instead, used a principal and his teachers, and if they discussed what was "taught" during the week, and why, our playlet would have been a documentary, and not a heavy-handed one, either. There are thousands of teachers who believe that there are certain subjects that are "inherently good," that are "good in themselves," that are "good for their own sake." When you ask "Good for whom?" or "Good for what purpose?" you will be dismissed as being "merely practical" and told that what they are talking about is literature *qua* literature, grammar *qua* grammar, and mathematics *per se*. Such people are commonly called "humanists."

There are thousands of teachers who teach "subjects" such as Shakespeare, or the Industrial Revolution, or geometry because *they* are inclined to enjoy talking about such matters. In fact, that is why they became teachers. It is also why their students fail to become competent learners. There are thousands of teachers who define a "bad" student as any student who doesn't respond to what has been prescribed for him. There are still thousands more who teach one thing or another under the supposition that the "subject" will do something for their students which, in fact, it does not do, and never did, and, indeed, which most evidence indicates, does just the opposite. And so on.

The third point we would like to make about our analogy is that the "trouble" with all these "reasons" is that they leave out the (patient) learner, which is really another way of saying, that they leave out reality. With full awareness of the limitations of our patient-learner metaphor, we would assert that it is insane (literally or metaphorically, take your pick) to perform a pilonidal-cyst excision unless your patient requires it to maintain his comfort and health; *and* it is also insane (again, take your pick as to how) for a teacher to "teach" something unless his students require it for some identifiable and important purpose, which is to say, for some purpose that is related to the life of the learner. *The survival of the learner's skill and interest in learning is at stake.* And we feel that, in saying this, we are not being melodramatic.

☆ ☆ ☆ ☆ ☆ ☆ ☆ ☆ ☆ ☆ ☆ ☆ ☆

reader: color this red → WHAT
leave this alone DID YOU LEARN
color this blue IN SHOOL TODAY

(neatness counts)   Song by Tom Paxton

What did you learn in school today
dear little boy of mine?
What did you learn in school today
dear little boy of mine?
I learned that Washington
never told a lie

I learned that soldiers seldom die
I learned that everybody's free
That's what the teacher said to me
And that's what I learned in school today
That's what I learned in school

What did you learn in school today. . .
I learned that policemen are my friends
I learned that justice never ends
I learned that murderers
die for their crimes

even if we make a mistake sometimes
And that's what I learned in school today
That's what I learned in school. . .

I learned our government must be strong
It's always right and never wrong
Our leaders are the finest men
and we elect them again and again
And that's what I learned in school today
That's what I learned in school. . .

I learned the wars are not so bad
I learned about the great ones
that we have had
We fought in Germany and in France
And someday I might get my chance
And that's what I learned in school today
That's what I learned in school. . .

☆ ☆ ☆ ☆ ☆ ☆ ☆

31

CRISIS
in the classroom
Charles E. Silberman

But how *do* the children learn, an American inevitably and quite naturally wants to know. Or as one American principal asked me, "How do the children get any work accomplished if they do nothing but play all day?" The question, and the view of education it reflects, is not unique to Americans: it is shared by formal educators in England, too. "There is a reason for coming to school, and that's work," a London head tartly remarked, indicating his disapproval of the very informal infant school across the playground from his junior school.

But play *is* a child's work; the distinction between work and play, so central to formal schooling, is not one that children make until adults force it upon them. On the contrary, play is one of the principal ways young children learn. In the words of the Plowden Report, "it is the way through which children reconcile their inner lives with external reality. In play, children gradually develop concepts of causal relationships, the power to discriminate, to make judgments, to analyze and synthesize, to imagine and to formulate. Children become absorbed in their play, and the satisfaction of bringing it to a satisfactory conclusion fixes habits of concentration which can be transferred to other learning."

It is a mistake, however, to assume children can learn through play alone, without any assistance or "teaching" by adults. On the contrary, children need feedback from people as well as things if their random play, their "messing around" — in early infancy, with movements of the eyes, hands, arms, legs, and with sounds, later on with objects, words, concepts — is to lead to more structured or purposeful activity. We are just beginning to appreciate the critical role the mother plays in language development, for example, and to understand that middle-class children's greater facility with language is the product, in large part, of the fact that middle-class mothers have more time for reciprocal play with their children than do lower-class mothers.

Classroom Countdown:
education at the
cross X roads

Max Rafferty

It happened about three decades ago, when John Dewey's permissive pragmatism became the unofficial philosophy of the American educational establishment. Here's how it's affected the schools:

(1) In regard to knowledge

To Dewey, knowledge equals experience. There are no self-evident truths, no universals, no absolutes of any kind. Anything that satisfies a want is a "good." Otherwise the word has no meaning. Life is a stream of sensations to which the child must be taught to respond successfully, nothing more.

Understand now why so many of the kids live it up with raw sex and cooked pot?

(2) In regard to the learning process

Dewey taught that the child learns only what he lives. Education must therefore be an exercise in living. "Learning by doing" thus becomes one of the ritual responses in the litany of Progressive Education. The fundamentals of learning – the "Three R's" – are taught only as the child finds them necessary in helping him lead a "good" life.

Wonder any longer why the hippies stress the "back to nature" routine? And why so many of their protest placards are misspelled?

(3) In regard to curriculum

The Progressive Educationists term the curriculum the whole living experience of the child. So the school must interest itself in verything about the child and take the steps necessary to remedy any gaps in his experience that a foolish or shortsighted parent may refuse to fill up. The accumulation of knowledge for the mere sake of knowledge is not only unnecessary; it is probably actively harmful. Development of creativity is the important thing. The child must feel completely unrepressed and free from inhibitions so that his natural creativity will blossom and flourish.

Help you figure out why some of our teen-agers go around looking like unmade beds and exuding an almost visible aura of unwashed disinhibition?

(4) In regard to education's aims

The two main goals of Progressive Education are to aid the child to live the life of the group and to enable him to "adjust" to a constantly changing environment. The child is constantly reminded that he is merely one member of the group and that his success is being measured **by** how well he is accepted by his companions.

Remind you of the S.D.S. zombies prior to their recent split, all salivating together on cue like Pavlov's dogs, all breathing the same obscenities, all mouthing the same party line, knowing no life as individuals, experiencing only what the group experiences?

Indeed the Progressive Educationists have much to answer for. Most dangerous when they are most dedicated, they war against your children in the firm belief that they are helping them. They treat parents as though they were retarded first-graders, glaciating all over them in a fine mixture of contemptuous kindness and smug superiority.

But isn't Progressive Education as dead as Moses? That's what you've been told, isn't it?

Judge for yourself. Visit your local school. Look around. Listen closely. Above all, ask questions. Questions like these:

Do the people running your school believe "life adjustment" is the main goal of the instructional program? If they do, this is Progressive Education.

Does your school place primary emphasis upon the happy, easy, comfortable acceptance of your child by his "peer group"? If it does, your school is "progressively" oriented.

Is subject matter in your school paid lip service but relegated to a back seat? Are things like "social studies" and "language arts" and "orientation" being taught instead of history and geography and English? If these things are being done, it doesn't much matter what they call it. What you've got is Progressivism.

On the first day of the new school year, all the teachers in one private school received the following note from their principal:

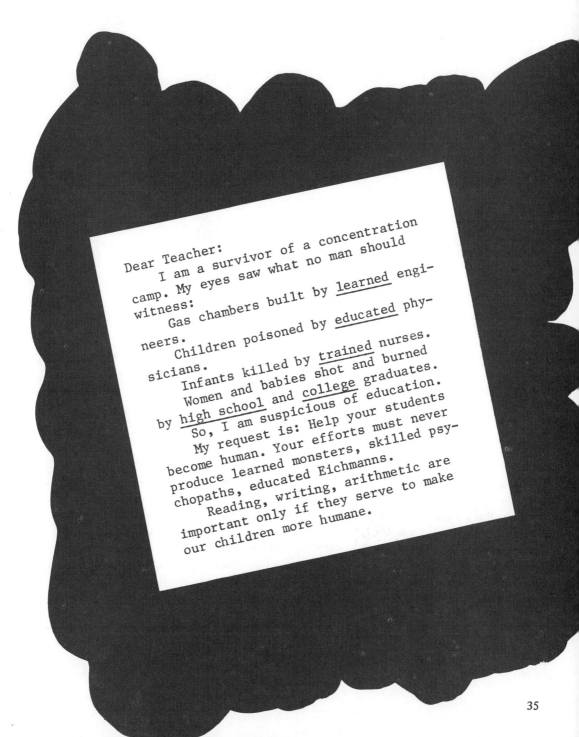

Dear Teacher:
    I am a survivor of a concentration camp. My eyes saw what no man should witness:
    Gas chambers built by <u>learned</u> engineers.
    Children poisoned by <u>educated</u> physicians.
    Infants killed by <u>trained</u> nurses.
    Women and babies shot and burned by <u>high school</u> and <u>college</u> graduates.
    So, I am suspicious of education.
    My request is: Help your students become human. Your efforts must never produce learned monsters, skilled psychopaths, educated Eichmanns.
    Reading, writing, arithmetic are important only if they serve to make our children more humane.

FROM

PREPARING
instructional objectives
Robert F. Mager

Once upon a time a Sea Horse gathered up his seven pieces of eight and cantered out to find his fortune. Before he had traveled very far he met an Eel, who said,

"Psst. Hey, bud. Where 'ya goin'?"

"I'm going out to find my fortune," replied the Sea Horse, proudly.

"You're in luck," said the Eel. "For four pieces of eight you can have this speedy flipper, and then you'll be able to get there a lot faster."

"Gee, that's swell," said the Sea Horse, and paid the money and put on the flipper and slithered off at twice the speed. Soon he came upon a Sponge, who said,

"Psst. Hey, bud. Where 'ya goin'?"

"I'm going out to find my fortune," replied the Sea Horse.

"You're in luck," said the Sponge, "For a small fee I will let you have this jet-propelled scooter so that you will be able to travel a lot faster."

So the Sea Horse bought the scooter with his remaining money and went zooming through the sea five times as fast. Soon he came upon a Shark, who said,

"Psst. Hey, bud. Where 'ya goin'?"

"I'm going out to find my fortune," replied the Sea Horse.

"You're in luck. If you'll take this short cut," said the Shark, pointing to his open mouth, "you'll save yourself a lot of time."

"Gee, thanks," said the Sea Horse, and zoomed off into the interior of the Shark, there to be devoured.

The moral of this fable is that if you're not sure where you're going, you're liable to end up someplace else — and not even know it.

Before you prepare instruction, before you choose material, machine, or method, it is important to be able to state clearly what your goals are. . . .

36

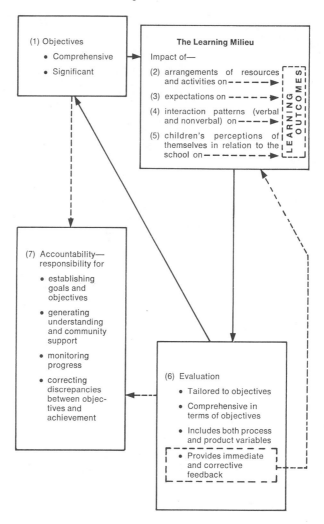

Performance based criteria is the method of big business, a technique of management, and we are now in the process of applying these industrial techniques to education everywhere. We ought to know better. When industry developed the assembly line and other systematic techniques to increase efficiency, what happened? The workers felt dehumanized by the system and formed unions to fight it. And that is precisely what is happening with our young people today. They feel increasingly dehumanized by the system, so they are fighting it at every possible level. Applying industrial techniques to human problems just won't work. A systems approach, it should be understood, is only a method of making sure you accomplish your objectives. Applied to the wrong objectives, systems approaches only guarantee that your errors will be colossal.

— Roscoe L. Davidson

Ɏoᴜᴘ Eᴅᴜᴄᵃᴛᵢoɴ

from THE MEDIUM IS THE MASSAGE

Marshall McLuhan & Quentin Fiore

There is a world of difference between the modern home environment of integrated electric information and the classroom. Today's television child is attuned to up-to-the-minute "adult" news — inflation, rioting, war, taxes, crime, bathing beauties — and is bewildered when he enters the nineteenth-century environment that still characterizes the educational establishment where information is scarce but ordered and structured by fragmented, classified patterns, subjects, and schedules. It is naturally an environment much like any factory set-up with its inventories and assembly lines.

The "child" was an invention of the seventeenth century; he did not exist in, say, Shakespeare's day. He had, up until that time, been merged in the adult world and there was nothing that could be called childhood in our sense.

Today's child is growing up absurd, because he lives in two worlds, and neither of them inclines him to grow up. Growing up — that is our new work, and it is *total*. Mere instruction will not suffice.

✿✿✿

The youth of today are not permitted to approach the traditional heritage of mankind through the door of technological awareness. This only possible door for them is slammed in their faces by a rear-view-mirror society.

The young today live mythically and in depth. But they encounter instruction in situations organized by means of classified information — subjects are unrelated, they are visually conceived in terms of a blueprint. Many of our institutions suppress all the natural direct experience of youth, who respond with untaught delight to the poetry and the beauty of the new technological environment, the environment of popular culture. It could be their door to all past achievement if studied as an active (and not necessarily benign) force.

The student finds no means of involvement for himself and cannot discover how the educational scheme relates to his mythic world of electronically processed data and experience that his clear and direct responses report.

It is a matter of the greatest urgency that our educational institutions realize that we now have civil war among these environments created by media other than the printed word. The classroom is now in a vital struggle for survival with the immensely persuasive "outside" world created by new informational media. Education must shift from instruction, from imposing of stencils, to discovery — to probing and exploration and to the recognition of the language of forms.

The young today reject goals. They want roles — R-O-L-E-S. That is, total involvement. They do not want fragmented, specialized goals or jobs.

We now experience simultaneously the dropout and the teach-in. The two forms are correlative. They belong together. The teach-in represents an attempt to shift education from instruction to discovery, from brainwashing students to brainwashing instructors. It is a big, dramatic reversal. Vietnam, as the content of the teach-in, is a very small and perhaps misleading Red Herring. It really has little to do with the teach-in, as such, anymore than with the dropout.

The dropout represents a rejection of nineteenth-century technology as manifested in our educational establishments. The teach-in represents a creative effort, switching the educational process from package to discovery. As the audience becomes a participant in the total electric drama, the classroom can become a scene in which the audience performs an enormous amount of work.

As for curriculum, the Councils of the Future, instead of assuming that every subject taught today is taught for a reason, should begin from the reverse premise: nothing should be included in a required curriculum unless it can be strongly justified in terms of the future. If this means scrapping a substantial part of the formal curriculum, so be it.

This is not intended as an "anti-cultural" statement or a plea for total destruction of the past. Nor does it suggest that we can ignore such basics as reading, writing and math. What it does mean is that tens of millions of children today are forced by law to spend precious hours of their lives grinding away at material whose future utility is highly questionable. (Nobody even claims it has much present utility.) Should they spend as

FUTURE

much time as they do learning French, or Spanish or German? Are the hours spent on English maximally useful? Should all children be required to study algebra? Might they not benefit more from studying probability? Logic? Computer programming? Philosophy? Aesthetics? Mass communications?

Anyone who thinks the present curriculum makes sense is invited to explain to an intelligent fourteen-year-old why algebra or French or any other subject is essential for him. Adult answers are almost always evasive. The reason is simple: the present curriculum is a mindless holdover from the past.

Why, for example, must teaching be organized around such fixed disciplines as English, economics, mathematics or biology? Why not around stages of the human life cycle: a course on birth, childhood, adolescence, marriage, career, retirement, death. Or around contemporary social problems? Or around significant technologies of the past and future? Or around countless other imaginable alternatives?

The present curriculum and its division into airtight compartments is not based on any well thought out conception of contemporary human needs. Still less is it based on any grasp of the future, any understanding of what skills Johnny will require to live in the hurricane's eye of change. It is based on inertia — and a bloody clash of academic guilds, each bent on aggrandizing its budget, pay scales and status.

This obsolete curriculum, furthermore, imposes standardization on the elementary and secondary schools. Youngsters are given little choice in determining what they wish

SHOCK

to learn. Variations from school to school are minimal. The curriculum is nailed into place by the rigid entrance requirements of the colleges, which in turn, reflect the vocational and social requirements of a vanishing society. . . .

. . . .Given further acceleration, we can conclude that knowledge will grow increasingly perishable. Today's "fact" becomes tomorrow's "misinformation." This is no argument against learning facts or data — far from it. But a society in which the individual constantly changes his job, his place of residence, his social ties and so forth, places an enormous premium on learning efficiency. Tomorrow's schools must therefore teach not merely data, but ways to manipulate it. Students must learn how to discard old ideas, how and when to replace them. They must, in short, learn how to learn.

ALVIN TOFFLER

Schools

Excess
Is Not
The Way

Experienced and respected child development experts are beginning to warn against two widely different educational concepts that have gained popularity and support over the years.

One of the concepts is the traditional "pressure cooker" theory that the best school is the one that teaches the most in the shortest time. Thus, the pressure is on to teach reading and writing at an ever earlier age, often skipping phases of understanding in the process. If the results are unsatisfactory, it is the fault of either a dumb child or of a bad teacher.

The other concept is the "permissiveness" theory usually associated with "free" schools. It rejects not only pressures but even discernible structures of teaching content. Children move haphazardly from one activity to another, guided largely by what interests them at the moment.

Last week, in New York, two men who have devoted a lifetime to the study of human growth, and who have often disagreed with each other, challenged some of the prevailing shibboleths.

Harvard's B. F. Skinner, the behaviorist best known for his controversial experiments in conditioning human development by controlling the child's environment, lashed out against what he considered the mistaken attempt to create "free and happy students" through permissiveness—a "do-it-yourself educational policy."

The result, Professor Skinner told an assembly of educators at New York University, is that a far from happy student "plays truant as never before . . . drops out of high school . . . attacks the very teachers and vandalizes the very schools that have set him free . . . And when he discovers that his education has not prepared him to play a part in the world . . . he drops out of that world, too."

Jean Piaget, the 76-year-old Swiss dean of the child psychologists, speaking at the Graduate Center of the City University, reaffirmed his life-long disagreement with the "American dilemma" of trying artificially to speed up a child's learning process.

Not unlike Mr. Skinner, Mr. Piaget believes that background and environment will to a large extent determine the pace at which a child learns. But, he warns, no matter how fast that pace, all children must pass through the same phases of understanding. Skipping or reversing those phases poses a risk to the child's development.

An everyday example of how pushy parents' attempt to skip a natural phase for one that seems to them more important was offered by a first-grade teacher. Too many parents, she said, drill their five-year-old children in the alphabet in the effort to teach reading, but send them to school without teaching them to tie their shoe laces. The children are doubly frustrated by not being able to cope with the reading, for which they are not ready, and by not being able to cope with their shoe laces—something useful to them — for which they are ready.

But what also emerges from the Piaget approach is that the acceptance of a different speed—for example, for children from the slums and children from highly literate, affluent homes — should not be allowed to lead to the uncontrolled, unstructured classroom.

While Mr. Piaget rejects Professor Skinner's controls as a means of conditioning the child for the future, he insists that unless children are given a continuing chance to use and test their developing abilities, their intellectual growth will be stunted.

"We need pupils," Mr. Piaget has written, "who are active, who learn early to find out by themselves, partly by their own spontaneous activity and partly through materials we set up for them." The principal goal is to "create men who are capable of doing new things. . . ." This is attained by a mixture of discovery and subtly controlled structure, leading through the natural succession of phases, Mr. Piaget says.

An even more impassioned plea against the excessive rushing of the natural stages of development was made by Louise Bates Ames and her associates of the Gesell Institute of Child Development in her recent book, "Stop School Failure."

There are many Americans, Dr. Ames writes, "who feel that their child *ought* to do what parents and school desire at the time *they* feel it should be done. So they teach and train and urge and argue. . . ."

The result of premature instruction, Dr. Ames warns, "tends to be that the child who is started too soon either is put off reading entirely . . . or he persists with it, tries hard, and becomes hopelessly confused."

—FRED M. HECHINGER

good teachers

2

People hate those who make them feel their own inferiority. – Lord Chesterfield

The vanity of teaching often tempteth a man to forget he is a blockhead. – Lord Halifax

In teaching, the greatest sin is to be boring. – J. F. Herbart

The most advanced teacher of the most advanced school believes nothing more profound than that the best way of teaching a boy is to leave him to his own devices.

– Aubrey Menen

It's heartbreaking to be a teacher because one is fighting Nature most of the time. – E. V. Lucas

The secret of education lies in respecting the pupil. – Emerson

The average schoolmaster is and always must be essentially an ass, for how can one imagine an intelligent man engaging in so puerile an avocation? – H. L. Mencken

Everybody who is incapable of learning has taken to teaching. – Oscar Wilde

& bad teachers

The object of teaching a child is to enable him to get along without his teacher.

— *Elbert Hubbard*

The true teacher defends his pupils against his own personal influence. — *A. B. Alcott*

What nobler employment, or more valuable to the state than that of the man who instructs the rising generation? — *Cicero*

It is when the gods hate a man with uncommon abhorrence that they drive him into the profession of a schoolmaster. — *Seneca*

The scholarship which consists in the memorization of facts does not qualify one to be a teacher. — *Confucius*

A teacher affects eternity. He never knows where his influence stops. — *Henry Adams*

Let such teach others who themselves excel. — *Alexander Pope*

Notes for INTERN survival

DAVID MESIROW

Your first task is to determine who your advising teacher *really* is. Each advising teacher's position is unlike that of any other advising teacher; his "advice" and his performance will depend on who you are, on his school, and on his own individuality. Therefore, it is imperative that you get a sense of his World View, that you find out what his position is in the power-structure of the school and find out how influential he is with other teachers and administrators. Quickly develop the technique of asking leading but discreet questions of and about your advising teacher and about the school; the history of previous interns is a good place to begin.

Having acquainted yourself with your advising teacher, you must now come to grips with the place in which you are performing. It is an Institution. It has bureaucratic priorities that supersede the stated purpose of the place. All kinds of records are kept: enrollment, attendance, grades, and other evaluations of students. This function of public education will not disappear in the foreseeable future. You have a contractual obligation to perform administrative tasks; each has its own rationale. For instance, your attendance book is a legal record for determining the whereabouts of any student assigned to you during that class time. Moreover, the recording of daily attendance plays a crucial part in the distribution of state money to school districts. There is nothing you can do about such bureaucratic functions in the sense of immediately changing the machinery — especially if you attempt to do so by yourself. You will be better off to accommodate yourself to the routine in order to minimize its effect on your teaching.

If you are discharged from your post, it will not be for teaching inability but for some "grave" reason, like inability to get along with others on the faculty, or unwillingness to follow instructions, or stupidity, or unprofessional conduct, but not, your first year, for inability to teach.

> — *Abraham Bernstein*
> Teaching English in
> High School

Identifying yourself is the next task. Most interns are mistaken, at one time or another, for students in the school. Depending on how you feel about this, you can allow the illusion to continue or you can accompany your advising teacher as he makes his rounds of colleagues in the days before school officially opens and be introduced as a Teacher. The latter has some advantages. It will reduce the number of challenges you will receive walking into the faculty lounge or other sanctuaries reserved for teachers. One clear advantage of being introduced as a teacher is that it will permit you to begin the immediate cultivation of those people who exercise power in the school: the secretaries in the main office, the janitors, the librarian, and the bookroom clerk.

In many schools (the number, happily, is shrinking), your physical appearance influences what administrators, teachers, students, clerks, aides, secretaries, and parents think of you and often has a decisive effect on how you are treated. Education needs bright, competent people to make substantive changes. Choose carefully the types of changes you wish to bring about; unorthodoxy in clothing, hair, and adornments may be too peripheral to expend much energy and risk on.

Above all, do not try to bring about changes single-handed. The road you are traveling is littered with many who have tried by themselves.

Be cool and positive in your relations with other adults in the school. Some people cannot resist attacking (even in the guise of sympathy) those who make themselves vulnerable; discussing your successes with other teachers is better than relating your failures — most people forget the former, and frequently, in the course of conversation, relate the latter to their colleagues, and somehow it always gets to the administration.

As rapidly as possible you need to learn the subtle art of self-defense as a teacher. An intern has to develop a sixth sense — anticipation of complaints by parents to the school over material used in his classroom. When you plan to deal with something that really smacks of controversy, have a chat with your advising teacher first. Be sure to have handy — preferably on a piece of paper — a rationale for the use of the material, and prior to the lesson. Also, any papers you hand out that seem to have controversial overtones ought to be collected before the end of the period or day. A fragment of a lesson or some words, taken out of the context of the lesson, can become an item to inflame those who have a narrow understanding of the purpose of education. Difficulties arise even for experienced teachers in these matters; however, interns are especially vulnerable. Your advising teacher should be sensitive to this aspect of teaching and be able to serve as an effective liaison between you and the administration. Administrators find it particularly disconcerting to be called by complaining parents when they have no foreknowledge of an event which generates a complaint. If forewarned, the administrator is forearmed and the complaints is likely to die on the phone.

Keep in mind, also, that whenever you are asked to see the principal or some other administrative person, you should alert your advising teacher and determine if it would be wise to have him accompany you.

One note about your students. The degree of your personal involvement with students is a matter you must decide. You should know, however, that some students are voracious consumers of your time and you will want to determine the value such expenditure of time has for your student and for you — and what effect it has on your other responsibilities.

WATCH FOR CHILDREN ▷ SCHOOL'S OPEN

B the eginning teacher

Following are questions and excerpts from four interviews. The teachers are Rosa Lee Colo, fourth grade teacher, Edison Elementary School, Empire, Ohio, who at the time of her interview was a second grade teacher at Como Elementary School, Columbus, Ohio; Ernest Ellis, mathematics and science teacher, McArthur High School, Hollywood, Florida; Judy Hall, first grade teacher, Milo (Maine) Elementary School; and Wallace King, U.S. Navy, who at the time of his interview was an algebra teacher at Capitol Hill High School, Oklahoma City.

What were your most difficult problems your first year of teaching?

Mr. Ellis Planning! I would plan lessons that were either too long or too short. At first it was difficult for me to judge how much time I should devote to one particular topic in an entire unit and how I should coordinate the units with our six-week schedule and final examinations.

As far as classroom control and discipline were concerned, I didn't really have any particular problem — perhaps because of my military background.

Mr. King Classroom control was my biggest problem. I was probably too lenient at the beginning because this problem seemed to mushroom as the year went along. I found out that getting a little bit stricter with a student after I'd been easy on him was out of the question.

Rules and regulations of the school and district presented no big problem, but preparing lesson plans was something else. I had to teach classes varying in length from fifty minutes to two-hours-and-twenty-five minutes. So in some classes I would run over and in some I might run a little short. But after a while I was able to adjust to these varying time blocks.

I found helping students challenging because each student has unique problems, and I had to use a completely different approach with each one.

Miss Colo   One problem I ran into was the size of my class. I've had at least thirty-three children in my room at all times and sometimes as many as thirty-six. A class that size is difficult for any teacher but for a beginning teacher it's even harder.

Another thing that's difficult for a first year teacher in an elementary classroom is grouping children for reading and math. I did my student teaching with first graders, so I was afraid I wouldn't expect enough from my second graders.

But whereas in the beginning I thought I could group the children once and keep those groups for the rest of the year, I found as the year went on that grouping has to be flexible.

Are you the only second grade teacher in your building?

Miss Colo   No, there are two others, and each of us has a reading group. One has the high group; one, the middle; one, the low. So, we have parts of three rooms of children together, which I've enjoyed.

Did you run into problems with parents?
Miss Colo   It's difficult for a first year teacher to meet parents. I would say that it's best not to mention that you're a beginner. Some parents feel insecure if they think their children have a first year teacher.

Before this year, I never believed there were parents who would really give a teacher a hard time or blame her for their child's problems. But I had a traumatic experience with parents this year.

The ones I'm talking about have several children with learning problems. The youngest is in my class. So, over the years these parents have been hearing about their children's problems and they just don't want to hear the same story any more. I didn't understand this at first. If I had, I might have softened what I said. But I learned the hard way, and I think maybe all teachers do that in their first year.

Miss Hall   Well, you see I went to a very, very conservative college, and, if nothing else, it prepared me to conform. So, as far as adjusting to the rules of my school and assuming the duties that go with being a schoolteacher, I have had no problem.

I do feel that I've played this whole school year by ear, though. My training didn't prepare me to be a teacher. Oh, I had courses on putting up bulletin boards, my professors gave me advice like "Join all three education associations, local, state, and national," and I have frequently drawn upon information learned in music and reading courses, but for the most part, my methods courses provided no practical information on how to run a class-room. Most of my instructors hadn't taught in elementary schools.

Do you understand what I mean? I had very little that was specific to fall back on except one good quarter of student teaching. For example, in our science methods course, we taught a lesson to our peer group. But you can't present a project on birds to eighteen- or twenty-year-olds and get perspective on how that lesson will go over with six- or seven-year-olds.

I was lectured at in high school and I was lectured at in college. But when I stepped in front of those twenty children of mine, I knew

I could not reach them by lecturing. So I didn't attempt it.

In what ways could your preparation for teaching have been improved?

Miss Colo We should have had more time observing and teaching in an elementary classroom. Education majors should start observing classes in their sophomore year. In the junior year maybe they could be in some kind of cooperative program in which they would take regular classes at college part of the time and work with students in a classroom — observing and teaching — part of the time.

Just observing is not enough. Sitting in the back of a room is so different from being in the front of the class. You don't understand what's really happening unless you're up there teaching.

Was your first year of teaching as difficult as you had anticipated?

Mr. King About what I had anticipated — with a few exceptions. For example, my white students sometimes accused me of being partial to the black students because I, too, am black. I hadn't expected that.

Why did the white students make that charge?

Mr. King The black kids in one of my classes were leaving fifteen minutes early to catch the bus. When a white student confronted me about the blacks leaving early, I explained that the administration had approved it. I tried to point out that she should take her complaint to the persons responsible for making the decision. But I still think there was a block between us because of this situation.

Mr. Ellis Yes, I must say it was as difficult as I had anticipated. I thought I would have the most trouble in the preparation phase of teaching and I did have problems in that area.

Miss Colo No, it wasn't as difficult as I had expected. Of course the first few months were hard for me because I couldn't get over the number of children in my room. I was crushed because I couldn't remember all their names. I thought, How can I ever do anything with these children when I can't even remember who they are!

But I learned to really enjoy my children. At first I was scared to. That's one thing about a beginning teacher. You're miserable at first because you're afraid you're losing control and you can't relax with the children.

Miss Hall You've really got to dig, you've got to work. I don't like a teacher-oriented room, but in the first grade you have to push, push, push to get the children ready for second grade. It's the system.

Charley may not be ready for second grade, but there's a new group coming into first grade. So, out! Push him out! And you hope and pray he'll be able to somehow grasp whatever he needs in order to meet some measure of success.

I don't go along with that. But I'm conforming again. My district says that these children must be ready for second grade, and so I push — reading the most. My principal and my supervisor said: "I don't care whatever else you do this year, do the reading." But I try to let the children direct the other things — art and music and social studies.

Is there anything to that bit of advice, "Don't smile until Christmas"?

Miss Colo I think so. At first you have to set up basic control and then you can ease up and give the children an extra pat on the shoulder and an extra grin. If I had been everybody's buddy at the beginning of the year, a few of my students would have really taken advantage of me.

Miss Hall I guess I'm a middle-of-the-roader. I didn't want to come on like an ogre. I've seen some teachers who go into class on the first day and snap, "Now you sit down!" or "Get in that line!" If I were six years old, I'd be terrified.

Mr. Ellis I would say the teacher shouldn't smile until after he's midway through the second semester. I just began to get into the swing of things about March. I felt I had everything under control then and that I would make it to June.

I was more relaxed with the students and by that time they had gotten used to me. We could communicate better; we seemed to get even more done. Previously, I'd had to use a lot of pressure to get them to accomplish what needed to be done.

Mr. King In any relationship with people, a smile is always needed — even if it's used just to encourage or to say a friendly hello. But in the light of my experience, I do think the beginning teacher should come in very strict and not wait until later in the year to try to get classroom control. He can always relax a little later on in the year.

Did you learn from your students this year an important lesson you'll never forget?

Miss Colo I've learned that teachers shouldn't generalize about families. For example, one day I was discussing families — mother and father and brother and sister — and a little girl burst into tears because she didn't have a father.

I've also learned that the child who can't make friends is sometimes a severe discipline problem. I never understood all the different reasons for discipline problems before. I also learned there's only so much a teacher can do to help the child who is not liked by the class. If you try to make the class accept this child, it has just the opposite effect.

I've also learned to consider children's feelings. The record on one of my boys says he's a low achiever who never does anything and doesn't care. Well, he burst into tears one day because he couldn't complete a paper. That's not a child who doesn't care.

Mr. King One thing I've learned is that you can trust people about as much as you demonstrate trust in them. If you give the impression you don't trust them, they'll likely become untrustworthy.

Mr. Ellis I think one of the first things I learned is that you must be very fair with students — especially those at the level I'm teaching. I teach math to ninth graders and physical science to tenth, eleventh, and twelfth graders. They don't like to be led on.

Take the ninth graders, for instance. If I offered some gimmick reward to try to con them into doing a long assignment, they would say, "No tricks! If this is what you want us to do, then just tell us and we'll do it."

As far as getting the tenth, eleventh, and twelfth graders to become interested in the science area, you have to sort of glamorize the subject. To give you an idea of what I mean, my physical science course is primarily in the curriculum to satisfy science requirements for senior high graduation. Normally students who take this course do not plan to enter professions where they'll need a scientific background. So I have to sell them on the importance of the course and the importance of learning some science. I have to keep the course interesting — and simple.

What new ideas — learned the hard way in your beginning year — will help to make next year easier?

Miss Colo I got some new ideas about the physical arrangement of the room. I didn't like seating the children in straight rows, so I've tried several different arrangements. I don't keep the same groupings all the time either; I used to think this was necessary because I thought sitting in the same place was a kind of security for a child.

Grouping the children in threes and fours to work together has helped my shy children build friendships. One little boy who was *so* shy is thrilled now because the kids in his group accept him. They pat him on the back, and he knows they're his friends.

Mr. Ellis I learned to simplify my tests. At first most of my examinations had four different kinds of questions: true and false, multiple choice, completion, and essay. But I found that the tests were difficult for me to grade and that the students, in some cases, didn't perform as well as I thought they could. However, when I give a test with only two types of questions, the students seem to do better and the grading is easier for me.

What advice would you give to a new teacher?

Miss Colo Spend as much time in a classroom as possible before you take over your own class and collect as much resource material as you can.

Mr. Ellis Start planning before September!

Find out as soon as possible what textbooks you'll be using and what library facilities the school and county has. Then begin making master plans and subdividing them into units.

Mr. King Start off with a firm attitude and continue it throughout the year.

Miss Hall To new teachers I would say that all that book learning and all those courses don't amount to a thing unless you have the soul, or the human understanding, to deal with children. Don't think just because you've got that B.S. or M.S. or whatever that you've got it made. Remember, you're working with human beings.

The Day They Locked Up the Textbooks

Mildred J. Fischle

It was the **first** day of school. The usual first day faculty meeting had just begun. The old were welcomed back; the new were introduced and told what a fine addition they would be to this, the best faculty in the school system. Those who had traveled to Europe were assured that they would have an opportunity to share their slides at a forthcoming faculty meeting. The principal was sure everyone was eager to see them.

Then it was time to enumerate the myriad school policies, procedures, and more procedures. The old had ample opportunity to exhibit the patience of Job, for they had heard this same presentation nigh unto five, ten, and twenty or more times already. But the new had to be informed, so all suffered through the recitation.

The principal announced that there was an ample supply of pencils, one quart of paste per semester, one role of tape to be shared by each floor, and the usual supplies to be found in the usual places.

At this point, there were numerous games of tic-tac-toe going on in various corners of the room. Some teachers were writing grocery lists. The more concerned were writing lists of supplies they would try to cop before anyone else got to the backroom. Others were looking over class lists and wondering what was in store for them. One teacher was commenting to a friend about the children he was getting, which parents to beware of, and so on.

Suddenly, in the same droning voice, the principal announced that during the summer the textbooks had been locked up in the storeroom and somehow the keys had been lost. Therefore, it would be necessary for the teachers to teach without textbooks.

"Impossible!" the teachers cried. "Teach without textbooks? I can't do it!" "They can't blame me if the kids don't learn!"

"Why don't they buy some new texts?"

"We can't teach like that." After the tempest in the teapot had simmered down, the principal told the teachers that he and the assistant principal had made a list of concepts for each teacher to introduce to their students and use as a basis for their curriculum that year. Many library books would be made available, and one or two copies of textbooks would be borrowed from another school. This would really be an opportunity for the teachers to learn how to teach. But to complicate matters, the ditto machine was broken and would not be repaired for at least a month. Again chaos broke out: "I spent half the summer making out masters!" "I have all the masters I used during the last five years!" The principal wondered, "What will they do? Will they strike? Will they be able to teach?"

The teachers were dismissed, and by the time the principal returned to his office there was a long line outside his door, each teacher with a tale of defense just in case he didn't do his usual superior job. One said she always had all the children reading from the same reader at the same time and didn't know *how* she could operate without the books. Another said he would be happy to ditto portions of the text if only the ditto machine worked. And so it went. The principal listened to each tale of woe with compassion, but also with curiosity about what would happen in the classrooms in the days ahead.

He was very careful not to hold any schoolwide faculty meetings the first month for fear the teachers might gang up and dethrone him. But he did meet with small groups of teachers to find out what they were doing, what kinds of lessons they were planning, and how they were presenting concepts to the children.

One teacher was using the community as a source of meaningful curriculum. She asked the children where they could find something in the neighborhood that used pounds and ounces. Yes, there was a supermarket down the street, so off went the class to visit the supermarket. As a dividend the butcher let the class go into the meat-cutting room, and they learned much more than that one pound equals sixteen ounces. What about gallons? Oh, there was a gas station next door. Again the visit suggested more than quarts and gallons. There were words to define, stories to be written, discussions to be held, things to be looked up in books.

"Where does the gas come from?" "That's where I put air in my bicycle tires — too much pressure and bang!" Back in the classroom there were library books and a few textbooks that were used to explain what the class had seen.

The teacher discovered that the children were reading, but not all were reading the same book. As she listened to them read individually, she found herself getting to know the children as never before. She started asking them where in the community more information could be found, and they began to help plan new excursions. They learned about the machines in the laundromat, how many pounds in a wash load, how many coins were needed to start the machine, and how to care for different kinds of materials.

After their first negative reactions, more teachers began to come alive. This was a different approach. Each teacher was beginning to put his own self into the teaching/learning process. The children were teaching them how to teach. More wondrous than that, the children were learning! What they were doing had meaning. They were part of the planning, the doing, and the evaluating. The teacher was there to guide, to pull knowledge from the children that would turn that list of concepts into usable ideas ideas that were alive because they were a part of life.

Teachers began to share experiments and results with each other. "This is what I did!" "How did it go?" "Did you know about the spaghetti factory?" Soon the complaining was replaced with a new enthusiasm. Perhaps it could be called teaching and discovering.

In February the principal announced tersely that the key to the storeroom had been found under somewhat mysterious circumstances. A few of the teachers galloped to the room to bring back their textbook security. Most merely cantered over and brought back a few copies of each book to add to the library collection.

What happened the day the textbooks were locked up? The teachers learned to stretch themselves and to use themselves as instruments; they learned the joy of teaching. The children learned to reach into themselves and the community around them; they experienced the wonder of learning. The textbooks were now in proper perspective — aids to learning!

Ann Landers' Advice

Dear Ann Landers: I didn't think much of Toronto Reader's advice on how to spot a drug user. I especially want to speak out against Hint Number Two which said: "Take notice if a student falls asleep in class."

Ann, baby, I've got two classes during which I fall asleep every chance I get and I am not blowing grass or tripping out on acid. One is Civics and it bores me out of my gourd.

The other class is English Literature. The teacher's voice is so monotonous she puts me to sleep in five minutes. If she could bottle it, it would make the best sedative known to mankind.

So please, Annie, cancel that counsel, I don't want to be grabbed for a junkie just because I *doze* off during boring lectures.

Beautiful Dreamer

Hey Jerry - how can you stand it. I can hardly stay awake. Do you think she'll ever stop talking & give us a chance. I think I'll kill myself.

S.

Hey Max,
I don't know what's keeping you awake. I'm so bored I could stretch out and fall asleep. Do you believe she can stand there and talk so long? I wish she'd let us talk once in a while.

J.J.

THE MEMOIRS OF JESSE JAMES

Richard Brautigan

I remember all those thousands of hours
that I spent in grade school watching the clock,
waiting for recess or lunch or to go home.
    Waiting: for anything but school.
My teachers could easily have ridden with Jesse James
    for all the time they stole from me.

Yellow Vans, 8:15

Buzzzz

"I pledge allegiance, to . . ."

". . . The morning announcements . . ."

". . . Of the . . ."

". . . Senior dues . . ."

". . . Of America."

Buzzzz . . .

Tramp. Tramp. Tramp.

I see Tommy and Bonnie and Billy and Sue.

Good little do bees who know what to do.

Buzzzz . . .

Where is the old screw? If she thinks I did that homework

She's out of her sweet bippy.

"Oh, good morning, Miss Roseicheekt.

No, mam, I couldn't get that one."

Buzzzz . . .

"Get me an ice cream."

"How many periods did they get you for?"

"No. 9, No. 9, No. 9, No. 9, No. 9."

"Why don't we do it in the . . ."

"Spinach, and the orange stuff must be carrots."

". . . Hard to explain, sir. I'd just rather sit down in the lobby.

Where I can think, than come up and sit in the midst of this mass

Lunacy. I know that's hard to understand, but . . ."

"Let's go get a smoke, man."

Buzzzz . . .

   Tick, tock. Tick, tock.

   It's never going to end, I'm going to die in here.

   I wonder if he'd give me a pass to the nurse.

   Or the bathroom. Anywhere.

Buzzzz . . .

Buzzzz . . .

Buzzzz . . .

Buzzzz . . .

   Yellow Vans, 2:45

   4 more days left.

               — *Gregg Shaw*

On Education

He always wanted to explain things.
But no one cared.
So he drew.
Sometimes he would draw and it wasn't anything.
He wanted to carve it in stone or write it in the sky.
He would lie out on the grass and look up in the sky.
And it would be only him and the sky and the things inside him that needed saying.
And it was after that he drew the picture.
It was a beautiful picture.
He kept it under his pillow and would let no one see it.
And he would look at it every night and think about it.
And when it was dark, and his eyes were closed, he could still see it.
And it was all of him.
And he loved it.
When he started school he brought it with him.
Not to show anyone but just to have with him like a friend.
It was funny about school.
He sat in a square, brown desk
Like all the other square, brown desks
And he thought it should be red.
And his room was a square, brown room,
Like all the other rooms.
And it was tight and close.
And stiff.
He hated to hold the pencil and chalk,
With his arm stiff and his feet flat on the floor,
Stiff,
With the teacher watching and watching.
The teacher came and spoke to him.
She told him to wear a tie like all the other boys.
He said he didn't like them.
And she said it didn't matter!
After that they drew.
And he drew all yellow and it was the way he felt about morning.
And it was beautiful.
The teacher came and smiled at him.
"What's this?" she said. "Why don't you draw something like Ken's drawing?
Isn't that beautiful?"
After that his mother bought him a tie.
And he always drew airplanes and rocketships like everyone else.
And he threw the old picture away.
And when he lay alone looking at the sky,
It was big and blue and all of everything,
But he wasn't anymore.
He was square inside
And brown.
And his hands were stiff.
And he was like everyone else.
And the things inside him that needed saying didn't need it anymore.
It had stopped pushing,
It was crushed.
Stiff.
Like everything else.

(This was written by a high school senior, two weeks before he committed suicide.)

SEX

MY DARLING, MY HAMBURGER - Paul Zindel

"It was Marie Kazinski who asked how to stop a boy if he wants to go all the way," Maggie whispered.

Liz dragged her trig book along the wall tiles so it clicked at every crack.

"I'll bet she didn't ask it like that," Liz said.

" 'Sexually stimulated' was how she said it, if you must know the sordid details."

"Go on."

"She simply raised her hand," Maggie said "and asked Miss Fanuzzi in front of the whole class."

"What'd she say?"

"Who?"

"Miss Fanuzzi."

Maggie shifted her books from one arm to the other. "Oh, something dumb. Miss Fanuzzi knows a lot about puberty and mitosis, but I think she needs a little more experience with men." . . .

Liz lowered herself again. She opened her looseleaf notebook and started reading a love comic hidden inside.

"Miss Fanuzzi said we're going to discuss masturbation tomorrow." Maggie put the mirror back in her pocketbook.

"That's nice." Liz waited a moment, then asked, "What advice did she give for stopping a guy on the make?"

"Who?"

"Miss Fanuzzi," Liz snapped.

"You mean about what to do when things get out of control?" Maggie could tell when Liz Carstensen really wanted to know something because she would start tapping her fingers.

"Yes, stupid."

"Well" — Maggie lowered her voice — "Miss Fanuzzi's advice was that you're supposed to suggest going to get a hamburger."

TWO

The teachers can really hurt you if they want to. Like we had a teacher who would write up on the board before we even came in. All the boards would be filled with writing. And he wouldn't explain a thing to us. Every day the same thing – writing but no explanation for the things he wrote. And when the tests came, everybody failed.

BLOCKS Apart

And then he would criticize us, give us zeros, demerits and all these kinds of crazy things, and there was no way of getting to him. So we all got in a little group and went down to the principal's office. He didn't believe us. So what we did is, we stopped work. We never worked in that class and the teacher called the principal. We told him, "We won't work because he won't explain the things he writes up on the board and we can't learn unless he explains."

Finally they threw out that teacher and they brought in another one. That new one, all he ever did was explain. He never wrote anything on the board.

I mean, you get aggravated. All of these teachers are just too much for the boys. So there was only one way out. You play hooky, you cut out of that class, you sleep, you get even on him, you hate it. You live through it to get out of school.

The biggest difference between the first year and the second was that I was really beginning to teach now. Part of the change in me was simply that I'd learned to shut up. My lessons were less entertaining, of course — I didn't rant and rave so much. But the kids were learning more since I'd learned to keep them active. I was catching on to the difference between feeding them material and motivating them to seek it themselves. They seemed to be working more independently — and they seemed to be working. It was the greatest.

I'd learned to keep quiet in the face of problems, too. I didn't feel compelled to solve their troubles — no stranger ever solved mine. The kids seemed just as happy and open. I guess all they wanted was an ear.

an empty SPOON

"I have no place to stay. I couldn't do my homework in the subway; the light wasn't no good."

"I think I'm pregnant because I spit up some again this morning. But maybe it was the hot dogs and gravy on the rice. This food ain't even what I'd feed my cat. It gets you if you're pregnant."

"Do you ever wonder what it's like? Being me, I mean? I think about it a lot. When my father hit me, I cry. I can't tell my mother, she be mad at that."

"Please excuse me for last week. I went down South to some funerals. My uncle killed his wife and baby and then hisself. I liked it in the country. It was different."

Sunny Decker

There is nothing easier than being yourself. Which is why, if you play it right, teaching is such a joy. It's a tactic that occasionally proves disastrous, but on the whole, anything's better than being a phony. Grownups I knew as a kid were always so busy role-playing that they didn't seem to be people. They were parent types, teacher types, and so on. It's incredible that no amount of failure in handling their charges prompted them to try any new tactics. Like honesty, for instance. It was a cardinal sin for my parents to say, "Gee, I just don't know"; or for my teachers to say, "I was wrong — I feel like a heel." They felt it incumbent upon themselves to be the last word. And because they weren't, their answers were pat answers, empty answers. Grownups had scripts that they'd memorized, consisting of phrases like when-you're-older-you'll-change-your-mind. They gave orders: Wear your boots; raise your hand; for God's sake remember to flush the toilet. For all their talk about manners, they never really thought it necessary to treat us with common courtesy. Grownups don't *respect* children. I might have been cute, talented, or precocious, but I was a curio to adults — not a person.

I'm very bitter about the whole thing. And I nurture my hostility. I want to remember every injustice I suffered, so that maybe I can avoid growing up to be a grownup. There are better things to be.

It's hard to deal with each kid and every situation as though it's a first. But once you say, "I've met his type before," or "That's typical of adolescents," you're dangerously close to falling back on the script. If you can keep from generalizing — from robbing kids of their uniqueness — it's an easy ride. Without even trying, you meet kids as individuals; you establish dynamic relationships; you work *with* them, instead of banging at doors and bemoaning the lack of communication between generations.

Repeat: There is nothing easier than being yourself. When I'm mad, I yell. When something's funny, I laugh. And I saw no reason why the kids shouldn't have as much fun as I did. I tried to see to it that they succeeded. Success is great fun.

Because I'm not a role player, the kids had a hard time. It's easy to work for a teacher type. It's hard when you're dealing with a real person. Real people are inconsistent. My kids responded well to familiar structure. They really *wanted* Monday to be vocabulary day and Tuesday to be composition. I can't work that way. So they were nervous wrecks, which I loved — it made for a nice, noisy classroom.

placing
BLAME
for poor school work

When some children do poorly in school, some people place the blame on the children, some on the children's home life, some on the school, and some on the teachers. Of course, all of these thing share the blame, but where would you place the *chief* blame?

	National totals 1,790 %	No. children in schools 996 %	Public school parents 698 %	Private school parents 144 %	Profes- sional educators 270 %
N=					
On children	14	11	20	12	8
On children's home life	57	61	53	58	67
On schools	6	5	7	10	9
On teachers	12	11	13	12	7
No opinion	13	15	12	14	10

Note: Columns add to more than 100% because of some multiple responses.

The crux of using a plan book is to think of it as a resource rather than as "the gospel." If one wants to remember the essence of a plan for use the following week, what's wrong with writing it down? *–Blanche Wintringham,* first grade teacher. School No. 1, Little Falls, N.J.

I like to use a plan book. It gives me confidence, makes the class period move more smoothly, and results in greater acomplishment. *– Nathal R. Weston.* teacher of French, Dirigo High School, Dixfield, Me.

If there is a spark of creativity or originality in the teacher, any resemblance between his actual classroom activities and his plan book is accidental. *– Roy Higginbotham,* principal, Minor Elementary School, Birmingham, Ala.

Teachers without plans too often waste major portions of class time in irrelevant activity or discussion. Flexibility may come to mean sloppiness, and spontaneity can turn out to be the coach discussing his newest football play with his math class. *– Kaye H. Wittwer,* former teacher of English, Ronan, Mont.

What good lawyer would argue a case without having prepared a brief? What good clergyman would speak from the pulpit without having prepared a sermon? What good engineer would direct the construction of a bridge without having planned beforehand? What good surgeon would operate without having charted his course? What *good* teacher would enter his classroom without having carefully prepared plans? *– Robert S. Bailey,* principal, Hamilton Terrace School, Berkeley Heights, N.J.

I wouldn't be without my plan book. I deviate whenever and wherever class discussions and interests pull us in a valuable way. Most activities are in my head, but my plan book helps me keep organized. *Mary Ney,* fourth grade teacher, Wildwood School, Mahtomedi, Minn.

Plan books are as passé as the pot-bellied stove in the one room school. — *Alice MacKenzie,* junior high school social studies teacher, River Edge, N.J.

It takes me only about 10 minutes to fill in one of those neat looking sheets. This keeps the principal happy, and when he is happy, I teach better. How's that for indirect benefits? — *Sarah Yoder,* second grade teacher, Caernarvon Elementary School, Churchtown, Pa.

The thinking that takes place during planning is a necessary and valuable element in effective teaching. Whether or not the plans are written down for others to see is inconsequential. —*Maribeth Henney,* assistant professor, Department of Elementary Education, Iowa State University, Ames.

The issue is: What about the less-than-good teacher? Lesson plans can help him. — *Sarah A. Hulett,* eighth grade English teacher, Landrum Junior High School, Spring Branch District, Houston.

Good plan books reveal only that the teacher can prepare and write good plans. — *Pamela I. Jarrett,* fourth grade teacher, Floyd School, Montgomery, Ala.

All good teachers, good principals, and good department heads realize that a well-prepared plan book makes an excellent *guide* for the teacher. He will be prepared to add, delete, or change his plans to keep his students interested in the subject at hand. — *Shirley B. Kosmo,* first grade teacher, Lehigh Acres (Fla.) Elementary School.

A teacher who finds it "difficult to predict . . . what will go on in class at the beginning of the period — much less what will happen tomorrow" is ill-prepared. If he does not consistently plan for good things to happen, they won't. — *John E. Morris,* assistant professor of professional laboratory experiences, Georgia Southern College, Statesboro.

Every teacher must play by ear once in a while; but without some sort of plan book, a teacher may find he is constantly playing it by ear. This makes evaluation an impossibility. — *Ellen Kersey,* teacher of English and journalism, Blackstock Junior High School, Oxnard, Calif.

It is doubtful that many administrators are so lacking in understanding of the teaching process that their primary judgment of a teacher rests upon the quality of his plan book. — *Rolland Dewing,* chairman, Division of the Social Sciences, Chadron (Neb.) State College.

The superior teacher knows that plans for instruction are both necessary and tentative. However, like attendance records and other clerical tasks, lesson plans are more often a bludgeon to enforce conformity than a tool of supervision. — *John F. Ohles,* professor of secondary education, Pennsylvania State University.

PLAN AND RECORD OF WORK

Grade 4   Room 12   For week ending January 12

	Reading	Language, Spelling, writing	Mathematics	Science, social studies
WEDNESDAY	_Tom's grp._ _Sue's grp._ _whole class_ Reread story from Fri. Pract. using primary accent in 3 syll. words. Read a Scand. fairy tale. Wkbk. pp. 62-63. Wkbk. p. 71	Review what makes a good paragraph. Write a good paragraph on your favorite TV prog.	Introduce "the nines" Discover multiplication facts about the nines	Teach longitude, lat. Compare climate in Norway + Colombia. Discuss differences in climate
TUESDAY	Chk. wkbks. Rd. a S. Am. folk tale How to use a pronunc. teaching guide in dict. Regrp. for re-teaching primary accent. Prac. with word list. Begin next story	Read and show paragraphs to each other in pairs. Correct as necessary Hand in today	Review and practice facts Begin examples, p. 102 Homework: finish p. 102	Discuss differences in life styles due to diff. in climate Read in text, pp. 216-22 Summarize
MONDAY	Check dict. ditto Prim. & Sec. accent pract. in longer wds. Free reading Regrp. Wkbk. p. 72 for tchg. as needed	Teach "Point of view" Read bk., play, movie reviews in _Time_, _Newsweek_, _TV Guide_, _Hartford Courant_, _Meadowbrook School News_, etc. Summarize	Chk. p. 102 Begin solving probs. with nines, p. 477 Homework: finish p. 477	Show film "Weather or not" - discuss. Meet in groups to plan projects "How Climate Affects Us."

Groton Public Schools

Conference Summary

Teacher Evaluation Program

Teacher___Ruth Enders_____

Supervisor___Lawrence Hopen_____

Date____January 26,1972_____

Note: Conference Summaries should number at least three per year for probationary (two by February 1) and one per year for tenure teachers.

Summarize Areas of Strength

Miss Enders is currently completing her first year of teaching in the fourth grade at William Hartley School. She has an excellent grasp of subject matter as demonstrated by her ability to interest children in ideas and in what is going on around them. She is well aware of children's abilities and needs and gears her program accordingly. She plans well and has set definite goals for herself and her charges. She has demonstrated her ability to relate to parents and has been able to help them understand her program, the school,and its aims. She is available to parents at all times. She is professionally mature for a beginning teacher and budgets her time well. She is an asset to the professional staff of the Town of Groton.

Summarize Areas that Need Improvement

Miss Enders' only shortcoming seems to be a tendency to favor highly verbal pupils at the expense of those who are less outspoken. I would stress that this is by no means an acute problem. At this point it is a very minor consideration, but one that should, nevertheless, be attended to.

Indicate Plan of Action

Miss Enders was open to suggestion when I pointed out her neglect of some of the quieter students. I suggested some things she might try that would involve such students in oral language activities. Miss Enders was most responsive and came up with several good ideas that she will try.

Form T.E.2

TEACHER: *Socrates*

A. PERSONAL QUALIFICATIONS RATING (high to low)

1 2 3 4 5

	Rating	Comment
Personal appearance	— — — — X	Dresses in an old sheet draped about his body
Self-confidence	— — — — X	Not sure of himself — always asking questions
Use of English	— — — X —	Speaks with a heavy Greek accent.
Adaptability	— — — — X	Prone to suicide by poison when under duress

B. CLASS MANAGEMENT

Organization	— — — — X	Does not keep a seating chart
Room appearance	— — — X —	Does not have eye-catching bulletin boards
Utilization of supplies	X — — — —	Does not use supplies

C. TEACHER-PUPIL RELATIONSHIPS

	Rating	Comment
Tact and consideration	— — — — X	Places students in embarrassing situation by asking questions
Attitude of class	— X — — —	Class is friendly

D. TECHNIQUES OF TEACHING

	Rating	Comment
Daily preparations	— X — — —	Does not keep daily lesson plans
Attention to course of study	— — X — —	Quite flexible — allows students to wander to different topics
Knowledge of subject matter	— — — — X	Does not know material — has to question pupils to gain knowledge

E. PROFESSIONAL ATTITUDE

	Rating	Comment
Professional ethics	— — — — X	Does not belong to professional association or PTA
In-service training	— — — — X	Complete failure here has not even bothered to attend college
Parent relationships	— — — — X	Needs to improve in this area — parents are trying to get rid of him

We're from Webster,
Couldn't be prouder.
If you can't hear us now,
Then we'll yell a little louder.
We're from Webster.
yeah!

KILL KILL KILL!

We're from Webster,
Couldn't be prouder.
If you can't hear us now,
Then we'll yell a little louder.
We're from Webster!

...AND FINALLY, EITHER YOU BUMS MASH THOSE OTHER CREEPS AND WIN THE SPORTSMANSHIP AWARD, OR YOU CAN ALL TAKE COLD SHOWERS AND WALK HOME TONIGHT!
17
23

the REAL teacher

What do you think a real teacher is? A real teacher ———

A real teacher is on my side.

A real teacher
lets me be me and tries to understand what it's like to be me.

A real teacher
accepts me whether he likes me or not.

A real teacher
doesn't have expectations of me because of what I've been or what he's been.

A real teacher
is more interested in how I learn than what I learn.

A real teacher
doesn't make me feel anxious and afraid.

A real teacher
provides many choices.

A real teacher
lets me teach myself even if it takes longer.

A real teacher
talks so I can understand what he means to say.

A real teacher
can make mistakes and admit it.

A real teacher
can show his feelings and let me show mine.

A real teacher
wants me to evaluate my own work.

IS TEACHING **your** THING?

Would you like to have a child of yours take up teaching in the public schools as a career?

	National totals	No. children in schools	Public school parents	Private school parents	Profes-sional educators
N=	1,790	996	698	144	270
	%	%	%	%	%
Yes	67	65	71	61	72
No	22	21	21	31	22
Don't know	11	14	8	8	6
% totals	100	100	100	100	100

"My arithmetic teacher was crammed with knowledge but he managed to make me feel ignorant. He was extremely erudite but his tongue was a sword. He was a virtuoso of the verbal slap. In his class, we knew how it felt to be a zero."

STUDENTS RECALL

"Our history teacher had a magic touch. His classes set our minds on fire. We emerged from them as if from a dream. He understood our longing for adventure and led us into a labyrinth of legends, myths, and mysteries. He was funny in his imitation of historic figures; each era was evoked vividly. His lectures were lucid; the specific and the symbolic emerged with clarity. One lesson he drove home: Historical truth is never final. It is discovered, forgotten, and must be rediscovered endlessly."

THEIR

"Our teacher, Mr. Greco, was a painter with a poetic soul. Mystical and idiosyncratic in his art, he was real and direct in life. We thrived on this vital contrast. Most teachers warned us to face reality; Mr. Greco endowed us with a sense of mystery. Tragedy and joy were personal acquaintances of his. A refugee, he had known sorrow. Suffering brought him wisdom, which he imparted with grace and nobility."

TEACHERS

from Teacher and Child
Haim G. Ginott

"Our English teacher had a unique talent for complicating life. After an explanation of his, even a simple subject sounded complex. His main interest was in logistics: tests taken on time, papers typed properly, homework handed in promptly. The psychology of teaching and learning escaped him. He took special pains, or perhaps pleasure, to confront us with our bitter reality, as he saw it: 'How is the vacuum of your mind today?' he would ask casually. His corrosive sarcasm painted a bleak picture of our future. 'Soon enough,' he would warn, 'you will knock your head on the ceiling of your ability.'"

"We were the luckiest class in school. We had a homeroom teacher who knew the core truth of education: 'Self-hate destroys, self-esteem saves.' This principle guided all her efforts on our behalf. She always minimized our deficiencies, neutralized our rage, and enhanced our natural gifts. She never, so to speak, forced a dancer to sing or a singer to dance. She allowed each of us to light his own lamp. We loved her, but the school board thought her dangerous. She defied too many official orthodoxies. She did not use tests and grades, and she was against punishment. She did not believe that academic achievement necessarily leads to individual fulfillment, or even to financial success.

" 'Stupid idiot!'
" 'Silly fool!'
" 'Dumb Blockhead!'
"Like a rattlesnake, he always had fresh venom. He used to tell us that in his mind he had a picture of a perfect pupil. Compared to this brainchild, we were a dismal disappointment. We were 'ignorant illiterates' wasting professional time and public money. His relentless diatribes undercut our self-respect and ignited our hatred. When he finally fell ill, the whole class celebrated in Thanksgiving."
"As long as I live I'll loathe my English teacher. He was the meanest man I knew before I was ten. He was a master of the double insult."

"What angered me most about our French teacher was his partiality toward some students. He had different laws for rich and poor, powerful and meek. Physical punishment was reserved for the weak and defenseless. The rich children were never smacked; he treated them with deference. It was obvious that he feared their parents. The poor had no such protection. In his eyes we were white trash, undeserving of common courtesy. He resented having to teach us. He was too good for the common people."

"Then I met Mr. Benjamin, my sixth-grade teacher. He was different. He delighted in our company. In his presence, we felt important; what we thought made a difference. He believed in us and guided us, appealing to our pride and imagination. 'The world needs your talents,' he would assure us. 'There is suffering and sickness and slums. You can be your brother's keeper or his killer. You can bring hell or help. You are each other's agents of agony or of comfort. In every situation, you can become part of the solution, or part of the problem.' His words still ring true in my heart and affect my life for the better."

"Our biology teacher was a most memorable man. He was a scientist whose credo was 'Scientific progress *not* at the expense of humanity.' His reverence for life radiated into his daily dealings with students. His lessons were a delight — he was fresh and funny and devoid of sarcasm. He was the dramatic opposite of the antiseptic teacher who preached peace in the world while creating dissension in the classroom."

"Mr. Jacobs won our hearts, because he treated us as though we were already what we could only hope to become. Through his eyes we saw ourselves as capable and decent and destined for greatness. He gave direction to our longings and left us with the conviction that our fate can be forged by our hopes and deeds; that our lives need not be shaped by accident; that our happiness does not depend upon happenstance. Mr. Jacobs introduced us to ourselves. We learned who we were and what we wanted to be. No longer strangers to ourselves, we felt at home in the world.

Dr. Haim Ginott is also the author of *Group Psychotherapy with Children*; of *Between Parent and Child*; and of *Between Parent and Teenager*.

FACULTY

LOUNGE

students

E
V
A
L
U
A
T
E

their
teachers

I first must say that I have thoroughly enjoyed this class. During this year, I have learned how to really express myself without feeling inferior. Without the feeling that the teacher wasn't even listening to what I have to say no matter how trite it may be.

I liked the loose classroom atmosphere because you had the feeling you could say anything that you wanted. You didn't have to be afraid that if you said something that wasn't right everyone would laugh at you. Also something which I liked in your classroom was that you didn't have to be afraid to disagree with the teacher. In so many of my past classes kids would keep quiet if they didn't agree with the teacher because they were afraid it would affect their marks.

On the whole I enjoyed this year a great deal and I feel I've also learned something, which I can honestly say is more than what I've done in other classes.

If only a few more people would be more open, loose and unafraid to express their ideas more would be accomplished. Our study on humor and what actually made people laugh was great. I really began to understand what made people tick. On the whole it was an interesting and thought provoking year filled with many more worthwhile topics.

I found our class on the whole beneficial as well as enjoyable, due to the loose classroom atmosphere. I have learned much more in this way than I would have if I was "under pressure," or in a stiff, unflexible daily routine class, which to me would be very boring. My independent study has proven to me that I *can* read on my own, and enjoy it. Before, I would only read a book unless I had to.

SILENCE MAKES THE HEART GROW LOUDER

bud church

... The bell for the class hadn't rung yet. Ron was outside the door talking quickly to the students as they entered the room. Each one nodded his head. Some smiled a little. Something was up.

I casually pressed myself against the wall and worked my way near the door. "Don't say anything, even if Mr. Church calls on you." Ron was telling them. So that was it. An old trick on teachers. And a neat one. Every teacher deserves to have it happen now and then.

The class sat down and looked at me, absolutely quiet. The bell blasted for a second, then died. No one stirred. I stood in the center of the semicircle I taught in, saying nothing. I slowly turned my head studying each stiff face a few seconds, looking for a crack. No one flinched. They had me.

Well, time to go to PLAN B, as my colleagues in the car pool put it when our wives suddenly decide they all need a car the same day. I sat in an empty seat in the semicircle and waited. I waited, and they waited. And it was perfectly still. I had never experienced such a calm. I confess I couldn't take it. Suddenly I went to the board and without looking at any of them wrote: "Silence is beautiful." Then I sat down with them.

A girl was looking at me curiously, a girl who never contributed much to class, who was considered dull-average. On an impulse I tossed the chalk to her. She looked at it a second, and I waited for her to scoff and throw it back. But she didn't. She went to the board and slowly wrote something like "I don't like to talk." As she was walking to her seat a boy jumped up and grabbed the chalk from her and wrote under my sentence, "That's a lot of crap." He placed the chalk on a desk. It didn't sit there long. Ron jumped forward and swept up the chalk with a deft movement as he skipped past the desk toward the board.

I don't exactly remember what was put up, but every member of that class put something on the board. Many put several things. Two dozen different kinds of handwritings — tiny cursive scrawls, bold square manuscript, sweeping loops of letters, one written painfully upside down, others in circles and mushrooms and rainbows. A few were obviously connected in a chalky conversation; others were just scraps of poems or song verses or graffiti. Never a word was spoken.

The end of the period came. We were at a high anyway. Every bit of board was covered. There was much crammed in, for reading between the lines. The students left as quietly as they had come. I'm not sure how long it was before I said anything to anyone. When I did the words came stumbling·and harsh.

The teacher in me wasn't able to let such precious possibilities rest. I had to try it on a class. That, I knew, would be another bucket of bullfrogs altogether. Contrived, artificial, phoney — it would only work once, I warned myself; but I pushed the advice away as teachers so often do, determined to ruin a good thing if I must.

I selected an entirely different kind of class, an advanced class, the hot-shots of the school — always talking, always testing and parrying and stumping and in general flapping their verbal banners in front of their squads of studied reflections.

They came in jabbering, some arguing about whether student council really was a viable force in the school and others convinced that Hamlet's problem was Freudian and even Shakespeare probably didn't know it.

When the bell rang they obeyed smoothly, turning with rapt attentiveness to the business of the class. I looked at the students carefully, touching the eyes of each one briefly, then went and sat among them. I said nothing. They waited. It was always my move in this class for then they'd know how to gauge a successful response, (something they were masters at for they had spent eleven years learning it). I at least had that going for me. This time it was my conspiracy.

Finally I gave the chalk to a girl conspicuously two desks away from me. She took it. It was very quiet. She sensed that breaking the silence was inappropriate, for even advanced students underneath all those years of achievement are sensitive human beings. I didn't look at her. Finally she went to the board and wrote, "I don't know why, but I know how." She brought the chalk back to me. I gave it to someone else. He went up and wrote, "What is the sound of one hand clapping," stolen but appropriate. Then it happened again, all over the board — in corners, at angles, shared thoughts and private quips, anger and tenderness. A few in this class, unlike the other one, didn't go up (which says something, I think, in its silent way). I joined in, too, answering a comment I couldn't resist, or just balancing out the composition with smudges of chalk in empty spaces.

In the last ten minutes of this class we talked about it. It's funny how that had to happen. No one really wanted to, but I told them what had occurred in the other class and none of them told me to shut up; and they, too, couldn't help but verbally reflect on the experience. It was kind of a shame.

Something similar happened the next time I tried it. A friend of mine, David Kranes in the English Department at the University of Utah, had arranged for me to visit the University to talk about teaching. Most of my role was informal. I went from class to class, usually made up of undergraduates, getting feedback about how they looked at the years of schooling they had gone through, sharing some of my frustrations at getting kids to be more alive, and in general elated by the responsiveness of these young people to the prospect of education in America being someday something more than eulogized drudgery.

One evening over beers I told Dave about the silent lessons, and he urged me to try it in one of his classes. So the next day Dave introduced me to the group he had selected, mumbling something about how I was going to take the class for the period, and I got up and went to the board. I looked out at the class for a minute, scattered around an old biology room in which the seats were bolted to the floor in ancient rows, and then I wrote: "I am Mr. Church. 'Bud' will do. Who are you?" I picked out a coed who looked both alert and pretty and walked over to her seat and gave her the chalk. She got up, more on reflex than anything else, and I sat in her place. She went slowly to the board, paused for a moment, then wrote, "I'm Theresa. What's going on?"

She came back to me and gave me the chalk. I got up. Everyone was watching me closely. No one had spoken. I walked way to the back of the room and gave the chalk to a boy sprawled over two or three chairs. He got up as casually as he had been sitting and shuffled up to the board and wrote."I'm suspicious." Then he came back and gave me the chalk.

So this one was going to be a chess game for awhile, I thought, moves between me and the class. Well, that's the college game, so let's play it. I gave the chalk to another girl. She wrote, "I'm Shauna, but I'm suspicious too." She gave the chalk back to me. I went up and wrote, "Is everyone at U. of U. suspicious? All I want to do is get to know you." I left the chalk up in the front of the room this time. Without much pause a boy went up and wrote, "I'm not suspicious but I'm curious." Another boy took the chalk and wrote, "I'm curious, too, about why we don't use the board on the other wall? The next person went to the board on the other wall. Before we were through most of the board space on both walls was filled up, and arrows were drawn all over, including across a painted wall from one board to the other.

Finally a boy got up and stomped up to the chalk board and began collecting all the chalk, even an almost full box of it that was on a table. Then climbing over chairs and desks he went in a straight line for an open window, extended his hands out of it ceremoniously, and dumped every piece of chalk down two stories on whatever was below.

The class laughed heartily but no one said a word. A boy near me wrote on a piece of paper, "Can we continue with pencil and paper?" and passed it to me. As I was writing, "Go ahead!" Dave jumped up and found one tiny stub of chalk on the floor that had been missed, a piece bigger in diameter than length. He hastily wrote on the board, "What the hell is going on!" I went over to a far corner of one of the boards and wrote, 'Make Love, Not Grades." Meanwhile the paper was going around the room, and other students took the scrap of chalk and were still going, ignoring my attempt to be cute, picking up more thoughtful or witty threads.

Finally Dave interrupted. He felt that in the final ten minutes the class ought to know me and how all this had started. The class was upset at the interference. This college class was upset! It was beautiful. They didn't care about who I was, at least not via the noises we call "speech." They felt that the sounds of words were flat after what had gone on. We looked at the board. Again, all kinds of messages were there for him who had eyes to see. As one boy put it, for the first time in his experience in a college class he felt he had gotten to know the anonymous students who sit around him, the ones with whom he had engaged in classroom skirmishes but seldom communication, as well as the ones who never spoke. Their walks to the board, their handwriting, the look in the eyes after as they walked back, the set of their mouths, said things. Something had sprung open in unique messages. The students were almost sad when it ended. So was I.

I teach fourth grade now. Naturally I have tried the silent treatment. It came one day when I had put a four line poem on an overhead transparency and had projected it on the screen at the beginning of the class without saying anything. I simply put it up there for them to read aloud, to comment on if they wished, to wonder about. I hadn't planned to do anything but that for a minute or two, perhaps fielding questions if they had any, but in general just starting off the morning.

But it became silent very quickly, and stayed that way. Each student read it to himself and then waited. And I wondered, do I dare try? I went to the board and wrote: What word do you like best in the poem?" Hands went shooting up, and even a couple of words were called out, but I went to a boy and gave him the chalk and sat in an empty chair. He got up and went to the board without any hesitation and wrote, "Dragon." I went up and wrote "Why" and he wrote, "Because it's neat." By then some students were asking each other if I had laryngitis, and some students were clamoring about wanting the chalk so they could write

on the board, and I wrote, "Mark, would you be willing to read the poem aloud?" He did. One boy was very confused and kept asking, "Why isn't he talking?" I gave the chalk to him. He shook his head and gave it back. I think he was sorry later.

I turned off the overhead and wrote on the board a question I had gotten from somewhere: "Which are you more sure of, tomorrow or gravity?" A boy named Jimmy Holman, an itchy boy who finds it hard at any time to stay still, darting in and out of ideas and trouble, the kind our education system creates and will break or alienate before grade 8, ran up and took the chalk from me and carefully wrote, "Gravity." Then Jimmy tapped the pointer on the board and began to lecture: First I have to draw two pictures like this," ("Yes, Mr. Holman" someone chided.) and he drew one picture of a man standing on earth, and another of a man upside down above the earth. "This is gravity," he said pointing to the first one and, turning to the second, he said, "this isn't."

I still didn't say anything. When I was pressed again about why didn't I talk I went to the board, spanked Jimmy away with the pointer, and wrote, "Words are walls." "That doesn't make sense," a girl commented. I wrote, "If it makes sense to you, thumbs up. If it doesn't, thumbs down." (By now as I wrote each word on the board the class was saying it in unison.) I put my thumb up. About half the class put their thumbs up. I put my thumb down, and the other half put theirs down. So I wrote, "Can words say I love you?" A girl came up and wrote, "I love you means I love you." I guess even Gertrude Stein would be proud of that at nine years old.

THE
free
AND
happy
STUDENT

The natural, logical outcome of the struggle for personal freedom in education is that the teacher should improve his control of the student rather than abandon it. The free school is no school at all.

B.F. Skinner

His name is Emile. He was born in the middle of the eighteenth century in the first flush of the modern concern for personal freedom. His father was Jean-Jacques Rousseau, but he has had many foster parents, among them Pestalozzi, Froebel, and Montessori, down to A. S. Neill and Ivan Illich. He is an ideal student. Full of goodwill toward his teachers and his peers, he needs no discipline. He studies because he is naturally curious. He learns things because they interest him.

Unfortunately, he is imaginary. He was quite explicitly so with Rousseau, who put his own children in an orphanage and preferred to say how he would teach his fictional hero; but the modern version of the free and happy student to be found in books by Paul Goodman, John Holt, Jonathan Kozol, or Charles Silberman is also imaginary. Occasionally a real example seems to turn up. There are teachers who would be successful in dealing with people anywhere — as statesmen, therapists, businessmen, or friends — and there are students who scarcely need to be taught, and together they sometimes seem to bring Emile to life. And unfortunately they do so just often enough to sustain the old dream. But Emile is a will-o'-the-wisp, who has led many teachers into a conception of their role which could prove disastrous.

The student who has been taught *as if he were Emile* is, however, almost too painfully real. It has taken a long time for him to make his appearance. Children were first made free and happy in kindergarten, where there seemed to be no danger in freedom, and for a long time they were found nowhere else, because the rigid discipline of the grade schools blocked progress. But eventually they broke through — moving from kindergarten into grade school, taking over grade after grade, moving into secondary school and on into college and, very recently, into graduate school. Step by step they have insisted upon their rights, justifying their demands with the slogans that philosophers of education have supplied. If sitting in rows restricts personal freedom, unscrew the seats. If order can be maintained only through coercion, let chaos reign. If one cannot be really free while worrying about examinations and grades, down with examinations and grades! The whole establishment is now awash with free and happy students.

Dropping out of school, dropping out of life

If they are what Rousseau's Emile would really have been like, we must confess to some disappointment. The Emile we know doesn't work very hard. "Curiosity" is evidently a moderate sort of thing. Hard work is frowned upon because it implies a "work ethic," which has something to do with discipline.

The Emile we know doesn't learn very much. His "interests" are evidently of limited scope. Subjects that do not appeal to him he calls irrelevant. (We should not be surprised at this since Rousseau's Emile, like the boys in Summerhill, never got past the stage of a knowledgeable craftsman.) He may defend himself by questioning the value of knowledge. Knowledge is always in flux, so why bother to acquire any particular stage of it? It will be enough to remain curious and interested. In any case the life of feeling and emotion is to be preferred to the life of intellect; let us be governed by the heart rather than the head.

The Emile we know doesn't think very clearly. He has had little or no chance to learn to think logically or scientifically and is easily taken in by the mystical and the superstitious. Reason is irrelevant to feeling and emotion.

And, alas, the Emile we know doesn't seem particularly happy. He doesn't like his education any more than his predecessors liked theirs. Indeed, he seems to like it less. He is much more inclined to play truant (big cities have given up enforcing truancy laws), and he drops out as soon as he legally can, or a little sooner. If he goes to college, he probably takes a year off at some time in his four-year program. And after that his dissatisfaction takes the form of anti-intellectualism and a refusal to support education.

Are there offsetting advantages? Is the free and happy student less aggressive, kinder, more loving? Certainly not toward the schools and teachers that have set him free, as increasing vandalism and personal attacks on teachers seem to show. Nor is he particularly well disposed toward his peers. He seems perfectly at home in a world of unprecedented domestic violence.

Is he perhaps more creative? Traditional practices were said to suppress individuality; what kind of individuality has now emerged; Free and happy students are certainly different from the students of a generation ago, but they are not very different from each other. Their own culture is a severely regimented one, and their creative works — in art, music, and literature — are confined to primitive and elemental materials. They have very little to be creative with, for they have never taken the trouble to explore the fields in which they are now to be front-runners.

Is the free and happy student at least more effective as a citizen? Is he a better person? The evidence is not very reassuring. Having dropped out of school, he is likely to drop out of life too. It would be unfair to let the hippie culture represent young people today, but it does serve to clarify an extreme. The members of that culture do not accept responsibility for their own lives; they sponge on the contributions of those who have not yet been made free and happy — who have gone to medical school and become doctors, or who have become the farmers who raise the food or the workers who produce the goods they consume.

These are no doubt overstatements. Things are not that bad, nor is education to be blamed for all the trouble. Nevertheless, there is a trend in a well-defined direction, and it is particularly clear in education. Our failure to create a truly free and happy student is symptomatic of a more general problem.

The illusion of freedom

What we may call the struggle for freedom in the Western world can be analyzed as a struggle to escape from or avoid punitive or coercive treatment. It is characteristic of the human species to act in such a way as to reduce or terminate irritating, painful, or dangerous stimuli, and the struggle for freedom has been directed toward those who would control others with stimuli of that sort. Education has had a long and shameful part in the history of that struggle. The Egyptians, Greeks, and Romans all whipped their students. Medieval sculpture showed the carpenter with his hammer and the schoolmaster with the tool of his trade too, and it was the cane or rod. We are not yet in the clear. Corporal punishment is still used in many schools, and there are calls for its return where it has been abandoned.

A system in which students study primarily to avoid the consequences of not studying is neither humane nor very productive. Its by-products include truancy, vandalism, and apathy. Any effort to eliminate punishment in education is certainly commendable. We ourselves act to escape from aversive control, and our students should escape from it too. They should study because they want to, because they like to, because they are interested in what they are doing. The mistake — a classical mistake in the literature of freedom — is to suppose that they will do so as soon as we stop punishing them. Students are not literally free when they have been freed from their teachers. They then simply come under the control of other conditions, and we must look at those conditions and their effects if we are to improve teaching.

Those who have attacked the "servility" of students, as Montessori called it, have often put their faith in the possibility that young people will learn what they need to know from the "world of things," which includes the world of people who are not teachers. Montessori saw possibly useful behavior being suppressed by schoolroom discipline. Could it not be salvaged? And could the environment of the schoolroom not be changed so that other useful behavior would occur? Could the teacher not simply guide the student's natural development? Or could he not accelerate it by teasing out behavior which would occur naturally but not so quickly if he did not help? In other words, could we not bring the real world into the classroom, as John Dewey put it, or destroy the classroom and turn the student over to the real world, as Ivan Illich has recommended. All these possibilities can be presented in an attractive light, but they neglect two vital points:

(*a*) No one learns very much from the real world without help. The only evidence we have of what can be learned from a nonsocial world has been supplied by those wild boys said to have been raised without contact with other members of their own species. Much more can be learned without formal instruction in a social world, but not without a good deal of teaching, even so. Formal education has made a tremendous difference in the extent of the skills and knowledge which can be acquired by a person in a single lifetime.

(*b*) A much more important principle is that the real world teaches only what is relevant to the present; it makes no explicit preparation for the future. Those who would minimize teaching have contended that no preparation is needed, that the student will follow a natural line of development and move into the future in the normal course of events. We should be content, as Carl Rogers has put it, to trust

the insatiable curiosity which drives the adolescent boy to absorb everything he can see or hear or read about gasoline engines in order to improve the efficiency and speed of his "hot rod." I am talking about the student who says, "I am discovering, drawing in from the outside, and making that which is drawn in a real part of me." I am talking about my learning in which the experience of the learner progresses along the line: "No, no, that's not what I want"; "Wait! This is closer to what I'm interested in, what I need." "Ah, here it is! Now I'm grasping and comprehending what I need and what I want to know!"

Rogers is recommending a total commitment to the present moment, or at best to an immediate future.

Formal education as preparation for future rewards

But it has always been the task of formal education to set up behavior which would prove useful or enjoyable *later* in the student's life. Punitive methods had at least the merit of providing current reasons for learning things

that would be rewarding in the future. We object to the punitive reasons, but we should not forget their function in making the future important.

It is not enough to give the student advice – to explain that he will have a future, and that to enjoy himself and be more successful in it, he must acquire certain skills and knowledge now. Mere advice is ineffective because it is not supported by current rewards. The positive consequences that generate a useful behavioral repertoire need not be any more explicitly relevant to the future than were the punitive consequences of the past. The student needs current reasons, positive or negative, but only the educational policy maker who supplies them need take the future into account. It follows that many instructional arrangements seem "contrived," but there is nothing wrong with that. It is the teacher's function to contrive conditions under which students learn. Their relevance to a future usefulness need not be obvious.

It is a difficult assignment. The conditions the teacher arranges must be powerful enough to compete with those under which the student tends to behave in distracting ways. In what has come to be called "contingency management in the classroom" tokens are sometimes used as rewards or reinforcers. They become reinforcing when they are exchanged for reinforcers that are already effective. There is no "natural" relation between what is learned and what is received. The token is simply a reinforcer that can be made clearly contingent upon behavior. To straighten out a wholly disrupted classroom something as obvious as a token economy may be needed, but less conspicuous contingencies – as in a credit-point system, perhaps, or possibly in the long run merely expressions of approval on the part of teacher or peer – may take over.

The teacher can often make the change from punishment to positive reinforcement in a surprisingly simple way – by responding to the student's successes rather than his failures. Teachers have too often supposed that their role is to point out what students are doing wrong, but pointing to what they are doing *right* will often make an enormous difference in the atmosphere of a classroom and in the efficiency of instruction. Programmed materials are helpful in bringing about these changes, because they increase the frequency with which the student enjoys the satisfaction of being right, and they supply a valuable intrinsic reward in providing a clear indication of progress. A good program makes a step in the direction of competence almost as conspicuous as a token.

Programmed instruction is perhaps most successful in attacking punitive methods by allowing the student to move at his own pace. The slow student is released from the punishment which inevitably follows when he is forced to move on to material for which he is not ready, and the fast student escapes the boredom of being forced to go too slow. These principles have recently been extended to college education, with dramatic results, in the Keller system of personalized instruction.

The responsibility of setting educational policy

There is little doubt that a student can be given non-punitive reasons for acquiring behavior that will become useful or otherwise reinforcing at some later date. He can be prepared for the future. But what *is* that future? Who is to say what the student should learn? Those who have sponsored the free and happy student have argued that it is the student himself who should say. His current interests should be the source of an effective educational policy. Certainly they will reflect his idiosyncrasies, and that is good, but how much can he know about the world in which he will eventually play a part? The things he is "naturally" curious about are of current and often temporary interest. How many things must he possess besides his "hot rod" to provide the insatiable

curiosity relevant to, say, a course in physics?

It must be admitted that the teacher is not always in a better position. Again and again education has gone out of date as teachers have continued to teach subjects which were no longer relevant at any time in the student's life. Teachers often teach simply what they know. (Much of what is taught in private schools is determined by what available teachers can teach.) Teachers tend to teach what they can teach easily. Their current interests, like those of students, may not be a reliable guide.

Nevertheless, in recognizing the mistakes that have been made in the past in specifying what students are to learn, we do not absolve ourselves from the responsibility of setting educational policy. We should say, we should be *willing* to say, what we believe students will need to know, taking the individual student into account wherever possible, but otherwise making our best prediction with respect to students in general. Value judgments of this sort are not as hard to make as is often argued. Suppose we undertake to prepare the student to produce his share of the goods he will consume and the services he will use, to get on well with his fellows, and to enjoy his life. In doing so are we imposing *our* values on someone else? No, we are merely choosing a set of specifications which, so far as we can tell, will at some time in the future prove valuable to the student and his culture. Who is any more likely to be right?

The natural, logical outcome of the struggle for personal freedom in education is that the teacher should improve his control of the student rather than abandon it. The free school is no school at all. Its philosophy signalizes the abdication of the teacher. The teacher who understands his assignment and is familiar with the behavioral processes needed to fulfill it can have students who not only feel free and happy while they are being taught but who will continue to feel free and happy when their formal education comes to an end. They will do so because they will be successful in their work (having acquired useful productive repertoires), because they will get on well with their fellows (having learned to understand themselves and others), because they will enjoy what they do (having acquired the necessary knowledge and skills), and because they will from time to time make an occasional creative contribution toward an even more effective and enjoyable way of life. Possibly the most important consequence is that the teacher will then feel free and happy too.

We must choose today between Cassandran and Utopian prognostications. Are we to work to avoid disaster or to achieve a better world? Again, it is a question of punishment or reward. Must we act because we are frightened, or are there positive reasons for changing our cultural practices? The issue goes far beyond education, but it is one with respect to which education has much to offer. To escape from or avoid disaster, people are likely to turn to the punitive measures of a police state. To work for a better world, they may turn instead to the positive methods of education. When it finds its most effective methods, education will be almost uniquely relevant to the task of setting up and maintaining a better way of life.

behaving

3

Nothing so needs reforming as other people's habits. — *Mark Twain*

To be good is noble, but to teach others how to be good is nobler — and less trouble.

— *Mark Twain*

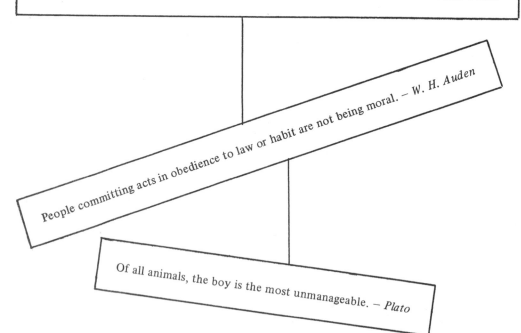

People committing acts in obedience to law or habit are not being moral. — *W. H. Auden*

Of all animals, the boy is the most unmanageable. — *Plato*

& misbehaving

My son, if sinners entice thee, consent thou not. — *Proverbs 1:10*

A little neglect may breed mischief. — *Benjamin Franklin*

The dominant trait of the students of today is their short span of attention — their inability to know or believe anything for more than half-an-hour. — *Jerzy Kosinski*

Distrust all in whom the impulse to punish is powerful. — *Friedrich Nietzsche*

FROM UP THE DOWN STAIRCASE

BEL KAUFMAN

Hi, teach!

Looka *her!* She's a teacher?

Who she?

Is this 304? Are you Mr. Barringer?

No. I'm Miss Barrett.

I'm supposed to have Mr. Barringer.

I'm Miss Barrett.

You the teacher? You so young.

Hey she's cute! Hey, teach, can I be in your class?

Please don't block the doorway. Please come in.

Good afternoon, Miss Barnet.

Miss Barrett. My name is on the blackboard. Good morning.

O, no! A *dame* for homeroom?

You want I should slug him, teach?

Is this homeroom period?

Yes. Sit down, please.

I don't belong here.

We gonna have you all term? Are you a regular or a sub?

There's not enough chairs!

Take any seat at all.

Hey, where do we sit?

Is this 309?

Someone swiped the pass. Can I have a pass?

What's your name?

My name is on the board.

I can't read your writing.

I gotta go to the nurse. I'm dying.

Don't believe him, teach. He ain't dying!

Can I sharpen my pencil in the office?

Why don't you leave the teacher alone, you bums?

Can we sit on the radiator? That's what we did last term.

Hi, teach! You the homeroom?

Pipe down, you morons! Don't you see the teacher's trying to say something?

Please sit down. I'd like to –

Hey, the bell just rung!

How come Mrs. Singer's not here? She was in this room last term.

When do we go home?

The first day of school, he wants to go home already!

That bell is your signal to come to order. Will you please –

Can I have a pass to a drink of water?

You want me to alphabetize for you?

What room is this?

This is room 304. My name is on the board: Miss Barrett. I'll have you for homeroom all term, and I hope to meet some of you in my English classes. Now, someone once said that first impressions –

English! No wonder!

Who needs it?

You give homework?

First impressions, they say, are lasting. What do we base our first – Yes? Do you belong in this class?

No. Mr. McHabe wants Ferone right away.

Who?

McHabe.

Whom does he want?

Joe Ferone

Is Joe Ferone here?

Him? That's a laugh!

He'll show up when he feels like it.

Put down that window-pole, please. We all know that first impressions — Yes?

Is this 304?

Yes. You're late.

I'm not late. I'm absent.

You are?

I was absent all last term.

Well — sit down.

I can't. I'm dropping out. You're supposed to sign my Book Clearance from last term.

Do you owe any books?

I'm not on the Blacklist! That's a yellow slip. This here is a green!

Hey, isn't the pass back yet?

Quit your shoving!

He started it, teach!

I'd like you to come to order, please. I'm afraid we won't have time for the discussion on first impressions I had planned. I'm passing out —

Hey, she's passing out!

Give her air!

— Delaney cards. You are to fill them out at once while I take attendance from the Roll Book. Standees — line up in back of the room; you may lean on the wall to write. Print, in ink, your last name first, your parent's name, your date of birth, your address, my name — it's on the board — and the same upside down. I'll make out a seating plan in the Delaney Book. Any questions;

In ink or pencil?

I got no ink — can I use pencil? Who's got a pencil to loan me?

I don't remember when I was born.

Don't mind him — he's a comic.

Print or write?

When do we go to lunch?

I can't write upside down!

Ha-ha. He kills me laughing!

What do you need my address for? My father can't come.

Someone robbed my ball-point!

I can't do it — I lost my glasses.

Are these going to be our regular seats — the *radiator?*

I don't know my address — we're moving.

Where are you moving?

I don't know where.

Where do you live?

I don't live no place.

Any place. You, young man, why are you late?

I'm not even here. I'm in Mr. Loomis. My uncle's in this class. He forgot his lunch. Hi, Tony — catch!

Please don't throw — Yes, what is it?

This Mrs. Singer's room?

Yes. No. Not anymore.

Anyone find a sneaker from last term?

Hey, teach, can we use a pencil?

You want these filled out *now?*

There's chewing gum on my seat!

First name last or last name first?

I *gotta* have a pass to the Men's Room. I know my rights; this is a democracy, ain't it?

Isn't. What's the trouble now?

There's glass all over my desk from the window.

Please don't do that. Don't touch that broken window. It should be reported to the custodian. Does anyone —

I'll go!

Me! Let me go! That's Mr. Grayson — I know where he is in the basement!

All right. Tell him it's urgent. And who are you?

I'm sorry I'm late. I was in Detention.

The what?

The Late Room. Where they make you sit to make up your lateness when you come late.

All right, sit down. I mean, stand up — over there, against the wall.

For parent's name, can I use my aunt?

Put down your mother's name.

I got no mother.

Well — do the best you can. Yes, young lady?

The office sent me. Read this to your class and sign here.

May I have your attention, please. Please, class! There's been a change in today's assembly schedule. Listen carefully:

PLEASE IGNORE PREVIOUS IN-STRUCTIONS IN CIRCULAR #3, PARAGRAPHS 5 AND 6, AND FOL-LOW THE FOLLOWING:

THIS MORNING THERE WILL BE A LONG HOMEROOM PERIOD EXTEND-ING INTO THE FIRST HALF OF THE SECOND PERIOD. ALL X2 SECTIONS ARE TO REPORT TO ASSEMBLY THE SECOND HALF OF THE SECOND PER-IOD. FIRST PERIOD CLASSES WILL BEGIN THE FOURTH PERIOD, SECOND PERIOD CLASSES WILL BEGIN THE FIFTH PERIOD, THIRD PERIOD CLASS-ES WILL BEGIN THE SIXTH PERIOD, AND SO ON, SUBJECT CLASSES BEING SHORTENED TO 23 MINUTES IN LENGTH, EXCEPT LUNCH, WHICH WILL BE NORMAL.

I can't hear you — what did you say?

They're drilling on the street!

Close the window.

I can't — I'll suffocate!

This a long homeroom?

What's today's date?

It's September, stupid!

Where We Stand

A Weekly Column of Comment on Public Education

by Albert Shanker

President, United Federation of Teachers

For Many New Teachers, the First Days Are Rough

A new school year has begun in communities throughout the country. Millions of students and millions of teachers are streaming into classrooms to share the special experience of the first day. For many in both ranks, the experience will be entirely new. For some it will be a shocking one. Students attending school for the first time in their lives must adjust themselves to being part of a large group of 25, 30 or 35 — a class in which their own wishes and impulses as individuals are subject to restraints. The rules of classroom procedure make severe demands on their self-control. For some, the adjustment is painful. Painful, too — and shockingly so — will be the experience of many new teachers facing classes for the first time.

The overwhelming majority of new teachers have been looking forward eagerly to opening day as the start of their teaching careers. Most of them chose to become teachers because they themselves had enjoyed school when they were students. Their most vivid memories are of classes they attended that did well; whose students, for the most part, met the expectations of their teachers. It is their hope, as they begin their new careers, that their classes will respond similarly. Of course they have been told in their education courses at college that things will not be the same, and not to be surprised if their actual experience does not quite conform to their imaginings. But, no matter how severely they have been warned of the difficulties they may encounter, their own past experiences as students determine their expectations.

In the few days before schools open for the students, teachers attend conferences where they are deluged with clerical forms — attendance cards, roll books, health records, emergency information, fire drill procedures, milk money collection forms and what not. They are also regaled with grim messages from the school administration: "Be sure to provide for the individual needs of your students.". . ."If you are having disciplinary problems, it means that you are not motivating the students properly." The conferences usually conclude with supervisory assurances to the teachers that if they have any problems, "My door is always open."

On the weekend before meeting their classes for the first time, new teachers spend hours and hours in careful preparation of lesson plans for the first week. They look through their college course notebooks for ideas. They make trips to libraries in quest of model lesson plans. They consult more experienced teacher friends. A busy, purposeful weekend, for

they know that first impressions are important. This will be the week they have been waiting for. They are so eager to succeed.

Unfortunately, for all too many, the first day or the first week will be an acutely disheartening experience. Thirty students enter the room. The teacher writes his or her name on the blackboard — and immediately hears five or ten student voices shouting out ugly variations on the name. The teacher calls for order, and the response is a combination of noise, pranks and derisive laughter. The teacher, not yet knowing the students' names, undertakes to seat them according to some plan, so that they can be called by name. She calls out the names. Some students refuse to respond; others give a wrong identity. Disorder and pandemonium. The teacher at this moment is swept by a sense of utter helplessness — all the education, the preparation, the effort torn to shreds by pushing, howling students out of control. In her mind is the awful question, "Will I ever be able to reach them?" And there is the fear of what might happen if the principal should chance to walk by and witness the disorder. "Will I be reprimanded? Fired?" It is hard, at that moment, for the teacher not to view the students as enemies, as threats to her capacity to do the job or hold the job.

A New Approach to the Crucial First Week

Over the next few days the teacher will desperately re-study the techniques and methods learned in college, will desperately seek to recall those she benefited from in her own student days. Most of these, she finds, simply don't work. She also finds that the supervisor whose door is always open can't help much. The supervisor has a thousand jobs — adjusting schedules, signing purchase orders, dealing with parent complaints, finding new teachers to replace those who didn't show because of some last minute change of plan. Instead of teaching techniques, the new teacher, in the first few weeks, will resort to techniques of mere survival.

Such experiences are quite widespread, yet nothing is being done to minimize them. With thousands of new teachers facing this ordeal tomorrow in New York, perhaps this might be a good time to say

that next year things could be different. Perhaps, as a way of precluding the shock of sudden confrontation of new teacher and 30 nameless students on Monday morning, the first week of school could be devoted to having the students (and their parents) meet the teacher one or two at a time. When the entire class later assembles, the teacher would know each student by name and would herself seem more human to the students — not just a name on the board and a voice pleading for order. And perhaps we could find a way to provide real help and training for new teachers, on the job, during the first few weeks.

It may be that little changes like these — changes that make school more human and humane — will prove more important than some of the more radical reforms now being advocated.

Ten forty-three.
In exactly TWO MINUTES
I'll ring the
FIRST BELL and
they'll all
stand still!

All, that is, except
your potential DEVIATE!
Your fledgling REBEL!
Your incipient BOAT-
ROCKER! THEY'LL try
to move all right!
THEY'LL have to
learn the HARD
way not to move!

So I'LL SCREAM at 'em
and take their NAMES
and give them FIVE
DETENTIONS and EXTRA
HOMEWORK! NEXT time
they won't move
after the first
bell!

Because when they've
learned not to question
the FIRST BELL, they'll
learn not to question
their TEXTS! Their
TEACHERS! Their
COURSES!
EXAMINATIONS!

They'll grow up to accept
TAXES! HOUSING DEVELOP-
MENTS! INSURANCE! WAR!
MEN ON THE MOON! LIQUOR!
LAWS! POLITICAL SPEECHES!
PARKING METERS!
TELEVISION!
FUNERALS!

Non-movement
after
the first
bell is
the
backbone
of Western
Civilization!

—Something Else—
LNS

96

36 children HERBERT KOHL

I was afraid that if one child got out of my control the whole class would quickly follow, and I would be overwhelmed by chaos. It is the fear of all beginning teachers, and many never lose it. Instead they become rigid and brutal — everyone must always work or pretend to work. The pretense is fine so long as the semblance of control is maintained. Thus one finds the strange phenomena in ghetto schools of classes that seem well disciplined and at work all year long performing on tests as poorly as those that have made the fear and chaos overt.

This problem is particularly great if the children are strangers, that is if they couldn't possibly be your brothers, sisters, your own children or nieces or nephews. Then you don't know how their parents control them, and it is easy, in the grip of fear, to imagine that the children are never controlled — in fact uncontrollable. It is a short step from there to the belief that the children aren't really human at all but "animals," wild, undisciplined, formless, and chaotic. No animals are actually like that though — it is only human fear that is wild, undisciplined, formless, and chaotic. The myth of children as "animals," the fear that they may be uncontrollable, hangs over all the ghetto schools I have visited or taught in, and for a while it hung over my classroom. . . .

I have only known one successfully suppressive teacher. She taught down the hall from 6-1 and had a quiet, rigidly disciplined, clean and neat class. The first week she filtered out into other classes potential "problems," and by the second week, control was total. Her class marched in line, left the building in order, went regularly to the dental clinic, and drew nice pictures. When she retired at the end of twenty-five years, she truly felt she had done many children a great service by keeping them clean and quiet.

Fear is only overcome through risk and experimentation. As I became familiar with the children in 6-1, I became more willing to respond to the children individually and less dependent on the protection of the role of teacher. I let an insult pass and discovered that the rest of the class didn't take up the insult; I learned to say nothing when Ralph returned from pacing the halls, or when Alvin refused to do arithmetic. The children did not want to be defiant, insulting, idle; nor were they any less afraid of chaos than I was. They wanted more than anything to feel they were facing it with me and not against me. These discoveries were my greatest strength when I began to explore new things to teach the children. They were as impatient to learn something exciting as I was to find something that would excite them.

I have never solved the "discipline problem," but I no longer believe it needs solution. Children will disagree with each other and with the teacher; they will be irrational at times, and the teacher will be, too. An atmosphere must exist in the classroom where conflict, disagreement, and irrationality are accepted temporary occurrences. No child, because he defies, should thereby have to become "a defiant child," or because he refuses to work "a lazy child." Such labeling makes the classroom a harsh, unforgiving place, a world not fit for children or adults.

ART BUCHWALD

DON'T BE A PAL TO YOUR SON

PARIS

There are many different attitudes on how to treat American youth. One we heard comes from Al Capp, the cartoonist father of three, who told us:

"When I was six years old my parents put me in a clean shirt, pointed out the direction of school, and told me not to come back for eight years. They never expected to see my teachers, and the teachers never expected to see my parents. Each one had a function. My parents were supposed to feed and clothe me; my teacher was supposed to teach me how to read and write. Neither group had any effect on the other. The only thing my parents knew about my teacher was that 'she was always picking on me.' Every child's teacher was 'always picking on him.'

"My teachers graded me on arithmetic, English, history, and geography. Since I failed all of them, it was obvious I was going to be a cartoonist. But we were never graded for adjustment, emotional stability, or 'Does he get along with other children?' My parents knew I got along with other children just by virtue of the fact I came home every afternoon with a bloody nose or a black eye.

* * *

"In those days we didn't worry about emotional stability. All children were emotionally unstable. They were full of hatreds and frustrations. Wouldn't you be if you were half the size of the rest of the world and didn't have a nickel to your name?

"In my day it wasn't a question of which was the best school to send a kid to, it was which was the nearest one. All schools were good, just as all churches were good, and all teachers were good.

"We never heard of words like adjustment, environment, rejection, and community of children. Sure we were unloved. We took it for granted that it was natural for everyone to hate us. No one paid any attention to us. And we, in turn, didn't pick up our father's shotgun and wipe out the whole family.

"The child today is wise to the adult jargon, and as soon as he thinks his parents are paying any attention to him the monster swells up in him. The child who is held in proper contempt by his family is grateful for anything he gets. All he needs is food and shelter. If he's loved, he becomes drunk with power, flexes his muscles, and takes over.

"Those parents who concern themselves with their children's problems are crazy. The problems of a nine-year-old kid cannot be solved in any way except by becoming ten. The problems of a 16-year-old will only be solved by turning 17."

Mr. Capp believes that the emphasis on teen-agers has been damaging. "Teen-agers are repulsive to everybody except each other. We all know that children pass through various stages of insanity, so why try to understand them?"

"But aren't teen-agers unhappy?"

"Sure they are. Let them stay that way.

We've put too much emphasis on security. The teen-agers today have been told they have rights. Why should they have rights?

"In Europe kids have no rights. If they ever asked for any they'd get belted by their fathers. But in America, things have been switched around. Children used to try to please their parents — now the parents try to please the children.

* * *

"It is my humble belief that we should give American children something they desperately need and crave for — brutality. We must make them feel neglected, insecure, unwanted, and unloved. In return, we'll get courtesy, obedience, good scholastic records, and fewer parents will be killed. They'll be so eager to be wanted that they'll do everything in the world to please us."

"Is there anything else?"

"Yes, don't be a pal to your son. Be his father. What child needs a 40-year-old man for a friend? And forget about teaching him facts of life. There is nothing that a boy could discuss with his father that he couldn't discuss much more openly with his guttersnipe friends.

"Keep in mind we owe children nothing. We'll supply them food, shelter, and clothing only because we're gambling that some day these subhumans will turn into civilized beings and, possibly, make reasonable, honest citizens."

George Cruikshank

AGGRESSION
in the classroom

Fritz Redl

There's plenty of minor aggression in the classroom that nobody objects to. The real problem is the aggression that prevents good teaching and good classroom life. This aggression comes primarily from three areas.

First, it is an input from the home or from the community. A teen-ager gets hopping mad at his old man, but he doesn't dare let off steam until he gets to school. Now, the teacher didn't produce the aggression, but it's there and he's got to handle it.

Second, is the discharge from within. Some youngster sits there daydreaming, and all of a sudden during a wild fantasy, he thinks of

something that upsets him and he conks his neighbors on the head. None of them have done anything to him, and the teacher hasn't either. Something just burst out from within. (If youngsters are seriously disturbed, most of the aggression comes from way within, and neither they nor anyone else knows why.)

Third, the aggression is engendered right there in the classroom. It may be triggered either by what the teacher does that's right but that doesn't happen to fit the kid, or by God knows what — the kid's reaction to the group or to other kids, or to something that maybe the teacher wouldn't have done if he had stopped to think. But anyway, it's reactive to something in the environment at the moment.

Now, if I were a classroom teacher, I would like to know how much of which of those three packages is exploding before me, because it makes a difference in terms of long-range planning. It also makes some difference in terms of what to do at the moment. Most of the time we are not sure, but different sources of aggression smell different when we are confronted with them. Experienced teachers develop an uncanny skill at sensing "This is something the kid brought with him. I've got to help him recover from it before he acts it out." The outsider, though, wouldn't know.

Some aggression does not affect us directly because certain youngsters may be model pupils in the classroom, but then after school they may go out and rape or murder someone. So a youngster may be full of sick aggression without being a classroom problem.

On the other hand, there may be a great kid sitting over there who's bored stiff. He likes you a lot, but he gets mad at the fact that you bore him stiff. Finally, he's just had it, and he runs out and slams the door. A normal youngster like that whose aggression is classroom-produced is our problem. Too often, an article on aggression in the classroom concentrates on a few examples of youngsters who should have been in a mental hospital for the last 10 years anyway and ignores all the other kids who bother us.

The term *aggression* is so overused now, you've got to watch out for it. Don't ever let anybody trap you into discussing aggression without first asking him: "Listen, brother, which aggression are you talking about? What actually happened?" Because aggression has a wide range — all the way from reacting to boredom to wrestling at the wrong time in the wrong place with another pupil.

Discharge of surplus energy or of displaced needs from the home or neighborhood; loss of control in the face of seductive equipment like a slingshot or a knife or whatnot; personal battles with adults, other kids, the group, or the teacher — all these fall under the heading of aggression.

The way Joe or Jane expresses aggression, while not the end of what we're looking for, certainly should be the starting point. Unless you know what lies behind their behavior, you will have trouble knowing how to handle it. Sometimes you may understand perfectly well how come. So the question then is what do you do to help him, which is a separate matter from knowing what was cooking to begin with.

I want to give special warning here not to make aggression synonymous with violence. The two are not the same, although they are obviously related. There is a theme in violence that we can legitimately call aggression. On the other hand, not all violence comes from aggressive drives. The behavior is aggressive, but the basis may be quite different. Let me give a few illustrations of violence that does not spring from aggression.

Panic coping. A kid may get scared stiff, so scared that he doesn't know what to do anymore. So he does something violent; he tears something apart. The fact that the behavior is violent is important. But this child is not hyperaggressive; he is frightened and desperate.

The need to be heard. A frequent source of violence is the feeling that nobody listens. The child finally concludes that the only way to get someone to listen is to be violent enough. So when other avenues are blocked off, violence is a substitute for verbal and nonverbal communication.

The desire to display guts. If a kid is supposed to be tough, how can he show it? Who is going to believe it? "I'd better not let them know I'm scared. So I've got to find ways to show I'm brave." In order to do this in a peaceful life, he's got to create problems.

Demonstrating loyalty to the group code. This source of violence is not originally meant to be aggression for aggression's sake. ("If the rest of my gang thinks school is no good, I'd better show that I'm with them. So I put a thumbtack in the teacher's chair. I don't hate the teacher; too bad it's her rear that gets stung. But I'm a regular guy and I'm going to prove it.")

Risk taking – to study survival skills. For instance, how can a boy know if he can run fast enough to outrun the cop, unless he swipes something first? Or else picks a rat out of an ash can, swirls it by the tail, throws it in somebody's first-story window, and then hops over the garage roof fast before they can catch him? A kid has to know how good he is in handling a dangerous assignment.

The stink and the dust produced in the decay of group psychology. If a group suddenly gets anxious or panicky or wild or disorganized or elated or mad at each other, you get a lot of behavior that involves violence but that did not start as aggression. Although Joe and Jane may be doing something, they're not doing it as Joe and Jane but as members of a group.

Last on my list of violence that does not start with aggression but is secondary to it is, of course, *an invasion of societal turmoil from the outside.* Someone or something in the community ties a package of emotional TNT to the back of a kid and it blows up in the classroom. The kid responsible wasn't originally aggressive; he carries the whole load of community or neighborhood or subgroup aggression. As his teacher, you're just an innocent bystander. What he does has nothing to do with the way you taught him or whether you bawled him out or flunked him.

In short, there is some relationship between violence and aggression, but not a simple one. For teachers it's very important to begin to sense the difference between Joe's being loaded with personal anger at what you just did and the explosion that results when his TNT package goes off at a given time. They are different problems.

Now let me give a few abbreviated hints of what to do about various kinds of child behavior – hints that are not fancy enough to be written up much in books.

First, you sometimes need to get kids off the hook. The aggressive behavior is beginning but without having really been planned, and if you get pupils off the hook *now*, they don't have to continue. Another way of putting it is that you sometimes need to cut a contagion chain without making a big deal out of it. And in most cases knowing how to do this is very important in dealing with a normally well-behaved child as well as with a wild one.

Take Joe, for example. He's sitting over there shaking imaginary dice, and at the moment you're not too bothered. You catch his eye and he stops, but only momentarily. After a while everybody gets interested. You want to cut that contagion chain now, because if you wait another five minutes, you'll have a mass problem on your hands.

If you interfere too early, everyone thinks you're a fusspot, a dope, or chicken, and you only aggravate things. If you don't interfere at the right time, you'll have trouble. Getting Joe off the hook at the right moment will stop his behavior without a big scene, and the rest of the group will not be too heavily afflicted. This skill of cutting contagion chains without making too much of a mess is, I think, one of the most important for anybody who deals with groups.

A second important technique for the practical handling of aggression in the classroom is signal interference. Signal interference in time saves nine. Very often teachers underestimate the possibility of stopping minor forms of misbehavior quite casually before the kid gets too carried away by it. They don't take the behavior seriously, because it isn't bothersome enough. So they wait until it does get bothersome enough, and by that time the situation is tense, the kid is already off his noodle, and anything they do now will have an explosive effect.

The big problem is that most teachers lack a good inventory of preaggression signals for their pupils. In some youngsters, the signals are easy to spot. Others apparently go aggressive all of a sudden from nowhere. That's because the teacher's radar doesn't pick up their signals. But if the teacher works at it, after a while he begins to get the messages from all around the room. One kid, for example, gets glassy-eyed and sits there quietly in a certain rigid position. If the teacher goes over and taps him on the shoulder, he'll go up like a rocket. Two minutes ago, if the teacher had gone around and said, "Come on, let's start working," that would have been fine.

A good many teachers — particularly those who are new to the classroom — do not know enough about the physiological and gestural signals that indicate the work-up to aggressive behavior. Everybody with experience understands them, but conveying this understanding to the other guy is hard. Apparently we don't think it's important because we don't have any fancy lingo for it, but if I were a beginning teacher, that's the kind of information I would like to have.

If you send me a kid with an unknown aggression work-up potential, I'd like to get to know that kid and figure out what he looks like before he goes off the handle. After that, I can tell at a glance that this is the moment to go over to him.

In observing classrooms and watching teachers with disturbed youngsters, I am constantly amazed at the terrific skill people with experience develop, and they can't ever explain it. What's more, they don't even mention it. They think it isn't worth discussing.

Let me describe one incident I observed:

A kid is sitting stiffly at his desk, obviously determined that he "ain't gonna do *nothing*." The teacher walks over to him, pats him on the shoulder, and says: "Now, how about it? You don't feel so good, huh? And he doesn't say anything. What does she do then? She says: "OK, I'll come back in a while. Maybe by then you'll be feeling better." That's all. She doesn't push him. ("Why don't you . . . ? What's the matter with you? What kind of family do you come from, anyway?")

She uses her judgment, and sooner or later he's over the hump. His face clears up; his posture is relaxed. Then she comes over and puts the pencil in his hand and he starts working.

Now, number three: Watch out for the choreography of the dare. In our present society we all have an insatiable, unquenchable thirst for tribal rituals. We still perform tribal dances. Take this scene:

We have what looks like a relatively normal classroom at the moment. Here is Joe back there, who wishes I'd leave him alone. But he knows I'm a nice guy, that I've got to make a living, after all. And I'm pretty harmless, though a little crazy, maybe.

Still, somehow, the noise gets too loud, and I finally say: "Listen, you, you'd better stop that now." Then maybe things get worse; and maybe by this time I'm angry, too. So I say: "All right, now, if you can't be quiet here, why don't you go out and cool off?"

Let's assume I'm relatively lucky in my diagnosis, and the youngster gets up and moves to the door, but on the way he mumbles something under his breath. If I ask him what he said, he probably feels he has to lie — so I make a liar out of him. Or if he is decently honest, I have to send him to the principal.

The foregoing is one way the scene can be played. But it also can be played differently. If Joe is sensitive of his prestige in the group, and I happen to have adults looking over my shoulder, then both of us become involved in a tribal dance. He has to say, "Make me," and I have to say, "All right. I'll make you." So either I try to bounce him or I call the principal or whatnot. Then for three weeks, lots of procedures go on — all nonsensical and having nothing to do with the original issue. Joe's become a discipline case, almost.

What I've described here is a personal interaction, a limit-setting process of a very simple nature, really. Most of the time it works like a charm, but in the second instance it became a tribal dance. If I were a principal assigning teachers to study halls or other large groups, I would like to know how vulnerable they are to the tribal dance routine, because in a dare situation the pressure is terrific. If you send me a kid who is tough, I don't mind. But I would like to know how involved this kid is in a tribal dance.

You see, some kids who are plenty tough don't fall for that kind of nonsense. In fact, some of my best delinquents would never be so stupid as that. If I really challenged them, they would think, "All right, so let the guy have his little victory for a change. So what! So I go out. I'm tough enough. Nobody will think I gave in." If, however, the youngster isn't really tough enough, but has to pretend he is, then he has to do the tribal dance in order to impress the others with his plumage, or whatever.

This is a big danger. And many a teacher could avoid many a large discipline problem if he were able to recognize the first drum beats of a tribal dance. Very often we push relatively tough kids who mean well into tribal dances because we are unaware of the position they are in. At other times, we do not interfere when we should because we are too afraid we'll provoke a tribal dance when actually we wouldn't.

So the tribal dance is a whole phenomenon — separate from the usual problem of discipline — that is a rather deep psychological problem.

Number four: Watch out for the subsurface effect. Whatever I do also has a side effect, and it is not always visible right now. If we are aware of what else happens besides the immediate effect of what we do, we won't simply say, "Because I blamed him for being noisy or because I praised him for being quiet, everything is hunky-dory right now."

So it's important to look with one eye to the possible nonvisible side effect. I can do something about it afterwards, but only if I'm on the lookout for it. Like that boy we've been talking about. Let's say he leaves the room and doesn't start the tribal dance. In that case, I'll want to make sure we have a brief get-together afterwards to tell him that I appreciate his doing what I asked and that I'll defend his reputation with the rest of the kids. I'll say that there are no hard feelings; it was just that I couldn't let him get so loud in class. That's all; nothing more.

If you have to live with aggression, at least try not to breed it. We breed it, of course, by exposing even otherwise normal boys and girls to experiences, to space arrangements, to life situations that invariably produce inner frustration.

For instance, if I bore a youngster, I expose him to frustration. Or, if I have to delay giving help that is needed — say, a boy over there is stuck in the middle of a long division problem, and I can't get to him for a while because I have to be over here with the others. Sooner or later he's had it, and he gets mad.

Or I may breed aggression if I intervene with too little sympathy. If a youngster is doing something interesting, something he likes, do I say, "Get going this minute. Do you want to be late again?" when I could just as well say, "Look, I'm sorry to have to break that up, but you know we've got to get out now."

One final point: Don't forget that from time to time, your own aggression will start showing. As you probably are aware, your hostile feelings and how you deal with them make a story no less complex and touchy than the one just presented. That your anger may be righteous and justified is not the only issue. You must ask yourself some questions: How does my anger make me behave in the classroom? Which (if any) of the behaviors it produces in me seem helpful in reducing youngsters' aggressive feelings, and which ones just make matters worse? Figuring this out requires clear thinking and real objectivity, but it is worth the effort. Your professional obligation is to handle your own aggression in such a way that the individual pupil or the class can manage the spillover effect.

can't you hear ME talking to you?

Acting tough could sometimes help you. Acting tough could also destroy you if you didn't know. Acting tough means acting in a certain way so that you will get some respect. When you act tough usually you don't know what you are doing, maybe you go out of your mind and you do nothing but act tough.

But you can't always blame yourself for acting tough because sometimes people make you act tough. But sometimes acting tough could help you. Because for example in my school you've got to act tough to prevent fights. Because in my school if you don't act tough they think you're scare of everybody and everybody will pick on you. But acting tough could also destroy you because there is always somebody who can bring you down and if you act tough with them you're finish. So I'm gonna give you an advice watch out before you act tough.

— *Carmen*

Helping the MBD child achieve

his full potential

Here is a child who seems to get very little out of school.

He can't sit still. Doesn't take direction well. He's easily frustrated, excitable, often aggressive. And he's got a very short attention span.

The teacher may seek professional help because of his disturbing influence in the classroom. But the real tragedy is that he's simply not developing basic learning skills. And failure to learn in these early years could mean he'll never catch up.

Yet this tragic waste of human potential could be averted. For the problem is more than the mischief and hyperactivity that occur as a phase of normal growth. He is a victim of Minimal Brain Dysfunction, a diagnosable disease entity that generally responds to treatment programs.

And Ritalin can be an important part of the total rehabilitation program which includes remedial measures at home and at school. Ritalin, an effective and well-tolerated CNS stimulant, can help control hyperactivity and other symptoms that so often beset the MBD child.

Of course, Ritalin is not indicated for childhood personality and behavior disorders not associated with MBD.

Ritalin®
(methylphenidate)
when medication is indicated

Drug Dependence
Ritalin should be given cautiously to emotionally unstable patients, such as those with a history of drug dependence or alcoholism, because such patients may increase dosage on their own initiative.

Chronically abusive use can lead to marked tolerance and psychic dependence with varying degrees of abnormal behavior. Frank psychotic episodes can occur, especially with parenteral abuse. Careful supervision is required during drug withdrawal, since severe depression as well as the effects of chronic overactivity can be unmasked. Long-term follow-up may be required because of the patient's basic personality disturbances.

PRECAUTIONS
Patients with an element of agitation may react adversely; discontinue therapy if necessary. Periodic CBC and platelet counts are advised during prolonged therapy.

ADVERSE REACTIONS
Nervousness and insomnia are the most common adverse reactions but are usually controlled by reducing dosage and omitting the drug in the afternoon or evening. Other reactions include: hypersensitivity (including skin rash, urticaria, fever, arthralgia, exfoliative dermatitis, and erythema multiforme with histopathological findings of necrotizing vasculitis); anorexia; nausea; dizziness; palpitations; headache; dyskinesia; drowsiness; blood pressure and pulse changes, both up and down; tachycardia; angina; cardiac arrhythmias; abdominal pain; weight loss during prolonged therapy. In children, loss of appetite, abdominal pain, weight loss during prolonged therapy, insomnia, and tachycardia may occur more frequently. Toxic psychosis has been reported.

DOSAGE AND ADMINISTRATION
Children with Minimal Brain Dysfunction (6 years and over)
Start with small doses (eg, 5 mg before breakfast and lunch) with gradual increments of 5 to 10 mg weekly. Daily dosage above 60 mg is not recommended. If improvement is not observed after appropriate dosage adjustment over a one-month period, the drug should be discontinued.

If paradoxical aggravation of symptoms or other adverse effects occur, reduce dosage, or, if necessary, discontinue the drug.

Ritalin should be periodically discontinued to assess the child's condition. Improvement may be sustained when the drug is either temporarily or permanently discontinued.

Drug treatment should not and need not be indefinite and usually may be discontinued after puberty.

HOW SUPPLIED
Tablets, 20 mg (peach, scored); bottles of 100 and 1000.
Tablets, 10 mg (pale green, scored); bottles of 100, 500, 1000 and Strip Dispensers of 100.
Tablets, 5 mg (pale yellow); bottles of 100, 500, and 1000.

Consult complete product literature before prescribing.

CIBA Pharmaceutical Company
Division of CIBA-GEIGY Corporation
Summit, New Jersey 07901   2/4734-1

HIGH SCHOOL VANDALIZED

WINDSOR LOCKS — Police are investigating a break at the high school, South Elm Street, apparently committed sometime Sunday night or Monday morning.

Police said entrance to the school was gained through a broken window and at least four classrooms were ransacked, apparently in search of money. No major vandalism was reported.

Classrooms entered were located in the woodworking shop, the audio-visual department and distributive education department. The school store operated under the distributive education program was also entered.

Since schools were closed Monday for the holiday, police are awaiting the return of teachers to determine what items might have been taken.

109

WORK PUNISHMENT ASKED FOR VANDALS

NORWICH – Youngsters found guilty of damaging school property should be required to "swing a broom" in the school system as part of their punishment.

That's the feeling of Schools Supt. John M. Moriarty who said no useful purpose is served "only if parents pay the bill for the damage."

Moriarty contends that offenders should "lose some of their leisure time and it's up to the court to see that this is done."

His comments came after a report by John Caulfield, director of maintenance for the school department, on window breakage in city schools.

He estimated the loss so far this school year at about $4,000.

And, he has told the Board of Education, there were years when the total for glass damage did not exceed $600.

Caulfield said, "It's mostly young children that are involved." He said ages range from "six to 15."

In some cases, he said, welfare families are involved "and they don't have the money to pay for the damage."

Moriarty said, "we can't condone what is being done. Young people can drive at 16 . . . they now vote at 18 . . . it's not right to give them the easy way out in vandalism cases where someone pays the bill."

"People in the city who are paying taxes are paying enough for schools." he said "They should have some protection against these extra costs . . ."

Moriarty said he will look to judges to provide for work programs for offenders "regardless of what the labor laws say."

"Youngsters are able to swing a broom at 13 or 14," he commented.

At the suggestion of Edward Seder, a school board member, a suggestion in line with Moriarty's remarks will be sent to juvenile court officials.

A HANDBOOK

FOR TEACHING

IN THE

GHETTO SCHOOL

Sidney Trubowitz

Mr. M.'s start in the classroom was a combination of frustration, trauma, and learning. He described his initial meeting with the class as follows:

"The first day alone in the classroom I was so frightened it was amazing. And after each day for those first few weeks I can honestly say that I went home every afternoon muttering to myself that I wasn't coming back to that nonsense the next day. It used to take me until ten or eleven to unwind each night.

"I can remember trying to get the class down the stairway at three o'clock. It was unbelievable. They just wouldn't listen. They weren't hearing me. When I told them to stop at the landing, they ran around, they yelled things at me. They were out of the building before I knew it. I was just some guy up there saying some words. I said to myself, 'Hey, I'm your teacher.' I couldn't believe it. It was so frustrating. I didn't know what to do. I tried having them do it over. I tried keeping them in. I stood at the front of the line, at the end of the line, in the middle. Nothing worked.

"What helped? It improved when they got to know me as a person. They responded to me after I played ball with them, after I took one of the kids to buy a pair of sneakers on 125th Street, after I broke up a couple of fights."

Mr. M. had sufficient resources to overcome the shock of these initial encounters with the class and to look at the causes of his difficulty. He saw that his lack of knowledge and his inexperience contributed to the trouble he was having. He began to make changes. He described what happened in these words:

"I didn't have the routines set in my mind. I had even forgotten how to say the pledge to the flag. Every kind of movement was rough. I didn't know how to get the kids to hang up their coats. Distributing books was a problem. I had to work on getting the routines set in my mind.

"What helped was becoming more myself. I didn't lose the structure, but the way I gave directions changed. I stopped playing the sergeant. I became more natural and yet the structure was there.

"There was a period in which they tested me out. One day about five of them broke their pencil points and they started to go to the pencil sharpener one at a time. This was putting it up in front of me. I just casually walked over to one of them at the sharpener and took his pencil, not even stopping my talking as I did it. I had been told about being tested, so I didn't blow my cork.

"Another day one of the boys came over to talk to me with his hat on. I told him I wouldn't talk to him with his hat on. He got his back up and walked away. I didn't get excited. He came back later without his hat on."

Mr. M. sought curriculum approaches which would allow him to maintain effective control of the class and at the same time interest the children. "A trouble spot for me was handling transitions from one subject to the other. At first what I tried to do was give a brief introduction to the importance of the subject we were going to study. After a while I discovered a better way: to have each lesson grow out of the one before. For example, we'd move from a study of the prices of things in the stores to looking at transportation and how food came to New York from other parts of the country and the world.

"One of the hardest things was to have the children see the relationship between school and what happens in their own lives. I was forever on the lookout for opportunities to do this. For example, when someone talked about a policeman pushing someone around, I used this to move into a discussion of how they think a policeman feels working in the neighborhood. We went on to find out about civil service, about how someone gets to be a policeman, the preparation he needs, the salary he gets. When they began to see the whole scope of what it takes to be a policeman, it was a small start on changing their attitudes toward the cop on the corner."

The Way It

James Herndon

7H came charging and whooping up the stairs from where they had been studying mathematics with Mr. Brooks. Later I came to recognize their particular cries coming up my way. There's Roy, I'd think, there Harvey, there Vincent, Alexandra, picking their sounds out of the general outcry of the student body with a mixture of admiration and dread. 7H dashed in, flung themselves into seats and as quickly flung themselves out again. If 9D was willing to ignore me until doomsday, 7H didn't. They scattered from seat to seat, each trying to get as much free territory around him as possible, jumping up again as the area got overcrowded and ranging out to look for breathing space like Daniel Boone. From the seats, wherever they were, they confronted me with urgent and shouted questions, each kid, from his claim of several empty desks, demanding my complete attention to him: Are you a strict teacher? You going to make us write? When do we get to go home? Where our books? Our pencils? Paper? You going to give us them spellers? They were all finally outshouted by Roy, a boy about five feet six or seven inches tall with tremendous shoulders and arms, who stood in front of my desk, obscuring the view for all the rest, and just laughed as loud as he could for perhaps two minutes. Then he

stopped and told everyone to shut up, because he knew this teacher wanted to take the roll. After some more shouting I finally did call it, listed the names of those absent on absence slips and clipped them to the wall over the door where a monitor from the office was to pick them up. I went back to my desk, wondered if I ought to pass out pencils (I'd learned something), thought a bit about books, and decided to give out some spellers.

At that moment there came a tremendous outcry from over by the door. I looked over and three or four kids were standing there, looking up at the door and yelling their heads off. Naturally the rest of the class soon began shouting insults at them, without any idea of what the trouble was. Everyone was standing up; calls of "watermelon-head!" filled the room. The kids by the door wheeled and rushed up to me, furious and indignant. Vincent, who was one of them was crying. What the hell? I began to yell in turn for everyone to shut up, which they soon did, not from the effect of my order but out of a desire to find out what was the matter; they sat back to hear the story. The four were Roy, Harvey, Vincent and Alexandra, and what they demanded to know was why had I put their names up there on those absence slips? They weren't absent! Was I trying to get

114

SpOzEd TO Be

them into trouble? We here, Mr. Hern-don! They didn't want to get in no trouble! Alexandra began to threaten me with her mama. Roy, tempted beyond his own indignation, began to make remarks about the color and hair quality of Alexandra's mama. It shows how upset Alexandra was; it was fatal to ever mention your mother at GW, which Alexandra of all kids knew quite well.

For a moment I thought maybe I had put the wrong names up by mistake, but I checked them and saw that wasn't so. I displayed the slips, spread out on my desk. Their names weren't there. The names on those slips were not theirs, I told them. Right? They weren't satisfied. They demanded a closer look at them slips. I handed the slips around, whereupon it became a scene out of some old movie when Stepin Fetchit turns the letter upside down and sideways before giving it to Bob Hope to read, explaining he doesn't read Chinese. The fact was, Harvey, Roy, Vincent and Alexandra were having a little trouble reading their own names.

Finally Alexandra let out a screech and started for the back of the room, where a little tiny kid, black and scrawny, jumped smoothly out of her way, grinning at her, holding onto a desk in front of him ready to jump again. Alexandra was demanding something from him;

she was joined by Roy *et al*; and I finally made out that they were calling on him to verify my statement about their names and the slips. He wasn't doing that, apparently, so they all rushed back to me. All four now shouted that Virgil had told them their names were up there on them slips and they were getting into trouble for cutting school. The first day! The class began to hoot all over again. I started for Virgil, who left his chair and sped over by the windows.

I sped after him. Whooo-eee! Everything was great! Right away I saw I wasn't about to catch Virgil — I'd had some idea about making him recant in public — and stopped. Virgil promptly dashed out the door.

Just about then the monitor came along for the slips and I collected them and handed them over. The four kids still stood there. Were they in trouble or weren't they? They didn't know for sure, but probably they did know what they were up against here all of a sudden, just as I suddenly knew what I was going to be up against. As the monitor was leaving, a water bomb made from a folded sheet of school paper came flying through the open transom and exploded on the floor in the front of the room.

DISCIPLINARY REFERRAL
To be used only for serious discipline and class attendance cases.

Name _Michael Benton_ Home Room _317_ Class _9-14_

Sent to Office for _Insubordination, disturbing the class. Refuses to remain silent. Must have the last word. Comes on strong, using foul language to students and to me._

Signed _Ellen Fisher_

Do not write below this line

Disposition _Parental conference arranged for 9/21 at 10 a.m._

............TO BE DETACHED BY OFFICE ONLY............

This part to be returned to _Mrs. Fisher_
Teacher

Mike Benton _9/20/74_
Student's Name Date

Disposition _Talked with Mike and his mother. She is scheduled to meet with us tomorrow at 10 a.m. during your free time. Please plan to be with us._

By _J. Oliver_

17 PRECEPTS FOR CLASSROOM CONTROL...

Bernard Packin

1. *Set your standards early.* Good classroom control is established during the first days — in fact, during the first minutes — of school. Try to set this atmosphere by example, rather than by establishing a long list of "do's and don't's." Settle the first few incidents which arise quickly and firmly.

2. *Teach an interesting, varied lesson.* Involve the students in group work, panels and other activities. Teachers who talk and lecture a great deal are apt to become boring — whether they realize it or not. When students are busy, interested and satisfied they will rarely cause serious problems.

3. *Let students know you like them.* Good disciplinarians give children a feeling they are liked. Good teachers — like good parents — can still transmit this affection even when they find it necessary to reprimand children.

4. *Cultivate a pose which is friendly but which demands respect.* This manner may not come naturally to a beginning teacher, but it should be worked at diligently. Just as a clergyman can invoke feelings of warmth and respect, so should a teacher work for a similar relationship with his class. The teacher's demeanor should be firm but fair.

5. *Try to emphasize the positive.* Provide each child with some sort of success experiences. The old bromide that "nothing succeeds like success" is an integral part of good discipline. Students who consistently face failure will become dissatisfied. Such discontent leads to problems.

6. *Make your disciplinary actions quick, consistent, just, constructive — and inevitable.* Students understand and accept quick and fair action. They respect a predictable and consistent course of action. Actions that are deemed unacceptable by the teacher on Monday should also be deemed unacceptable by the teacher on Friday. Try to avoid threats — especially empty threats. But if you have threatened a pupil, be prepared to follow through. Students are perceptive enough to see through a bluff quickly.

7. *Avoid group punishment like the plague.* Group punishment — that is, the punishment of the many for the misdeeds of the few — is rarely, if ever, justified. Punish offenders, not the innocent.

8. *Do not humiliate students nor use sarcasm.* One can punish effectively without the use of sarcasm. When a child is humiliated or backed into a corner psychologically, he will lash back since, having lost self-respect in front of the class, he has little more to lose.

9. *Avoid using school grades as a threat.* Misbehavior may often influence a student's academic performance. But a teacher's threatening to lower grades as a means of punishment does not build good discipline.

10. *Know the background and problems of each child.* Students who are habitual

117

troublemakers may be socially and emotionally maladjusted. Such problems are often environmental, sometimes organic. Get to know the parents and home situation of problem children as soon as possible. Use your cumulative files immediately and refer recurrent problems to the appropriate personnel.

11. *Involve the parents of students who constantly misbehave.* Call in parents of troublemaking students for a conference (if this procedure is not contrary to your school policy). Such a meeting often contributes to the teacher's understanding of the child and his home. It also provides a way by which the teacher can enlist parental cooperation for solving problems readily. Many parents are only too happy to cooperate.

12. *Keep a simple record of incidents committed by recurrent offenders.* The simple technique of recording dates and incidents of recurrent offenders on an ordinary 3 x 5 card is an invaluable administrative technique. While the mind forgets, the card does not. This information proves useful in case of later referral to parents, the principal, the school psychologist or to other personnel.

13. *Have students write out a report on more serious infractions.* Such sheets prove helpful in dealing with a skeptical parent. They also provide a valuable cooling-off period for both the student and the teacher.

14. *Cultivate your own special disciplinary techniques.* A stern look or an effective pause are effective techniques used by many teachers. I have found code signals handy. In my school gum chewing is forbidden, so I give a person-to-person reminder by sign language. I rapidly close and open by thumb and forefinger imitating jaw motion. Then like a baseball umpire calling out the runner, I motion with my thumb toward the waste basket. If I wait until I catch the eye of the offender before giving my signal, I need not interrupt the rest of the class.

15. *Do not assign extra school work as punishment.* The teacher who assigns extra pages of homework as punishment may cause students to dislike the subject matter. This practice tends to defeat one of the teacher's main aims — the development of a love of learning. If the student comes to dislike the subject, he may indeed become a serious problem to the teacher.

16. *Use the principal as a resource person before problems get out of hand.* The role of the principal as disciplinarian has its place. But personally I prefer the role of the principal as a teacher-helper in problems of classroom management. As such he can do much to help the teacher implement the concept of preventive discipline.

17. *Know yourself.* Take a good look at yourself and your teaching procedures from time to time. Do not take out your own personal problems on your pupils. Realize your limitations, and try to correct them. Above all, bring to the school an honest feeling of liking for your work. This "mirror viewpoint" will bring you more understanding of your role as an educator.

can't you hear me talking to you?

my class has so many teachers that I would say you wouldn't like to see how the kids behave. They are horrible. They behave like animals. They jump and throw chairs across the room and they throw chalk at the teachers and the teacher does not do nothing. When the teachers is absent and we have a substitute the kids write on the board. They throw erasers across the room or chairs and hit the teachers. Then they bring boys from other classes. They come in and they start throwing clay on the ceiling and then it falls on whoever passes. The kids steal paper from the cabinets and right in front of the teachers and the teacher does not see them doing it so they keep on until there ain't no paper left in the closets.

Some of the kids in the school smoke. Some smoke pot and some sniff glue and I just feel like dying because that thing smells bad. They steal books and money from your coats and they break windows and they write dicks all over the blackboard and on the ceiling.

Sometimes some of the teachers start to argue and they can't stand one another and that ain't no good. And there is another riot in our school and the children did not go to school yesterday in the afternoon. Today I did not go to school because they won't let you in. Just because the Principal did not leave the white boy finish the speech because he did not want him to run for President [of the student body] Then Mr. J - - - [the guidance counselor] said that Puerto Ricans and Negroes are the same that they aren't no differences so they start a riot over that. I think it's terrible because we miss more school and we get dumber each minute that passes.

That's a danger school, man. One kid in my class started to play with matches and put one in the basket inside the room and flames started to come out and we went down to the principal and he said that if there was a fire inside the school no one would know because the alarms don't work and the fuses are all blown out.

— *Dolores*

an EMPTY SPOON

absentees

SUNNY DECKER

Cutting is a huge problem at North High. The kids cut something like four thousand classes a week, which isn't so awful if you realize they're keeping a staff of four employed. The sad part of our cutting problem is that so few kids do it as a prank. They don't begin to enjoy the thrill of getting away with something, as I did. Lavell Keller was like that.

He was the littlest boy I ever saw — little and fragile. His hair and eyes and skin were all the same soft color. I don't think I ever heard him speak. He began to cut my class the second day of school. I guess he came the first day to check out my legs.

The school has an elaborate system for reporting cuts that requires poring over a list of more than a thousand names every day. I liked to think that my class was so exciting that no one would cut — and those who did would not be worthy additions anyway. So, for a month, I never even checked the list.

I woke up, of course. To the fact that, given the chance, *I* would cut even the best of classes — my record attested to that; to the fact that I was allowing kids who were begging for discipline to hang themselves; to the fact that I was lazy.

I began to check. It was hard. I had to play a match game for every absentee on my roll of two hundred students. If they were really out of school, their names would be somewhere on The List. If they weren't on it, they were cutting. For each cutter, I had to fill out a slip and send it to the petty-crimes office. It was their job to track down the offenders and discipline them appropriately. A messy process.

But before long, I got compulsive about it. I came to school early just to find out who had cut me the day before. I reported the crimes with incredible efficiency. I must have written a pound of cut slips on poor Lavell Keller.

Months passed before I realized that attendance in my classes had increased. I hadn't looked for constructive ends. I took no joy in being an authoritarian, either. It's just that once I knew a kid cut my class, my feelings got hurt — and I wanted to get him back.

It wasn't easy to wage war with Lavell. He didn't mind the detentions (you just sit there) or suspensions (a three-day holiday with the school's blessing) that the cutting office assigned him. If he'd minded, he would have come to class.

I never saw him again until March, when I was asked to patrol the cafeteria. There he was, with a hot dog in his fist.

I was pretty nice, considering the months of humiliation I'd undergone because of him. I gave him the usual spiel, and asked the usual questions. Lavell said nothing. He looked way up at me and made me feel big and gawky, so I ended my harangue with an end-of-harangue-type summation, and walked away.

One of the counselors had seen me with Lavell, and asked if there were a problem. "A problem!" I was shrieky. "He hasn't been in English class since September!"

"But my dear, of course not," she said. "Don't you see — Lavell can't read a word."

I saw. I was not the object of hostility. I was only the mirror that would show Lavell his failures. And who wants to see failure every day at nine in the morning. I didn't bother to ask how he ever got to the tenth grade, or why no one ever told me he had a problem. That's an old bureaucratic story by now.

I tried to find him in the crowded lunchroom, to tell him that I might help him if he'd give me the chance. But he'd disappeared.

Though I still got mad at kids who cut me, I was a little more careful now, about checking reasons as well as cuts, and I was a little less ruthless. And though I'd learned something from Lavell, I felt crummy about making him an object lesson.

I still think about him from time to time. He got an F in English for the year. And then he dropped out of school.

DROPOUTS ARE LOSERS! SAYS WHO?

TWO

blocks apart

I had one very good teacher, in school. He was smart, too. He's young though and maybe he doesn't know as much as the old teachers who have been around for a long time and it shows in one way. He can get very hot-tempered, you know? And when he gets hot-tempered he really wants to smash somebody, though he doesn't do anything.

I guess he gets mad that he has been studying all this time to be a teacher and there are kids there, a whole class full, that don't want to learn, and I guess everybody would get mad at that. Like if you study to be a mechanic and nobody wants to bring their car to you, then what's the use? You know?

Like sometimes, him and me, right there in the class we start discussing something back and forth about history or like that. All right, it's good; we're both swinging. But those other kids, back there, in the back of the class? They are playing around. They're throwing papers at each other, or they're cursing, or they are talking about something else, or they're sleeping.

Like in hygiene, half of the kids are asleep. Or maybe even some of them drunk even before they came to school. A kid might sit there in the back of the class and he's a little bit up, you know. He thinks he's well off, but he's not. And he comes to school on a little tightrope. And before he gets to his third class, he's *out*.

Charlotte Leon Mayerson

The Lives
of Children

GEORGE DENNISON

I don't think the five boys learned anything at all during the period just covered by the journal. As I write these words, I experience something of the same defeat I felt at the time. Yes, it would have been a mistake to force classroom instruction upon them. That had been done in the past, and their appalling ignorance was one result of it. Nor would the smallness of our group have justified rigid discipline. The boys were far too unstable for that, too liable to collapse, too ready to rebel. Perhaps a more imaginative teacher than I would have hit upon some way of engaging them. Perhaps a more experienced one would have realized at once that the disorder was inevitable, and in the long run even desirable. Yet the sense of defeat lingers on. I mention it because it seems to belong intrinsically to the experience of teaching. There are many occasions when the best one can do is unsufficient, and may even be, from the point of view of the child – and in a deep and legitimate sense – quite superfluous. One even realizes that this very sense of defeat – given the magnitude of the problems faced by such children – conceals sizable quantities of vanity and impatience. Yet there it is. In libertarian schools it will be occasioned, as it was at First Street, by a break in relations and routines. In conventional schools it will be caused by the sullen resistance accompanying all the activities pursued under compulsion, in which case the teachers' sense of defeat may endure for months or even years.

smart kids

4

It is not every question that deserves any answer. — *Publius Syrus*

Them that asks no questions isn't told a lie. — *Rudyard Kipling*

The test of a first-rate intelligence is the ability to hold two opposed ideas in the mind at the same time, and still retain the ability to function. — *F. Scott Fitzgerald*

Difficulties are things that show what men are. — *Epictetus*

I have answered three questions, and that is enough. — *Lewis Carroll*

. . . very hard the task I find. — *Louisa May Alcott*

And though hard be the task, "Keep a stiff upper lip." — *Phoebe Cary*

&dumb kids

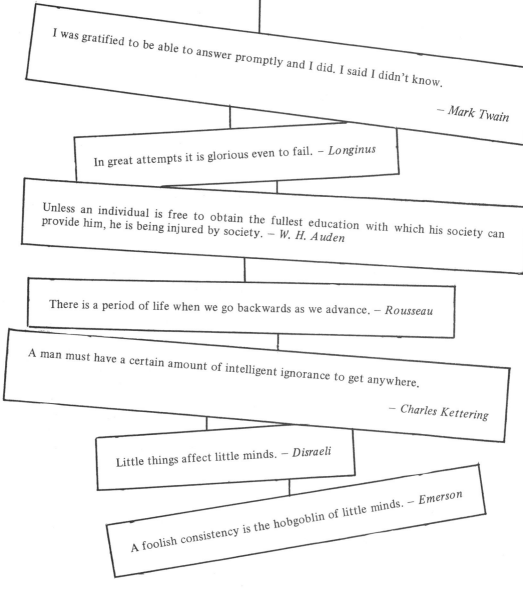

I was gratified to be able to answer promptly and I did. I said I didn't know.

— *Mark Twain*

In great attempts it is glorious even to fail. — *Longinus*

Unless an individual is free to obtain the fullest education with which his society can provide him, he is being injured by society. — *W. H. Auden*

There is a period of life when we go backwards as we advance. — *Rousseau*

A man must have a certain amount of intelligent ignorance to get anywhere.

— *Charles Kettering*

Little things affect little minds. — *Disraeli*

A foolish consistency is the hobgoblin of little minds. — *Emerson*

HOW
CHILDREN
FAIL

JOHN HOLT

Foreword

Most children in school fail.

For a great many, this failure is avowed and absolute. Close to forty percent of those who begin high school, drop out before they finish. For college, the figure is one in three.

Many others fail in fact if not in name. They complete their schooling only because we have agreed to push them up through the grades and out of the schools, whether they know anything or not. There are many more such children than we think. If we "raise our standards" much higher, as some would have us do, we will find out very soon just how many there are. Our classrooms will bulge with kids who can't pass the test to get into the next class.

But there is a more important sense in which almost all children fail: Except for a handful, who may or may not be good students, they fail to develop more than a tiny part of the tremendous capacity for learning, understanding, and creating with which they were born and of which they made full use during the first two or three years of their lives.

Why do they fail?

PROGRAMS

Sixteen in Webster Groves - WCBS TV

KURALT   "What do you worry about?" we asked the 16-year-olds of Webster Groves. Ninety-six percent answered, "What we worry about is getting good grades."

MRS. KOONS   This test is a six weeks' test and as far as I'm concerned this counts a third of your six weeks' grade. Your daily work counts two-thirds and this counts a third.

KURALT   To get a good job, they feel they must go to college. To reach college, they feel they must pass every test. To pass every test, a majority affirms, they will do anything.

BRIAN FAHEY   To many people, the pressures of school and from their parents to get these grades — the grades become all important. They have to get it. It's a drive. It's — it's not so much that they understand what the drive is; it's just that they've been told, this is what to do. And to many people, the pressure is just too much. They have to cheat, they feel, to get the good grades, to stay up with — with whoever's ahead of them.

KURALT   Fifty-four percent admit they have cheated in order to pass a test.

KIPSY WEISENFELS   You study for them and you're trying your hardest and you get flustered and then everything seems to go wrong and you start worrying about the tests and you start worrying about whether you're going to get the homework done and what's going to happen and what — if you get a bad grade, how it's going to hurt your — your semester grade. You really just start to get flustered and worried. Sometimes you — well, to counteract it, sometimes I — I go downstairs — why, I lift weights and that really does help take some of the pressure off because it just helps relax you because you work all your tension and anxieties off then with them.

BILL   For the last five years at least, the whole thing — everything that I've done has been geared to being accepted into the college because: "Son, if you don't go to college, you're not going to be anything in life."

CHIP COVINGTON   I'm sure each — the parents of each individual child are going to be proud if the student makes A-pluses all the way through and gets accepted to some fantastic university. They're going to be proud. And, on the other hand, they're going to be — also be disappointed if — if he doesn't. But I don't see any reason why a parent should shove a student into — into a school, or into a college, or into anything.

KURALT   If you ask them why they go through all this, 90 per cent of the 16-year-olds give as one reason: the chance to make my parents proud of me.

MRS. KOONS   I have a youngster in my class who is out now because she had a nervous breakdown. She's only 15. Now how could a kid — 15 years old — have a nervous breakdown?

KURALT   Webster High teachers.

MR. DAVEY   A student came in and told me that the keys to his own personal sports car would be taken away if he didn't get above a C.

MRS. McCONACHIE   I think that the basic problem with a lot of our kids is that their parents want them to get the grade. Society is valuing education at the present time, but the kid himself doesn't care if he gets a B or a C or an A. Oh, if he gets an A, it's fine, but otherwise he just couldn't care less. He's just getting the grade to take it away to get the diploma to get into college or to get a job. It's the piece of paper that signifies education. They're not interested in the learning.

MRS. BROWN   I think that this is one of the problems that teachers have to combat in the classroom, that students are getting pressures not only from home, but from society in general to achieve for that grade.

MRS. KOONS   They pressure themselves.

MRS. BROWN   Right. That's part of it. Yes.

MRS. McCONACHIE   I think this is a problem that may be more basic than that. Are they not able to let themselves go?

MRS. BROWN   Well, you can't — in the classroom, it's as if the teacher is up there with a bull whip and a stick and they just don't want to relax. I think it goes deeper than grades. I think that's just a symptom of an overall feeling.

MRS. McCONACHIE   Well, it's an inhibition that supposedly terrifies adolescents.

MRS. BROWN   Because in the classrooms, they're just tense as if the axe is going to fall any minute.

Ann Landers' Advice

DEAR ANN LANDERS: Our 12-year-old son is selling his homework and my husband thinks it is just terrific. He keeps saying, "That kid will make it big one of these days."

Albert has fixed prices (from what I gather when he talks on the telephone). He gets a dime for an arithmetic assignment and 25¢ for a book review. The boy is doing a very good business. He bragged at dinner tonight that he has saved up $21.

I think this is disgraceful but whenever I open my mouth I am shouted down. My husband insists that Albert has ingenuity, is smart and is making his brains pay off. If I am wrong, please tell me. If my husband is wrong, please tell him. I'm beginning to doubt my own sanity.

CHICAGO MOTHER

DEAR MOTHER: You are not wrong and I hope you'll keep talking. In this age of tax-chiseling, padded expense accounts and political pay-offs, it's a small wonder a kid would take to selling his homework. Someone should explain to the boy that it is admirable to help friends with their homework by showing them how to do it. But a person who sells "help" is supporting dishonesty in them and behaving dishonestly himself.

Jelly Side Down

by Nancy Stahl

Report cards written in 'teacherspeak'

When you receive your child's report card, you are often convinced that the school has him mixed up with someone else. In view of the 43 name tags you put on his shoes, boots, mittens, glasses, and space maintainer, this is hardly likely.

What has happened is that your child has fallen victim to the Jekyll and Hyde syndrome. As often as not, mother's little angel child is regarded by his teacher as Attila the Hun.

To confuse the issue further, report cards are written in "teacherspeak," the obscure foreign language required by education departments. Teacherspeak is composed of phrases like "Motivation," "Peer Group Pressure," "Individual Expression," and "Participation." Teacherspeak is a lot like saying "perspiration" instead of "sweat." It sounds nicer. Here are a few examples, with English translations:

Johnny lacks self discipline. Lack of self discipline in first grade usually means that Johnny wets his pants every afternoon. Check the clothes hamper.

John's oral expression needs improvement. If Johnny doesn't have a lisp, she is probably telling you that he has a dirty mouth.

Johnny lacks self confidence. This is an indirect reference to the security blanket that he makes you put in his lunchbox.

John's manual dexterity is below average. This means that he can't undo his coat buttons. No one in grade one can undo his coat buttons. It's often time for recess before the teacher gets all 322 children undone. By then, it's time to button them in again.

John lacks respect for personal property. He eats erasers.

Johnny contributes information. He told us how old you are and how much you weigh.

Johnny has a vivid imagination. He tried to make us believe that you were 22, weighed 105, and are a natural blonde.

I could spend a lot of time discussing teacherspeak, but its time to put on a perspiration shirt and rinse out the pants that Johnny lacked self discipline in.

Progress based on grade standard.

The grades in this section indicate your child's progress.

I – Improvement shown   S – Satisfactory   N – Need for improvement

A (√) check indicates point of weakness.

	Marking Period	
	1	2
READING		
Reads with understanding		
Reads smoothly & with expression		
Uses work book independently		
Phonics		
Level		
MATHEMATICS		
Learns new facts as presented		
Solves problems		
Accurate in computation		
LANGUAGE		
Oral expression		
Written expression		
SPELLING		
Weekly word list		
Everyday usage		
HANDWRITING		
*SOCIAL STUDIES		
*SCIENCE		
EFFORT		
CONDUCT		

Reading Levels

4. Helicopters & Gingerbread
5. May I Come In?
6. Seven is Magic
7. The Dog Next Door
8. How it is Nowadays
9. With Skies and Wings
10. All Sorts of Things
11. The Sun that Warms

*Not marked in Grade 2

	Marking Period	
	1	2
1. Social Habits		
Respects opinions of others		
Respects property		
Accepts constructive criticism		
Shares responsibility		
Gets along well with others		
2. Work Habits		
Works independently		
Listens and follows directions		
Has pride in daily work		
Completes assignments on time		
Makes wise use of time		
3. Health Habits		
Has pride in personal appearance		
Cooperation in safety		
4. Art effort		
5. Music effort		
6. Physical Education effort		

Days Absent	
1	2

September assignment: _____

Teacher _____   Grade _____

BULLETIN

Editor: Mortimer Smith

GRADES AND REPORT CARDS

A junior high principal writes: Most of the recent articles I have read on the subject of grades are against them. What is your view?

Our reply: We agree with you that most of the recent literature opposes the traditional A-B-C-D-F system of grading. But one should not infer from this that report cards with letter or number grades are passé. An NEA survey a year ago found that almost all teachers were still giving letter or number grades.

We favor grades, with all of their shortcomings. Parents have a right to know how their children are doing in school. No system achieves this perfectly, but many do a reasonably good job. There has been too much bad experience in the last three or four decades with the abolition of report cards to regard such a proposal with favor.

Reporting to parents should be done primarily in writing because oral communications alone are subject to misinterpretation. Many a parent has realized years too late that his child was not doing well in some subject or in all subjects. This can happen with written report cards, but it is not as likely to.

Ideally, we would tell parents how well their children are doing in terms of a grade standard. The problem of what the grade standard should be is a real one. Whatever one is adopted, it should be made clear to the parents. If the child receives a "C" the parents *and teachers* should know what this means. Is it average for that class in the school? For the school system? Or in terms of a standard of achievement adopted by the system?

We oppose the system of grading "on a curve," that is, in terms of others in the same class. It puts the child in the wrong competitive situation. The child will have to compete, but in the general society, not just with his classmates. In addition to letter grades, additional remarks can be made about deportment, improvement, special problems, special talents revealed, etc. But it is a great burden on teachers to make this section very long.

The most dangerous system of grading involves comparing the child "with himself" or "in terms of his potential." All too often the school underestimates the child's potential and gives him high marks which mislead his parents as to his attainments in comparison with average children.

In summary, the essential thing to bear in mind is that the report should be a meaningful and honest communication to the parents of the child.

grades,
Bah Humbug!!

Grades operate in a number of disguised ways. First they are the teacher's equivalent of the caveman's club. Since students need acceptable grades for desirable scholarships, jobs, and consequent social and economic prestige, the teacher's grading power is a penalty strong enough to give him the final voice in deciding the purpose, content and arrangement of instruction materials. Accordingly, to spend a number of years under the grading system is to be continuously conditioned to letting someone else decide which questions and data are important and almost unavoidably what answers are acceptable.

Teachers who favor this procedure of dictating usually state positively that it is a means of "transmitting a traditional body of knowledge." However, they fail to realize that a dictated selection of questions and information results in indoctrination in certain values. They come to think "these are the important questions to ask and this is the 'correct' way to answer them." When students are forced constantly to conform in their ideas to those of the system, they are conditioned into disinterested obedience, rather than responsible decision making and they are prevented from becoming questioning, searching, resolving persons.

Second, this system seeks to measure in terms of grades those qualities which cannot be measured in these terms. By limiting educational material to what can be measured in grades, they eliminate from the classroom such goals as the development of ability to know one's self, to enter into serious, mindbending conversation, to think independently, to relate knowledge to obligation and so on — all of which are necessary for responsible decision making.

On the other hand, by pretending to measure the immeasurable (many teachers, for example, try to rate the value of student effort when they make out grades) teachers, through grades, can falsely reduce all experience to a search for facts.

Third, grades teach students to compete against each other. Anyone who may attempt to justify such competition may say that it motivates and prepares students for the big competitive outside world. If grades do motivate, then they reinforce a value system that makes equal the acceptability of self with performing better than others. Further it states the belief that private reward must and should come at the expense of the wellbeing of others. The logical outcome of such a value system is precisely the war mentality of the "big competitive world" with self-interest groups pitted rifle-barrel to rifle-barrel.

Furthermore, if one accepts at all the idea that education is primarily to create a society of emotionally stable and fulfilled persons, then competition is apparently nonsense. There are simply no grounds for comparing the development of myself with the development of yourself. Then not only is this competition nonsense but obstruction. For as psychologists like Abrams Maslow have pointed out, self-realization occurs primarily through human relationships based on trust and acceptance rather than on fear and power struggle.

Thus, since grades teach students to compete with each other for power, status and rewards, they obstruct self-realization. The grading structure, then, by encouraging competition, confirms operation for self-interest and for individual power over peers.

Fourth, students who have been passive for 12 years in the face of established authority will be superbly fitted for colleges that are based on submission to authority, research production and scholarly pecking-orders. They fit very well in an economic system based on submission to bureaucratic organization, mass production and cutthroat economic self-interest.

This argument against grades is by no means an argument against evaluation. Evaluation that is for, and largely by, the students. If students, their thought enriched by class discussion and reading, are enabled to arrive at standards of measurement personally meaningful to them. If they can avail themselves of the teacher's orally-given insights about their personal progress in an area, if they are then in a position to choose what to pursue in light of their progress and interests, then evaluation educates rather than indoctrinates.

I have known teachers who declare that for social survival, students must be taught to obey, to compete, to focus on production. As totally as I disagree with their concepts about the possibilities of human beings, of human happiness, and of social organization, I grant them their honesty. For let us be clear: the current grading system precisely imposes the values of unquestioning acceptance of established authority, of unquestioning acceptance of the priority of products over persons, of unquestioning acceptance of organization. If one values in students independent, evaluatively critical thinking, if one values responsible decision-making, if one values cooperative behavior between persons based on trust and acceptance rather than competitive behavior based on fear and power-hunger, then one must judge grades as humanly degrading.

The Open Door
(student underground newspaper)

CONFIDENTIAL REPORTS
PROMPT DISCUSSION by SCHOOL BOARD

WATERFORD — Should the parents of students in Waterford's special services program be guaranteed the right to inspect confidential material about their own children?

The Board of Education learned Thursday night that no such guarantee presently exists in its policy book. One parent, who asked to remain anonymous, told the Day he had been denied inspection of a confidential report about his child.

Mrs. Charlotte M. Henderson, supervisor of special services in the Waterford school system, and some of the personnel who work in the program, offered explanations of current practices used to deal with "confidentiality."

A written description of existing practices was submitted to the board under the title "Proposed Policy for Confidentiality." The special services personnel requested the board to "put into writing" what is now common practice.

It was explained, "Parents can obtain a professional interpretation of a report, but they don't have access to the actual report." The possibility of "misinterpretation by a layman" was cited by board member John A. Scillieri.

The written presentation about special services lists "the core" of its planning-placement team: Assistant Schools Supt. Clarence A. Coogan, Mrs. Henderson, Mrs. Kathleen Laundy, school social worker (or some other social worker), and a psychologist.

This is the team's executive committee, faced with problems which range from psychiatric help to speech therapy. Waterford is providing these special services, as required in most cases by state statute, and with the aid of state funds.

Mrs. Henderson estimated that Waterford now has 300 students in the special services program, averaging 40 students from each of six elementary schools and Clark Lane Junior High, but less from Waterford High School.

The school board referred the request to draft the confidentiality policy to its Policy Committee. Principal J. Morgan Miner of Cohanzie School, who said he was "speaking as a parent," urged the board to "make this information available to parents, with interpretation, so that parents may obtain other interpretations from different qualified sources."

The board, generally, appeared to favor Miner's recommendation, but no vote was taken on it. Scillieri cautioned the board and the policy committee to "carefully consider" the consequences of allowing a layman to review a confidential report about his child "without professional interpretation."

The legal ramifications of a parent's right to inspect a report about his own child were mentioned briefly by Atty. Joseph Q. Koletsky and Atty. Joseph F. Segal, both members of the board.

The written information provided for the school board also was previously presented to staff members of all Waterford schools during in-service meetings last month. The planning-placement team is eager to "orient professionals to the function of special services," the report explains.

Mrs. Henderson said one purpose of the meeting with the school board was to clarify the position on confidential reports.

Last Name	First Name	Middle Name	Sex
LEVANTO	JEANNETTE	MARIE	F

Date of Birth **April 19, 1954** Birthplace **Attleboro, Mass.**

Mailing Address **84 Briar Hill Road,** Town of Legal Residence **Norwich**

Name of Parents or Guardian **Joseph and Dorothy Levanto**

Entered from **Kelly Jr. H. S.** Date **9/5/53**

Date of Withdrawal _____ Reason _____ Re-entered — Date _____

GRADE 9

	Course Number	1st Sem	2nd Sem	Credits
*ENGLISH 1	004	3	4	1.
*ALGEBRA	114	5	5	1.
*EARTH SCIENCE	204	3	3	1.
*SOCIAL STUDIES	304	2	3	1.
*SPANISH 1	424	3	4	1.
ART	675	5	5	.50
PHYS. ED.	790	4	4	.25

Days Absent 5 Tardy Total 5.75

GRADE 10

	Course Number	1st Sem	2nd Sem	Credits
*ENGLISH 2	014	3	3	1.
*PLANE GEOM.	134	5	4	1.
*BIOLOGY	224	4	4	1.
*WORLD HIST.	314	3	3	1.
*SPANISH 2	427	2	3	1.
DRAWING	683	4	4	.50
PHYS. ED.	792	4	4	.25

Days Absent 3 Tardy Total 5.75

GRADE 11

	Course Number	1st Sem	2nd Sem	Credits
*ENGLISH 3	024	4	4	1.
*ALGEBRA 2	154	5	5	1.
*CHEMISTRY	208	5	5	1.
*U.S. HISTORY	324	3	3	1.
*SPANISH 3	428	4	4	1.
POSTER	687	5	5	1.
PHYS. ED.	794	5	4	.25
DRIVER ED.	———	-	-	.25

Days Absent 1 Tardy Total 6.50

GRADE 12

	Course Number	1st Sem	2nd Sem	Credits
*WORLD LIT.	036	4	4	1.
*SENIOR MATH	174	5	4	1.
*PHYSICS	210	4	4	1.
TYPING	527	5	4	1.
POSTER	687	5	5	1.

Days Absent 4 Tardy Total 5.00

RANK IN CLASS — Rank includes all subjects for which both a semester grade and credit are earned in grades 10, 11, and 12. Physical Education is excluded. Accelerated subjects are not weighted.

2nd decile, for **6** semesters Number of students in class **654**

☐ Exact _____ ☐ Approximate _____

Graduation: Date **June 13, 1972**

STANDARD TESTS

GRADE 9 10/68

OTIS I.Q. 116 84%

DAT

VERBAL	75%
NUMERICAL	70%
SPACE	90%
ABSTRACT	90%
MECHANICAL	30%
VR & NA	75%

GRADE 11 10/70

OTIS-LENNON I.Q. 125 90%

HONORS

Grade 11	SECOND HONORS	1st SEMESTER
	SECOND HONORS	2nd SEMESTER
Grade 12	FIRST HONORS	1st SEMESTER
	SECOND HONORS	2nd SEMESTER

Abbreviations
  * — College Prep
  ** — Accelerated groups 8-10% of total class; selected by ability tests, achievement tests, past achievement and teacher recommendation; enriched; some independent study.
  T — Tutored
  S — Summer School

EXPLANATION OF ACHIEVEMENT GRADES
5 — Superior
4 — Above Average
3 — Average
2 — Below Average
1 — Failure

A — Absent from Exam
E — Excused
W — Withdrawn

College Recommendation Grade — 4
Class Period 50 minutes — 38 weeks
4 class periods per week — 1 credit per year.
Lab sciences are chemistry, physics, biology and physiology
1 period per week of Physical Education required in grades 9, 10, and 11.

72F256800

LEVANTO	JEANNETTE	MARIE	Class 19??
Last name	First name	Middle name	

STUDENT DESCRIPTION SUMMARY

Each figure represents the number of teachers rating the student at the indicated level on the rating scale. Each level is comparable to the descriptive scale specified by the N A S S P.

RATING SCALE

High ← Low → Not applicable

	A	B	C	D	E	N
Participation in discussion	1	–	3	1	1	
Involvement in classroom activities	1	1	4	–	–	
Pursuit of independent study	1	2	2	–	–	1
Evenness of performance	1	2	2	–	1	
Critical and questioning attitude	–	1	2	–	2	1
Depth of understanding	–	3	3	–	–	
Personal responsibility	3	3	–	–	–	
Consideration for others	4	2	–	–	–	

Date of rating 4/? by 6 teachers

	A	B	C	D	E	N
Participation in discussion	2	3	–	–	–	
Involvement in classroom activities	2	3	–	–	–	
Pursuit of independent study	1	3	–	–	–	
Evenness of performance	2	3	–	–	–	
Critical and questioning attitude	1	4	–	–	–	
Depth of understanding	2	3	–	–	–	
Personal responsibility	2	3	–	–	–	
Consideration for others	4	1	–	–	–	

Date of rating 4/?? by 5 teachers

PRIZES & AWARDS

Ann Strong Brown Prize – Mathematics

Student Guild Award – Poster

Connecticut Regional Scholastic
   Art Award – Certificate of Merit

NFA Blazer – Girls Sport

STUDENT ACTIVITIES

Grade 9

GIRLS' SPORTS
GIRLS' ATHLETIC ASSOC.

Grade 10

GIRLS' SPORTS
GIRLS' ATHLETIC ASSOC.
PEP SQUAD

Grade 11

GIRLS' SPORTS
GIRLS' ATHLETIC ASSOC.
GIRLS' CLASS LEADERS
STUDENT ADVISORY BOARD
FUTURE TEACHERS
INTERCULTURAL COMMITTEE

Grade 12

GIRLS' SPORTS
GIRLS' ATHLETIC ASSOC.
GIRLS' CLASS LEADERS
STUDENT ADVISORY BOARD
SPANISH CLUB
CAMPUS STORE
SENIOR ACTIVITIES

Post High School placement:

   Central Connecticut State College – New Britain, Conn.

Date_____ Signature_____ Title_____

139

The Learning Tree

GORDON PARKS

When the lunch bell sounded, he headed straight for the principal's office — expecting the worst. "I might even be expelled," he thought. When he arrived he was told to wait in the outer office until Mr. Hall could see him. And so he sat fretting, having no planned defense; only a feeling of determination burned within him. Before long Miss McClinock arrived. In somewhat of a flurry she swept into Mr. Hall's office without seeming to even notice Newt.

"Gettin' her story in first," Newt mumbled under his breath.

About five minutes later the secretary's buzzer sounded. She went to the principal's door, then turned to Newt. "You can go in now," she said.

Mr. Hall, a rather youngish, open-faced man wearing steel-rimmed glasses, leaned back in his swivel chair when Newt entered. Miss McClinock sat beside his desk, her fat hands resting firmly on her knees.

"Howdy do, sir," Newt said.

"Hello, Newton. Sit down there," Mr. Hall ordered. Newt sat down, and Mr. Hall twirled his chair in half circles for a few seconds before he spoke again. "Miss McClinock tells me you were rude and impudent last Friday. What have you to say for yourself?"

Newt picked nervously at a scab on his forefinger, looking at the principal. "Well — I guess it's all in the way you look at it, sir."

"What do you mean by that?"

"Well — I didn't mean to be rude when I went to see her. It was just because of things that happened between us a long time ago."

"As I distinctly remember, it was about your mark on the midterm test," Miss Mc-

Clinock snapped. "You felt I had down-graded you."

"That right, Newton?"

"In a way, yessir. But that ain't — wasn't all there was to it."

"What are you trying to say? Out with it."

"It's just that we — Miss McClinock and I — had a little fuss — or I don't know whether you call it fuss or not — but we didn't see things the same way after the first week or so."

"Miss McClinock happens to be your instructor — as well as your guidance teacher."

"I know, sir, but I didn't like the way she wanted to guide me."

Mr. Hall made a few more half turns, scratching his head. "This caused you to tell Miss McClinock that you hated her?"

"I didn't say I —"

"Don't lie, young man," Miss McClinock cut in, her cheeks glowing red. "You know you said it."

"I didn't say I did, alone. I said all the colored kids hated you — and they do."

"Why do you say this, Newton?" Hall asked.

"Because they all say so."

"Do they give reasons?"

"Yessir, they do. They say she tells them all the same thing — that they shouldn't go to college — that they're all goin' to turn out to be porters and cooks and maids. That's sure what she told me."

A frown came on Hall's face. He turned from Newt and Miss McClinock and looked out the window at the tree tops. "This true, Miss McClinock? Do you tell the Negro students such things?"

"Mr. Hall," she began, her nose twitching, "you've been at this school for just two years. I've been class advisor to these colored students for the last twenty years. What I've said to them was what I've been instructed to say to them."

The principal had turned to face her, and his frown was deeper now. "So this accusation of his is true?"

"To a certain extent — yes."

"Who instructed you to say such things?"

"Mr. Hornsby, our former principal. He —"

"Just a moment, Miss McClinock," Mr. Hall said, "just a moment, please. Newton, wait in the outer office until I call you."

Newt got up and went out, then Mr. Hall rose and shut the door behind him.

As he sat there on the bench, Newt began trying to imagine the conversation as it would go between Mr. Hall and Miss McClinock. He had been aware of the principal's surprise when she had confessed to the truth of his accusation, and he felt this was in his favor. His tension had eased somewhat, but he had already taken a pessimistic view of the outcome. He had decided that if he were expelled, he would say even more about what he felt was an injustice. If he won, then nothing more needed to be said. "But any way it goes," he decided, "Miss McClinock's goin' to have it in for me."

He sat there, time going slowly, recalling Washington Junior High, comparing it with this school of big, airy, sun-splashed classrooms, auditoriums and gymnasiums, remembering that there had been no microscopes and no chemical labs, and that their outdoor playground had been no more than a deserted garbage-strewn field adjoining the school property; retaining the memory of the little gym, the way it was used for just about everything, and the odor of stale sweat and smelly tennis shoes that clung to it even on graduation night — despite the thorough airing it was given the afternoon before.

His stomach growled from hunger, and the secretary glanced in his direction.

But he had known some wonderful moments back there too, warm, intimate and gay moments of easy pleasure and unrestrained laughter — moments that had not yet come to him here. He wondered, as he had often done before, what the whites' real reasons were for denying them a part of the school's athletic and social affairs. "Why does our color make such a difference? ... Didn't God know that we'd have a lot of trouble if he made us black? ... Since he's white, maybe he don't care either." He smiled wryly. "Never seen black angels ... even the chariot horses are white."

He gritted his teeth in defiance of the conspiracy he felt Miss McClinock and Mr. Hall must be forming against him; of the scorn he felt she held for his coloring. "If I turned white before they called me back in there, 'twould be a different story altogether...." He knotted his fist and watched the skin lighten under the pressure of the knuckle bones. "Wonder if you tore all the skin off, if it would all come back black? Guess it would ... don't think I'd like bein' white, anyway."

He dug into his pocket and brought out three large raisins; after picking lint and pocket dust from them, he popped them into his mouth. Then he got up and started across the room to the water cooler. At that moment, the door to the principal's office opened and Miss McClinock bustled out past Newt and into the hall.

"Come in, Winger," the principal said, and Newt followed him back into his office.

Mr. Hall began very slowly — uncertainly. "I just don't know — well, this is all sort of an unnecessary mistake — or maybe a misunderstanding. I'm speaking of Miss McClinock's attitude toward you and other Negro students — and her advice to you about college and so forth. For an explanation to make sense to you — or me — one would have to go much further back, to a period — a tragic one — before you or I existed." Hall walked to the window and gazed out at the campus, much the same way Newt had seen Miss McClinock do that evening after their argument. "Although she must share the blame for this awful wrong, Miss McClinock is somewhat a victim herself — having been eased into this wrong channel of

thought many years ago, not only because she thought it to be right but because it was a truth that existed during those same years."

Hall talked on, seeming to Newt to be addressing some unseen audience. "Mr. Hornsby was more to blame than she — but then, so is my father, my mother, Miss McClinock's father and mother and millions of others who helped shape the ideas that Miss McClinock so unwisely passed on to you — forgetting that time and progress must shake away such ideas." He turned slowly. "Are you following what I am saying? Do you understand, Newt?"

"Yessir — I think I do."

"Frankly, I was shocked at Miss McClinock's confession, but —" He shrugged, then paused for a second. "The valedictorian of my graduating class at college was a Negro, Curtis Mathews. But — do you want to know the ironic thing about this, Newt?" Hall shook his head. "When I came through the New York train station from a New England vacation last summer, there was Curtis Mathews — bearing out Miss McClinock's prophecy — asking me if I would like help with my bags. He was a redcap — a redcap, carrying bags for people who couldn't begin to compare with him in knowledge or social worth. 'What a waste!' I remember thinking when I left him that day."

"Did he know you, Mr. Hall?" Newt asked.

"Oh, yes. Yes indeed. He stopped work and we talked for nearly a half hour." Hall was quiet — remembering again. "He had seven children by then, Newt. I'll never forget it, a man with a master's degree, carrying bags, with seven children — and no hope."

They were both quiet for a moment.

"There are some things here at my own school that I don't like, son. For instance, I feel bad about the school board's keeping you boys off our football and basketball teams. It's a stupid, costly thing. Our white basketball team hasn't made the state championships in the last ten years. The colored team has not only done this, but it's held the championship of Kansas, Oklahoma and Missouri four times during the same period. Believe me — if it were left to me, or Coach Dennison, this would stop, but we are powerless."

"Yessir, I understand."

"I hope you do. And another thing — what I've told you is strictly between us. I had a long talk with Miss McClinock and I'm sure her thinking and attitudes will be different from now on. You continue to work hard. She will do the rest."

"Yessir."

"If you have any more problems, bring them to me. You're excused." As Newt started out, he added. "And you are to show Miss McClinock the highest respect. You understand that, don't you?"

"Yessir. Thanks, Mr. Hall."

"You're welcome."

A Report on Racial Imbalance in the Schools of Massachusetts

. . . . Our conclusions are clear. Racial imbalance represents a serious conflict with the American creed of equal opportunity. It is detrimental to sound education in the following ways: It does serious educational damage to Negro children by impairing their confidence, distorting their self-image, and lowering their motivation. It does moral damage by encouraging prejudice within children regardless of their color. It represents an inaccurate picture of life to both white and Negro children and prepares them inadequately for a multi-racial community, nation, and world. It too often produces inferior educational facilities in the predominantly Negro schools. It squanders valuable human resources by impairing the opportunities of many Negro children to prepare for the professional and vocational requirements of our technological society. It is imperative that we begin to end this harmful system of separation. The means are at hand. Each day of delay is a day of damage to the children of our Commonwealth. . . .

Educators and social scientists have produced a large body of evidence documenting the conclusion that racial separation has powerful and injurious impact on the self-image, confidence, motivation, and the school achievement of Negro children. It is not difficult to understand why racial separation is harmful to Negro children. Outside of the school the Negro child and his family too often have heard the message, "Keep out, stay back, you are not wanted." He and his family have too often been made to feel different and inferior. The racially imbalanced school reinforces that feeling. Inside the school, the young faces are almost all black. The older faces — those of the teachers, the ones in charge — are mostly white. Does the child wonder why only black children go to this school? A child cannot comprehend the subtle difference between illegal segregation in the South and racial imbalance in the North. He sees only that he is Negro and almost all his schoolmates are Negroes. The separation of some children "from others of similar age and qualification because of their race generates a feeling of inferiority as to their status that may affect their hearts and minds in a way unlikely ever to be undone."

Mr. Ostrowski, my English teacher. He was a tall, rather reddish white man and he had a thick mustache. I had gotten some of my best marks under him, and he had always made me feel that he liked me. He was, as I have mentioned, a natural-born "advisor," about what you ought to read, to do, or think — about any and everything. We used to make unkind jokes about him: why was he teaching in Mason instead of somewhere else, getting for himself some of the "success in life" that he kept telling us how to get?

I know that he probably meant well in what he happened to advise me that day. I doubt that he meant any harm. It was just in his nature as an American white man. I was one of his top students, one of the school's top students — but all he could see for me was the kind of future "in your place" that almost all white people see for black people.

He told me, "Malcolm, you ought to be thinking about a career. Have you been giving it thought?"

The truth is, I hadn't. I never have figured out why I told him, "Well, yes, sir, I've been thinking I'd like to be a lawyer." Lansing certainly had no Negro lawyers — or doctors either — in those days, to hold up an image I might have aspired to. All I really knew for certain was that a lawyer didn't wash dishes, as I was doing.

Mr. Ostrowski looked surprised, I remember, and leaned back in his chair and clasped his hands behind his head. He kind of half-smiled and said, "Malcolm, one of life's first needs is for us to be realistic. Don't misunderstand me, now. We all here like you, you know that. But you've got to be realistic about being a nigger. A lawyer — that's no realistic goal for a nigger. You need to think about something you can be. You're good with your hands — making things. Everybody admires your carpentry shop work. Why don't you plan on carpentry? People like you as a person — you'd get all kinds of work."

The more I thought afterwards about what he said, the more uneasy it made me. It just kept treading around in my mind.

What made it really begin to disturb me was Mr. Ostrowski's advice to others in my class — all of them white. Most of them had told him they were planning to become farmers. But those who wanted to strike out on their own, to try something new, he had encouraged. Some, mostly girls, wanted to be teachers. A few wanted other professions, such as one boy who wanted to become a county agent; another,

DOVE
COUNTER BALANCE
INTELLIGENCE TEST

This test might be useful in evaluating your verbal aptitude. The verbal aptitude test is not slanted towards middle-class experience, however, but to non-white, lower-class experience.

People from a non-white, lower-class background are required to do well on aptitude tests keyed to white, middle-class culture, before they are allowed to perform in that culture. By the same standard, it seems only fair that people of white, middle-class background should be required to do well on tests keyed to non-white, lower-class culture before they be allowed to perform in such a milieu.

The following test was developed by *Watts social worker Adrian Dove* to measure intelligence as the term applies in lower-class Black America.

If you score less than 20 (67%) on the test, you are virtually failing, and might therefore conclude that you have a low ghetto I.Q. As white middle-class educators put it, you are "culturally deprived."

1. "T-Bone Walker" got famous for playing what? (a) trombone (b) piano (c) "T-Flue" (d) guitar (e) "Hambone"

2. Who did Stagolee kill (in the famous blues legend)? (a) his mother (b) Frankie (c) Johnny (d) his girl friend (e) Billy

3. A "Gas Head" is a person who has a (a) fast moving car (b) stable of "lace" (c) habit of stealing cars (d) long jail record for arson

4. If a man is called a "Blood," then he is a (a) fighter (b) Mexican-American (c) Negro (d) hungry hemophile (e) Redman or Indian

5. If you throw the dice and "7" is showing on top, what is facing down? (a) "Seven" (b) "snake eyes" (c) Boxcars (d) "Little Joes" (e) "Eleven"

6. Jazz pianist Ahmad Jamal took an Arabic name after becoming really famous. Previously he had some fame with what he called his "slave name." What was his previous name? (a) Willie Lee Jackson (b) LeRoi Jones (c) Wilbur McDongal (d) Fritz Jones (e) Andy Johnson

7. In "C. C. Rider" what does "C. C." stand for? (a) Civil Service (b) Church Council (c) Country Circuit preacher or an old time rambler (d) Country Club (e) "Cheatin' Charlie" (the "Boxcar Gunsel")

8. Cheap "chitlings" (not the kind you purchase at a frozen food counter) will taste rubbery unless they are cooked long enough. How soon do you quit cooking them to eat and enjoy them? (a) 15 minutes (b) 2 hours (c) 24 hours (d) 1 week (on a low flame) (e) 1 hour

9. "Down Home" (the South) today, for the average "Soul Brother" who is picking cotton (in season from sunup until sundown), what is the average earning (take home) for one full day? (a) $0.75 (b) $1.65 (c) $3.50 (d) $5.00 (e) $12.00

10. If a judge finds you guilty of "holding weed" (in California), what's the most he can give you? (a) indeterminate (life) (b) a nickel (c) a dime (d) a year in County (e) $00.00

11. "Bird" or "Yardbird" was the "jacket" that jazz lovers from coast to coast hung on (a) Lester Young (b) Peggy Lee (c) Benny Goodman (d) Charlie Parker (e) "Birdman from Alcatraz"

12. A "Hype" is a person who (a) Always says he feels sickly (b) has water on the brain (c) uses heroin (d) is always ripping and running (e) is always sick

13. Hattie Mae Johnson is on the County. She has four children and her husband is now in jail for non-support, as he was unemployed and was not able to give her any money. Her welfare check is now $286.00 per month. Last night she went out with the biggest player in town. If she got pregnant, then nine months from now, how much more will her welfare check be? (a) $80.00 (b) $2.00 (c) $35.00 (d) $150.00 (e) $100.00

14. "Hully Gully" came from (a) "East Oakland" (b) Fillmore (c) Watts (d) Harlem (e) Motor City

15. What is Willie Mae's last name? (a) Schwartz (b) Matauda (c) Gomez (d) Turner (e) O'Flaherty

16. The opposite of square is (a) round (b) up (c) down (d) hip (e) lame

17. Do "The Beatles" have soul? (a) yes (b) no (c) Gee Whiz or maybe

18. A "Handkerchief head" is (a) a cool cat (b) a porter (c) an "Uncle Tom" (d) a heddi (e) a "preacher"

19. What are the "Dixie Hummingbirds"? (a) a part of the KKK (b) a swamp disease (c) a modern gospel group (d) a Mississippi Negro, para-military strike force (e) deacons

20. "Jet" is (a) an "East Oakland" motorcycle club (b) one of the gangs in West Side Story (c) a news, a gossip magazine (d) a way of life for the very rich

Fill in the missing word or words that sound best by putting the letter in the blank provided at the beginning of the sentence:

___ 21. "Tell it like it . . ." (a) thinks I am (b) baby (c) try (d) is (e) Y'all

___ 22. "You've got to get up early in the morning if you want to . . ." (a) catch the worms (b) be healthy, wealthy, and wise (c) try to fool me (d) farewell (e) be the first one on the street

___ 23. And Jesus said, "Walk together children . . ." (a) Don't you get weary. There's a great camp meeting (b) for we shall overcome (c) for the family that walks together talks together (d) by your patience you will win your souls (Luke 21:19) (e) find the things that are above, not the things that are on Earth (Col. 3:3)

148

___ 24. "Money don't get everything it's true ..." (a) but I don't have none and I'm so blue (b) but what it don't get I can't use (c) so make with what you've got (d) but I don't know that and neither do you

___ 25. "Bo Diddley" is a ... (a) camp for children (b) cheap wine (c) singer (d) new dance (e) mojo call

___ 26. Which word is out of place here? (a) Splib (b) blood (c) Grey (d) Spook (e) Black

___ 27. How much does a "short dog" cost? (a) $0.15 (b) $2.00 (c) $0.35 (d) $0.05 (e) $0.86 + tax

___ 28. True or False: A "pimp" is also a young man who lays around all day. (a) True (b) False

___ 29. If a pimp is uptight with a woman who gets state aid, what does he mean when he talks about "Mother's Day"? (a) second Sunday in May (b) third Sunday in June (c) first of every month (d) none of these (e) first and fifteenth of every month

___ 30. Many people say that Juneteenth (June 19) should be made a legal holiday because this was the day when ... (a) the slaves were freed in the USA (b) the slaves were freed in Texas (c) the slaves were freed in Jamaica (d) the slaves were freed in California (e) Martin Luther King was born (f) Booker T. Washington died

THE DOVE COUNTERBALANCE INTELLIGENCE TEST KEY

1. d	6. d	11. d	16. d	21. d	26. c
2. e	7. c	12. c	17. b	22. c	27. c
3. c	8. c	13. c	18. c	23. a	28. a
4. c	9. d	14. c	19. c	24. b	29. c
5. a	10. d	15. d	20. c	25. c	30. b

Teachers, like IQ tests, are biased against minorities and the poor, concludes a recent study by Pamela C. Rubovits and Martin L. Maher of the University of Illinois. They say white teachers have far different expectations for black and white students.

Their study examined the teaching behavior of 66 white, female teacher trainees with black and white seventh graders who had been randomly labeled "gifted" or "non-gifted." White students categorized as gifted were given more attention and praise and were criticized less than the white non-gifted students. The gifted whites were chosen most frequently as the students most liked by the teacher — the brightest, the all-but-certain leaders of the class. The blacks? Those labeled gifted got the least attention, the least praise and the most criticism of the entire class. The non-gifted blacks finished somewhere in between.

how **IS** intelligence tested?

J. RAYMOND GERBERICH

When your child's teacher tells you that your child has been given an intelligence test, just what does he mean? What kind of test is it? How many children take it at one time? How long does it take the child to complete the test? What does it actually measure?

In most cases, the test your child takes is one of the dozen or so widely used group intelligence tests. These are paper and pencil tests, given to your child and to many other children at the same time. Often the classroom teacher himself gives the test to his students. Sometimes, all the pupils in a grade are brought together in an auditorium and tested in a large group. In either case, the testing takes only from about a half-hour to an hour and a quarter depending on which test is used.

Special tests are available to test the intelligence of young children who are not yet able to read. These tests are made up almost entirely of pictures and figures. The teacher giving the test reads directions aloud to the children, and the children then draw X's or connecting lines as answers to the questions.

For example, the children might be asked to mark with an X the largest of several pictured objects, or to mark the pictures in a group that belong together. Or, the person giving the test will ask the children to mark the picture among several that shows an animal or an object named by the examiner. Children who haven't yet learned to read might also be asked to complete a picture that has missing parts.

When tests are given to children who are a bit older — those in fourth, fifth, and sixth grades — letters, numerals, and word forms are included as rapidly as the children learn in the classroom what these things mean.

Up to now, we have been explaining group tests. These are by far the most common. There are, however, tests given to one pupil at a time which take longer and are more accurate. They should be given only by persons especially trained to do so — a school psychologist, for example.

The intelligence test measures the mental age of a child in relationship to other children. (If seven-year-old Tommy, for example, gets the same score as the average score of children aged eight and a half, he has a mental age of 8-6.) The intelligence quotient is obtained by dividing mental age by chronological age and multiplying the result by 100 (just to get rid of decimals).

An IQ between 90 and 110 is considered normal or average. Scores above 130 imply superior intelligence: above 140, very superior intelligence. Some tests indicate to us more than this — they suggest, in addition to an over-all IQ, how capable a child is at the language or verbal parts of learning and also how capable he is at number learning.

Intelligence tests give a sampling of some of the ingredients that we think go into what we call intelligence. Different facets are measured at different ages and so the results will vary. Different tests designed for the same age level will also give varying scores.

In a general sense, intelligence tests indicate a pupil's ability to adapt to new situations or, to put it another way, his ability to learn the kinds of things he is expected to learn at school. Intelligence cannot be measured directly. We measure ability to perform tasks which we believe require intelligence.

Clearly, children cannot be asked to answer questions or do other tasks unless they deal with something they have already experienced, read about, or been told about. So, it is important that the various items on an intelligence test cover wide areas. Otherwise the test would be unfair.

As we have said, the score a child gets on an intelligence test is taken as an indication of his ability to learn or adapt. Roughly speaking, it is assumed that what a child has already learned will tell us to some degree what he is able to learn.

Since intelligence tests depend largely on knowledge and skills that have been learned, one might ask if they are just the same as achievement tests. Actually, they are not, although they do resemble them in some ways. In general the difference is that achievement tests are designed to measure what a child has actually *learned*. Intelligence tests, on the other hand, try to measure a child's *ability* to see relationships between things; to reason; to manipulate, compare, contrast, and otherwise handle materials which are so commonly known and so simple in themselves that almost any child can understand and take the test even though he may not do well on it.

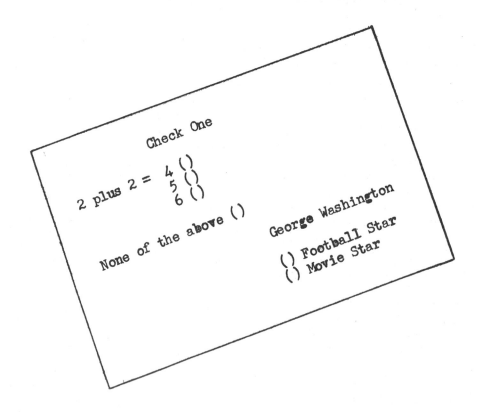

race,
intelligence & IQ
education

H.J.Eysenck

A psychologist asks why blacks consistently score lower on IQ tests than whites

The concepts in the title of this article tend to arouse an unusual degree of emotion. Many people may feel that even raising the possibility of the genetic determination of American Negro inferiority in IQ tests – let alone suggesting that it might have to be answered in the affirmative – is a form of racism and that anyone holding such views would automatically be in favor of segregation and other forms of discrimination. But it is important to realize that the *scientific problem* of the degree to which various groups are inferior (or superior) to one another on IQ tests, and the determination of the causes of such inferiority or superiority, is quite distinct from the *social and ethical problems* that confront us.

Even if it were a fact that American Negroes are genetically predisposed to score lower than whites or Orientals on such tests, it might still be argued that socially and ethically the right thing to do was to give special care, consideration and enriched education to Negro children in order to try, as far as possible, to bring them up to the average. But however we answer this second question (and my own answer would be emphatically against segregation and in favor of reparation), it is not the same question as the first; and answering the factual question should not be influenced by social and ethical considerations appropriate to the second.

153

Many researchers argue that the very notion of "race" is unscientific and that we should rather be talking about ethnic subgroups. Certainly it is erroneous to think of races as immutable types, qualitatively differentiated from each other. The discovery and elaboration of serological genetics, by means of which specific genes can be recognized by chemical reactions with the components of human blood, and the constant finding of new blood genes, has forced experts to expand the number of ethnic subgroups greatly.

Even apparently homogeneous groups, such as the American Negroes, can be shown to be quite heterogeneous in many ways. North American Negroes, to take but one example, are much more hybridized than South American Negroes, and it is even possible to assess the degree of hybridization quantitatively. Similarly, American Negroes are not identical with African Negroes, and these in turn constitute many different subgroups. Nevertheless, it is not meaningless to ask whether American Negroes, on the average, score lower on IQ tests than American whites do, or American Orientals or American Indians. These larger groups do show quite pronounced serological and morphological differences from each other that swamp intragroup differences.

However, we must be careful not to use American Negroes as a prototype for all Negroes, or American whites as the prototype for all whites. American Negroes score, on average, some 15 IQ points below American whites, but so do some white groups outside America. There is the possibility that the low scores of American Negroes on IQ tests may be due to selective immigration (the duller Negroes being captured and sold to slavery) and to the killing off of "uppity" bright negroes.

How can we account for the fact that, for some 60 years now, psychologists who have tested American Negroes have found them to average about 85 IQ points, compared with the white population's 100 points? Southern Negroes score somewhat lower even than this, northern Negroes somewhat higher, but, on the whole, the figure has remained remarkably steady.

Environmentalists maintain that this is due entirely to the poorer conditions under which Negroes are brought up and have to live: poor food, poor parental care, poor education, poor jobs, unemployment — the list is endless. They often add such factors as black children responding poorly to white testers; blacks doing poorly on tests because they are biased in favor of white culture; and poor motivation of black children due to pervasive experiences of failure.

Geneticists maintain that genetic factors are likely to play a part in addition to any environmental ones. Geneticists, these days, never maintain that genetic factors are all-important, and they admit without argument that *part* of the difference observed is likely to be due to environmental factors.

It is possible to test the value of each protagonist's arguments by arranging experiments that will tell us to what extent hypothesis is in accordance with fact. Deductions from the geneticist's theory are probably the weakest way to support that hypothesis. Demonstrations that individual differences in intelligence are strongly determined by heredity — while correct and important — apply only *within* a given racial group; they do not necessarily carry over to racial differences.

There are weaknesses in the contrary argument, too; the suggestion that what is true of white intelligence is not true of black intelligence implies even greater differences between white and black than purely quantitative ones. But as many geneticists have pointed out, the evidence at the moment is suggestive but not conclusive. At the moment, one can only say that the genetic evidence is in good agreement with the genetic hypothesis but is not compelling.

There is one interesting experiment that gives a kind of direct proof of racial differences in IQ based on genetic determinants and that could be extended to furnish such proof on a larger scale and in relation to other racial groups. M. M. de Lemos tested groups of aboriginal children in Australia. These children lived in mission compounds and were all educated in common and treated alike. Some of these children had one white great-grandparent, unbeknownst to the children. When the children were tested on a Piaget type of intelligence test, the children with part-white ancestry obtained significantly higher scores than the others did. In America, too, there has been a tendency for Negroes with lighter skins to do better on IQ tests. But it is possible that environmental conditions are somewhat more favorable for lighter-skinned Negroes.

It turns out to be more useful to test the deductions from the *environmentalist* theory, if only because these tests can be arranged fairly easily and without having to undertake impossible breeding experiments. Thus, it is easy to test groups of Negro children using white and black testers and show that the color of the tester is quite irrelevant; sometimes there is a slight advantage to the one, sometimes to the other.

Poor motivation, too, can be investigated. Arthur Jensen carried out one particularly interesting experiment in which two sets of tests were incorporated within a single format. To the testee the two tests looked alike. But while one was a test of cooperation and motivation, the other was a genuine IQ test. Negro children did as well on the motivational test as white children did, but they scored much lower on the IQ test.

When we turn to general socioeconomic status, we find other facts in disagreement with the environmentalistic viewpoint. We can compare American Negro and white children attending the same schools and coming from identical environments. When we do this, the differences in IQ are reduced a little, but not very much. In fact, when middle-class Negro children going to good schools in American middle-class neighborhoods are compared with working-class white children going to rather poor schools, it is found that, in spite of their inferiority in all aspects of socioeconomic status, the white children are still marginally ahead.

Such findings are difficult to explain by a purely environmentalistic hypothesis. Oriental children in California come from families distinctly inferior to white families in socioeconomic status, but they do better on IQ tests than white children. How is this possible on an environmentalistic theory? The relationship between IQ and socioeconomic status is complex and by no means as linear and straightforward as environmentalists suggest. Such simple theories fail to account for most of the observed facts.

We now turn to another argument, one that says that tests of IQ are not measures of intelligence at all but simply educational tests of cultural knowledge; that American Negroes do poorly because of their inferior education; and that if "culture-free" tests of intelligence could be devised, then Negroes would do as well as whites.

Alas, this argument, too, can be shown to be hopelessly wide of the truth. It is true that there are no culture-free tests, but tests differ in the degree to which they draw upon cultural knowledge. Typical tests of school knowledge contrast with such "culture-*fair*" tests as Raven's Matrices. In these the testee is not required to draw upon any school-taught knowledge but simply to deduce relations and correlates when he is confronted with simple nonrepresentational drawings.

Within white groups, heredity seems to contribute only about a third as much to individual differences on the less culture-fair tests as compared with the Raven's Matrices type of test. According to the environmental hypothesis, American Negroes would be less inferior to whites the more culture fair the test happened to be.

Exactly the opposite is true. Negroes do best — compared to whites — on tests heavily contaminated with school knowledge. They do poorest on culture-fair items involving the ability to think abstractly. The often repeated notion that Negroes are inferior only on verbal items and tests is simply wrong.

Another argument that goes against the environmentalist hypothesis is that if it were true that inferior schooling holds back the black child, then his inferiority on IQ tests should *increase* as he goes through school. Yet this is not so. The observed differences neither increase nor decrease, on the whole.

Why, despite all this evidence, are the environmentalist hypotheses so firmly held, defended with such tenacity, and given a charmed life where no experimentally ascertained facts are allowed to impinge on their sacred image? If we want to help the blacks achieve equality of *opportunity*, then we can do so only on a basis of factual knowledge.

This, I think, must be the answer to those who prefer not to experiment in this field for fear of what they might discover. If it is true that American Negroes are genetically predisposed to lower achievement on IQ tests, it is not doing them any favor to pretend otherwise. At the moment, many American universities are engaged in what might be called inverse racist policies of admission. Negroes are frequently admitted with qualifications very much below the minimum requirements for white students. This leads to their failure in orthodox courses and the demand for special "black studies" or more lenient marking systems.

It is wrong to refuse blacks admission on the grounds of color. It seems to me equally objectionable to grant blacks admission without the usual intellectual and educational qualifications. If the one is racism, so is the other.

Nor do such policies produce a lowering of racial barriers. Within the universities that practice this "inverse discrimination," the blacks tend to group together in opposition to the whites. This produces an exaggeration rather than an amelioration of the racial conflict.

By refusing to face the facts the black's alleged friends may turn out to be his worst enemies. Only factual research, carried out with the aim of helping the Negro achieve his rightful aspirations, can give us the answer to the problems that at the moment seem insuperable.

A court case in the San Francisco school district may spell the beginning of the end of IQ testing as a criterion for assigning students to advanced or retarded classes.

The suit was brought on behalf of seven black children who scored below 75 — the cutoff point for regular classes — on individual IQ tests administered by white school psychologists, but who scored significantly higher when given the same test by black psychologists who understood their language background.

The local association of black psychologists bringing the suit not only asked that the children be removed from special classes but also be awarded damages. The court indicated it saw some merit in the plaintiffs' position and issued a temporary injunction restraining the school district from using IQ tests as a basis for placing black schoolchildren in retarded classes.

The psychologists bringing the suit promise similar actions in other states.

how CHILDREN fail

John Holt

When we talk about intelligence, we do not mean the ability to get a good score on a certain kind of test, or even the ability to do well in school; these are at best only indicators of something larger, deeper, and far more important. By intelligence we mean a style of life, a way of behaving in various situations, and particularly in new, strange, and perplexing situations. The true test of intelligence is not how much we know how to do, but how we behave when we don't know what to do.

The intelligent person, young or old, meeting a new situation or problem, opens himself up to it; he tries to take in with mind and senses everything he can about it; he thinks about *it*, instead of about himself or what it might cause to happen to him; he grapples with it boldly, imaginatively, resourcefully, and if not confidently at least hopefully; if he fails to master it, he looks without shame or fear at his mistakes and learns what he can from them. This is intelligence. Clearly its roots lie in a certain feeling about life, and one's self with respect to life. Just as clearly, unintelligence is not what most psychologists seem to suppose, the same thing as intelligence only less of it. It is an entirely different style of behavior, arising out of an entirely different set of attitudes.

Years of watching and comparing bright children and the not-bright, or less bright, have shown that they are very different kinds of people. The bright child is curious about life and reality, eager to get in touch with it, embrace it, unite himself with it. There is no wall, no barrier between him and life. The dull child is far less curious, far less interested in what goes on and what is real, more inclined to live in worlds of fantasy. The bright child likes to experiment, to try things out. He lives by the maxim that there is more than one way to skin a cat. If he can't do something one way, he'll try another. The dull child is usually afraid to try at all. It takes a good deal of urging to get him to try even once; if that try fails, he is through.

The bright child is patient. He can tolerate uncertainty and failure, and will keep trying until he gets an answer. When all his experiments fail, he can even admit to himself and others that for the time being he is not going to get an answer. This may annoy him, but he can wait. Very often, he does not want to be told how to do the problem or solve the puzzle he has struggled with, because he does not want to be cheated out of the chance to figure it out for himself in the future. Not so the dull child. He cannot stand uncertainty or failure. To him, an unanswered question is not a challenge or an opportunity, but a threat. If he can't find the answer quickly, it must be given to him, and quickly; and he must have answers for everything. Such are the children of whom a second-grade teacher once said, "But my children *like* to have questions for which there is only one answer." They did; and by a mysterious coincidence, so did she.

The bright child is willing to go ahead on the basis of incomplete understanding and information. He will take risks, sail uncharted seas, explore when the landscape is dim, the landmarks few, the light poor. To give only one example, he will often read books he does not understand in the hope that after a while enough understanding will emerge to make it worth while to go on. In this spirit some of my fifth graders tried to read *Moby Dick*. But the dull child will go ahead only when he thinks he knows exactly where he stands and exactly what is ahead of him. If he does not feel he knows exactly what an experience will be like, and if it will not be exactly like other experiences he already knows, he wants no part of it. For while the bright child feels that the universe is, on the whole, a sensible, reasonable, and trustworthy place, the dull child feels that it is senseless, unpredictable, and treacherous. He feels that he can never tell what may happen, particularly in a new situation, except that it will probably be bad.

Nobody starts off stupid. You have only to watch babies and infants, and think seriously about what all of them learn and do, to see that, except for the most grossly retarded, they show a style of life, and a desire and ability to learn that in an older person we might well call genius. Hardly an adult in a thousand, or ten thousand, could in any three years of his life learn as much, grow as much in his understanding of the world around him, as every infant learns and grows in his first three years. But what happens, as we get older, to this extraordinary capacity for learning and intellectual growth?

What happens is that it is destroyed, and more than by any other one thing, by the process that we misname education — a process that goes on in most homes and schools. We adults destroy most of the intellectual and creative capacity of children by the things we do to them or make them do. We destroy this capacity above all by making them afraid, afraid of not doing what other people want, of not pleasing, of making mistakes, of failure, of being *wrong*. Thus we make them afraid to gamble, afraid to experiment, afraid to try the difficult and the unknown. Even when we do not create children's fears, when they come to us with fears ready-made and built-in, we use these fears as handles to manipulate them and get them to do what we want. Instead of trying to whittle down their fears, we build them up, often to monstrous size. For we like children who are a little afraid of us, docile, deferential children, though not, of course, if they are so obviously afraid that they threaten our image of ourselves as kind, lovable people whom there is no reason to fear. We find ideal the kind of "good" children who are just enough afraid of us to do everything we want, without making us feel that fear of us is what is making them do it.

We destroy the disinterested (I do *not* mean *un*interested) love of learning in children, which is so strong when they are small, by encouraging and compelling them to work for petty and contemptible rewards — gold stars, or papers marked 100 and tacked to the wall, or A's on report cards, or honor rolls, or dean's lists, or Phi Betta Kappa keys — in short, for the ignoble satisfaction of feeling that they are better than someone else. We encourage them to feel that the end and aim of all they do in school is nothing more than to get a good mark on a test, or to impress someone with what they seem to know. We kill, not only their curiosity, but their feeling that it is a good and admirable thing to be curious, so that by the age of ten most of them will not ask questions, and will show a good deal of scorn for the few who do.

In many ways, we break down children's convictions that things make sense, or their hope that things may prove to make sense. We do it, first of all, by breaking up life into arbitrary and disconnected hunks of subject matter, which we then try to "integrate" by such artificial and irrelevant devices as having children sing Swiss folk songs while they are studying the geography of Switzerland, or do arithmetic problems about rail splitting while they are studying the boyhood of Lincoln. Furthermore, we continually confront them with what is senseless, ambiguous and contradictory; worse, we do it without knowing that we are doing it, so that, hearing nonsense shoved at them as if it were sense, they come to feel that the source of their confusion lies not in the material but in their own stupidity. Still further, we cut children off from their own common sense and the world of reality by requiring them to play with and shove around words and symbols that have little or no meaning to them. Thus we turn the vast majority of our students into the kind of people for whom all symbols are meaningless; who cannot use symbols as a way of learning about and dealing with reality; who cannot understand written instructions; who, even if they read books, come out knowing no more than when they went in; who may have a few new words rattling around in their heads, but whose mental models of the world remain unchanged and, indeed impervious to change. The minority, the able and successful students, we are very likely to turn into something different but just as dangerous: the kind of people who can manipulate words and symbols fluently while keeping themselves largely divorced from the reality for which they stand; the kind of people who like to speak in large generalities but grow silent or indignant if someone asks for an example of what they are talking about; the kind of people who, in their

discussions of world affairs, coin and use such words as megadeaths and megacorpses, with scarcely a thought to the blood and suffering these words imply.

We encourage children to act stupidly, not only by scaring and confusing them, but by boring them, by filling up their days with dull, repetitive tasks that make little or no claim on their attention or demands on their intelligence. Our hearts leap for joy at the sight of a roomful of children all slogging away at some imposed task, and we are all the more pleased and satisfied if someone tells us that the children don't really like what they are doing. We tell ourselves that this drudgery, this endless busywork, is good preparation for life, and we fear that without it children would be hard to "control." But why must this busywork be so dull? Why not give tasks that are interesting and demanding? Because, in schools where every task must be completed and every answer must be right, if we give children more demanding tasks they will be fearful and will instantly insist that we show them how to do the job. When you have acres of paper to fill up with pencil marks, you have no time to waste on the luxury of thinking. By such means children are firmly established in the habit of using only a small part of their thinking capacity. They feel that school is a place where they must spend most of their time doing dull tasks in a dull way. Before long they are deeply settled in a rut of unintelligent behavior from which most of them could not escape even if they wanted to.

SØREN HANSEN and
JESPER JENSEN with
WALLACE ROBERTS

THE
LITTLE RED
SCHOOLBOOK

▊▍▎▏▊▍▎▏▊▍▎▏▊▍▎▏▊▍▎▏▊▍▎▏▊▍▎▏▊▍▎▏▊▍▎▏▊▍▎▏▊▍▎▏

Intelligence

People used to think that children who couldn't manage at school were stupid. It was also believed that babies were born with a particular level of intelligence, and that nothing could be done to change this level. Neither of these things is true, but there are still a lot of people who believe them.

It's obvious that everybody's not the same at birth. But the differences at birth are not nearly as big as they become later. A strange thing happens: children who find learn-ing difficult don't get *more* teaching at school, they get *less*. People say these children "can't cope with school" – instead of saying that school can't cope with them.

Many people disagree with this. They think that school is the one place where an effort should be made to cope with all children, including those who find learning difficult.

Intelligence can change

It's been shown that the sort of intelli-gence which is measured by intelligence tests can change. This sort of intelligence is often called "intelligence quotient" or IQ. The right conditions can improve a person's IQ.

If twins who are identical at birth are brought up in different surroundings, their IQ's will become different. The twin who is brought up in an interesting and lively home acquires a higher IQ than the twin who is brought up in a dull, boring home where his IQ is not stimu-lated.

People have also made studies of chil-dren's homes. Good children's homes where children got proper care and attention were compared with bad homes where children were just left to themselves. The children from the good homes acquired higher IQ's than children in the bad homes who started off on exactly the same level.

If a child can't cope at school, it's wrong to say that he's stupid. It may be that he hasn't had the right opportunities, or that not enough effort has been made to teach him anything. Perhaps more time should be spent on him than on the other children.

But there are some differences

A school should be able to take into account many sorts of differences between children – for example, how quickly they learn. Someone who learns slowly is capable of learning just as much and just as well as someone else who learns fast. But it's difficult

161

to allow for this because there are so many students in each class and because there is so much to do — and maybe because the teacher doesn't know how to tackle the problem. This is where the difficulties lie.

There may be other differences. Some arise because the school concerns itself only with certain things. The school is a world of its own, and people who can't manage the particular things which the school demands often manage very well outside school once they've left.

Nobody is bad at everything. There's always one thing you can do better than other things.

What a teacher expects of you

Do you know that what you learn and how quickly you learn it is very much influenced by what the teacher expects you to learn?

Do you know that teachers think middle-class students who are well-behaved and score well on IQ tests will learn more, and that they therefore teach them more?

Do you know that most teachers expect students with working-class accents or immigrant backgrounds or who are black, Mexican-American or Indian to learn less, and that they therefore teach them less?

Do you know that when teachers are given false information about their students they are fooled? In a recent experiment in New York, teachers were told that one group of students were very bright and that another group were not very bright. The first group enjoyed their lessons and learned a lot, the second group had less fun and learned a lot less. But in fact both groups of students were an equal mixture of all kinds of minds and abilities. What they got out of their lessons was determined not by their ability but by what the teacher expected of them.

Don't let a teacher make assumptions about you and your abilities.

What does "backward" mean?

Some children are so slow at learning that it's very difficult to give them the attention they need in ordinary classes. They are therefore put into special classes (called remedial classes) or into special schools. These children are not "mentally handicapped." They are called "backward" or "retarded." Backward children manage quite well for themselves later in life. If they get enough individual help and encouragement, they can learn as much as anybody else.

Being mentally handicapped usually means something quite different. Mentally handicapped children have brain damage or some illness. They find it terribly difficult to learn things and a great deal of work is needed to help them. Most mentally handicapped children can't manage on their own later in life. They often have to live in institutions for the rest of their lives.

Stupid or smart

If your teacher starts talking about who's stupid and who's smart, ask him what he means by intelligence. You'll find that he means the ability to cope with the demands *he* thinks school should make on you.

Fortunately there are many other, different demands in life than the ones made at school. People are good at different things. It's nonsense to call somebody dumb or stupid.

TESTS and EVALUATIONS

A Canadian social scientist has come up with what may be the closest thing yet to an objective intelligence test.

Where all previous intelligence tests have required the active participation of the testee, Dr. John Ertl's method is completely passive. He uses a brain-wave machine.

Electrodes are attached to the testee's scalp, and a computer directly measures the speed of response of the brain to a series of flashing lights. In minutes the computer prints out a three-digit "neural-efficiency" score.

Scores on the neural-efficiency analyzer correlates well with conventional IQ tests. More important, the machine has spotted a number of very bright children who had been labeled dull after conventional testing. Taken from slow-learning classes, these children adjusted satisfactorily to a faster pace.

The machine is also apparently able to factor out differences in social-economic backgrounds, environmental stress and similar variables. Ertl's supporters say the device demolishes the presumed 15-point IQ difference between blacks and whites reported by Arthur Jensen and William Shockley.

The machine's inventor, currently director of the Center of Cybernetic Studies at the University of Ottawa, believes the greatest value of the machine lies in its ability to diagnose reading difficulties (dyslexia) early and accurately. "There are no misses," he says.

RIGHTS AND

Not the violent conflict between parts of the truth, but the quiet suppression of half of it, is the formidable evil; there is always hope when people are forced to listen to both sides. It is when they attend only one that errors harden into prejudices, and truth itself ceases to have the effect of truth, by being exaggerated into falsehood. — *John Stewart Mill*

The surest way to corrupt a young man is to teach him to esteem more highly those who think alike than those who think differently. — *Friedrich Nietzsche*

It is better to debate a question without settling it than to settle a question without debating it. — *Joseph Joubert*

One of the greatest pains to human nature is the pain of a new idea. — *Walter Bagehot*

RESPONSIBILITIES

If we have a correct theory but merely prate about it, pigeonhole it, and do not put it into practice, then that theory, however good, is of no significance. — *Mao Tse-Tung*

Education makes a people easy to lead, but difficult to drive; easy to govern, but impossible to enslave. — *Lord Brougham*

To dedicate oneself to the defense of academic freedom is perhaps the most important thing an education can do. — *S. I. Hayakawa*

It is so easy to vote millions for ABMs and SSTs and then to reject money for the ABCs.

— *Anonymous*

In the first place god made idiots. This was for practice. Then he made school boards.

— *Mark Twain*

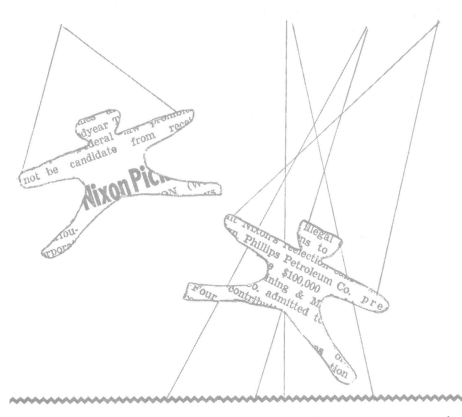

Is it not ironical that in a planned society of controlled workers given compulsory assignments, where religious expression is suppressed, the press controlled, and all media of communication censored, where a puppet government is encouraged but denied any real authority, where great attention is given to efficiency and character reports, and attendance at cultural assemblies is compulsory, where it is avowed that all will be administered to each according to his needs and performance required from each according to his abilities, and where those who flee are tracked down, returned, and punished for trying to escape — in short in the milieu of the typical large American secondary school — we attempt to teach "the democratic system"? *Royce Van Norman*

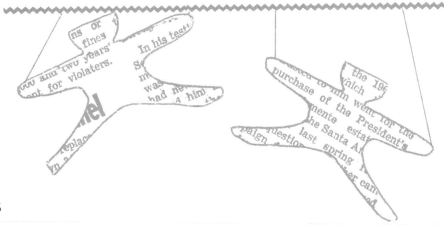

School officials do not possess absolute authority over their students. Students in school as well as out of school are "persons" under our Constitution. . . . in our system, students may not be regarded as closed-circuit recipients of only that which the State chooses to communicate. They may not be confined to the expression of those sentiments that are officially approved. In the absence of a specific showing of constitutionally valid reasons to regulate their speech, students are entitled to a free expression of their views. — US Supreme Court ruling in *Tinker* v. *Des Moines Independent Community School District*, 1969

NO!

CLIFTON, Ariz. — Eleanor Stacy, 13, was sent home from her junior high school graduation ceremony because her clothing did not conform with school rules. She was turned away because she wore a flowered dress. School officials had decided that girls should wear plain dresses.

PROPOSED STUDENT BILL OF RIGHTS

CANCELLED

PREAMBLE

Young people in the United States have the right to a full, free, and uninterrupted public education.

It is essential that schools provide students with real opportunities to function as participants in formulating and implementing rules of conduct in their school so that upon graduating they will be equipped and prepared to deal within our larger community as active and knowledgeable citizens.

The following regulations are illustrative of a reasonable code allowing for student rights and giving to the student a real part in dealing with his educational life.

I. DISTRIBUTION OF PRINTED MATERIALS

Students may distribute leaflets, newspapers, and other literature adjacent to school and on school property where normal flow of traffic will not be impeded. The time of such activity shall be limited to periods before school begins, after dismissal, and during lunch time, if such limitation is necessary to prevent interference with the school program. Such literature shall be protected by the same laws which apply to all other forms of expression in the community. Authorship and/or distribution may be done without fear of recrimination.

II. BULLETIN BOARDS

School authorities may restrict the use of certain bulletin boards to school announcements.

Ample bulletin board space shall be provided for the use of students and student organizations, including a reasonable area for notices relating to out-of-school activities or matters of general interest to students. There shall be no prior censorship or requirement of approval of the contents or wording of notices or other communications, but the following general limitations on posting may be applied.

1. School authorities may remove material which is obscene according to current legal definitions; which is libelous; or which inflames or incites students so as to create a clear and present danger of the commission of unlawful acts, or of physical disruption to the orderly operation of the school.
2. Identification on any posted notice shall be required of the student or student group including the name of at least one person of the group issuing same.
3. The school shall require that notices or other communications be dated before posting and that such material be removed after a prescribed reasonable time to assure full access of the bulletin board.

III. SYMBOLIC EXPRESSION

Students may wear or display buttons, armbands, flags, decals or other badges of symbolic expression, unless the manner of expression materially and substantially interferes with the orderly process of the school or the rights of others.

IV. CEREMONIES

All flag salutes, pledges of allegiance, and other ceremonies of political loyalty are optional.

V. SCHOOL RECORDS

Each student and/or parent may inspect his or her full school record upon reasonable notice and in the presence of a school official.

VI. DRESS CODE

No restrictions or requirements on length of hair or on clothing shall be adopted except by individual departments on the basis of safety or hygiene.

LEGALITY — Students are required to dress in compliance with local ordinance and state law. Prohibited are:

A.   Bathing suits — beach wear.
B.   Exposure of torso.
C.   Exposure of soles of feet.

VII. PREGNANCY

Pregnant students may remain in their regular school programs as long as physically possible.

VIII. UNREASONABLE PENALTIES

Students shall not be subject to:

(a)   Sarcastic remarks
(b)   Personal affront and indignity
(c)   School tasks imposed for punitive purposes
(d)   Frequent detentions without specific purpose
(e)   Forced apologies
(f)   Exclusion from the room without supervision
(g)   Grading reflecting other than academic performance

IX. NONSUSPENDABLE OFFENSES

The following offenses within the school shall be dealt with through administrative action other than suspension or expulsion:

1.   Abusive or obscene language
2.   Tardiness
3.   Fighting outside the classroom
4.   Smoking in prohibited areas
5.   Leaving school grounds without permission
6.   Truancy
7.   Vandalism
8.   Cumulative detention
9.   Other nondisruptive behavior

X. SUSPENDABLE OFFENSES

The deprivation of the right to an education may occur only for just cause and in accordance with due process of law. Suspensions shall not occur except upon substantial and material disruption of school activities or danger of physical injury to other students or teachers. An emergency must exist. Suspensions shall only be used to remove the disruptive cause and shall not be used as a form of punishment.

XI. PROCEDURES FOR SUSPENSION

In the event of suspension no student may be sent home without prior notification to parents or guardians and parent consent. Such notification, by telephone when practicable, must include the reason for suspension. If the parent cannot be reached, the student must remain in school until the end of the school day. The suspension shall last only so long as the emergency exists, but in no event more than five days. A letter mailed on the day of suspension to the parent or guardian must state the specific reasons for the suspensions and include a date for a conference as soon as possible within the suspension period. The letter should allow for the parent to arrange a more suitable date if necessary.

XII. CONFERENCE

In addition to the parent, there may be one or two persons selected by the student or parent to assist at the conference. There shall also be present a clinical member of the staff of the Board of Education, such as a psychologist or social worker. The principal or his representative may also bring to the conference two additional persons who are conversant with the problem under discussion. Such a meeting shall have two purposes: (1) to discuss the student's behavior and the reason for the suspension and (2) to plan with the parent and student the best way of helping the student toward a better school adjustment and prompt return to the regular school setting. If it is mutually agreed at the conference that the problem is medical or psychiatric, a formal referral shall be made to an appropriate medical or psychiatric resource for evaluation and recommendation. If the student maintains a denial of any wrongdoing and the matter is not resolved at the conference, a hearing shall be scheduled.

XIII. HEARING

The hearing may be held following the end of the suspension period. Its purpose is to determine whether the student was in fact guilty of suspendable behavior. The hearing may result only in erasure of the suspension from the student's record by majority vote.

The hearing board shall consist of three members: an elected student delegate, a member of the faculty or administration, and a disinterested member of the community, selected by the two first-named members. Each hearing board shall determine the procedural rules for its hearing. No individual may sit on more than three hearing boards within a school year.

CONCLUSION

This resolution recognizes the student's responsibility for his conduct and at the same time extends the range of his rights and responsibility. Greater understanding by all engaged in the educational process should result, and the outcome should be effective citizenship in our society.

The Rules*

1. No papers or notebooks will be accepted late.
2. All written work must be in ink.
3. All papers must be dated and show the section number.
4. Pencils may not be sharpened after the bell rings.
5. Students must be seated when the bell rings.
6. Students who arrive after the bell starts to ring must report to the principal's office for a pass.
7. Parents must sign student's papers if a failing grade has been assigned.
8. A student may not chew gum in the class.
9. A student may not go to the wastebasket during class.
10. Books must be stacked outside the classroom door when examinations are being taken.
11. No student may speak without being recognized by the teacher.
12. Everyone must sit in his assigned seat.
13. A boy may have only one button of his shirt unbuttoned.
14. Boys must have their hair neatly combed! Leroy, get a haircut. (crewcut)
15. Textbooks must be covered.
16. A student may not go to the water fountain during class.
17. A student may be permitted to go to the rest rooms, but a record will be kept of the dates, and, should the number of times be considered excessive, the student will be referred to the nurse.
18. When the bell rings, the students will sit quietly and await the instructions of the teacher.
19. A student may not borrow materials from another student.
20. A student who fails the final examination fails the course.

*Found in a student's desk.

. . . . we are witnessing the results of permissiveness, particularly on the part of some of our higher institutions of learning, which allow rights without obligations, demonstrations without restrictions, and lewd behavior without censure.

In addition to being skilled in the arts and sciences, particularly in the art of communication with clarity and conciseness, it is my hope that the youth of tomorrow will be fired with a patriotic zeal to adhere to the principles which have made America strong and will demonstrate a willingness to protect our free enterprise system and maintain a society based on fair play and equal justice.

LEGAL Advice to Principals

• It is doubtful if pupil personnel records can be kept confidential from the pupil and parent if the issue is challenged in the courts. Generally, common law gives persons with "real interest" the right to inspection. This is particularly true in those states not having legislation establishing matters of confidentiality of student records.

• As evidenced by the statutory material, court decisions, and school codes, the solution to the issue of smoking in the public schools is far from clear.

There is a general agreement that it is one thing to assume moral positions and another thing to implement those positions. Also, it is difficult to impose adult views on students and have significant behavioral changes in a practice like smoking. The 26th Amendment to the U.S. Constitution adds the further dimension of assigning legal adult status to 18-year-olds. However, it is also clear that principals and all educators are faced today with a question to which they must react.

• *Although the law generally* allows administrators to search lockers, this should not be viewed as a carte blanche right. As we have seen, students do have some ownership rights, particularly with regard to other students. School officials are charged by the state with operating the schools and safeguarding the health, welfare, and safety of students and school personnel; therefore, when drugs, weapons, or other dangerous materials are suspected, the principal not only has the right but duty to make a thorough investigation. Fishing expeditions as a matter of school policy are not advised. A general search of all lockers in reaction to a bomb threat or widespread drug abuse can be justified as a proper exercise of school authority.

• Student publications, always a vital concern for school administrators, is a subject area in which the judiciary continues to narrow the "in loco parentis" doctrine and concurrently to apply adult standards of "responsible" journalism.

• Guidelines of at least a general nature should be established clearly categorizing material which is libelous, obscene, scandalous, or clearly provocative as unacceptable. It may well be necessary for principals to insist upon the right of distribution, or prior review, to ensure that they have an opportunity to make this judgment. To avoid unnecessary legal confrontation, suspension, and/or disruption, school regulations should provide for the appeal of the principal's decision leading to final determination by the board.

• Every girl in the United States has a right to, and a need for, the education that will help her prepare herself for a career, for family life, and for citizenship. To be married or pregnant is not sufficient cause to deprive her of an education and the opportunity to become a contributing member of society. — *S. P. Marland, Jr.*, HEW Assistant Secretary for Education.

hOw to appraise a textbook

When examining a textbook that has been criticized it is wise to ask these questions.

1. What is the date of the copyright? Books inevitably reflect the climate of opinion at the time when they are written. A book written during World War II might well treat Russia, for example, in a manner markedly different from the one the same author would use now.

2. Is the material criticized unfairly? In other words, is the material being considered in terms of its subject matter and the author's intent?

3. Is it removed from context? Modern textbooks are carefully planned and the whole teaching unit must be considered, not merely isolated sentences or paragraphs.

4. When considered with full content what is the effect on the pupil liable to be? Will it be harmful or will it help him to achieve necessary insight and understanding of modern problems and events?

5. How is the material intended to be used in the schools? Is the student taught to accept unthinkingly everything he reads, or is he taught to evaluate and discriminate?

6. Does the book as a whole represent a fair and unbiased view? In other words, do the criticized sections represent the spirit and bias of the whole book?

The American Textbook Institute, which draws up the above criteria, adds "If we can treat the public as partners in this over-all job of public education and give them the opportunity to participate in the solution of school and textbook problems which is their right, much good may come out of the present controversy. Their criticisms will then be based on understanding rather than on emotion and propaganda, and such criticisms can well lead, not just to loyal public support, but to better books and better schools."

Citizen's Request for Reconsideration of a Work

Hardcover_____
Paperback_____

Author_____

Title_____

Publisher (if known)_____

Request initiated by_____

Telephone_____ Address_____

City_____ Zip code_____

Complainant represents

_____himself

_____(name organization)_____

_____(identify other group)_____

1. To what in the work do you object? Please be specific; cite pages._____

2. What of value is there in this work?_____

3. What do you feel might be the result of reading this work?_____

4. For what age group would you recommend this work?_____

5. Did you read the entire work?_____What pages or sections?_____

6. Are you aware of the judgment of this work by critics?_____

7. Are you aware of the teacher's purpose in using this work?_____

8. What do you believe is the theme or purpose of this work?_____

9. What would you prefer the school do about this work?

_____Do not assign or recommend it to my child.

_____Withdraw it from all students.

_____Send it back to the English department for reevaluation.

10. In its place, what work of equal value would you recommend that would convey as valuable a picture and perspective of a society or a set of values?_____

_____
(Signature of Complainant)

an immodest proposal

Frederica K. Bartz

In the columns of our local newspaper recently appeared a story about a mother whose concerned interest in better education led her to demand that an obscene and filthy book "about a girl who gets pregnant in the book by a minister" be removed from the classroom. The next day a nice lady, somebody's grandmother, who writes on the side of God, supported the first nice lady with a Letter to the Editor. Her letter was followed by more from other concerned and nice parents, one of whom protested the filth in a book assigned to his daughter, a book called "The Canterburry Tails." In the interests of these parents, of concerned parents and teachers everywhere, and of education generally, I would like to offer, in all modesty, my solution to the problem of obscenity in the classroom. The Fredrica Harry Golden Bartz Sanitary Plan for Displacing Obscene Literature.

Before presenting my plan, I would like to point out some previously unnoticed facts. The walls of every elementary, junior high, and senior high school in the country are covered with obscene sayings and filthy words. No parent has ever complained. No parent has ever demanded that these words be removed. No parent has ever refused to allow his child to go to the bathroom. It is obvious that obscenity does not poison the minds and morals of the young if it is read in these sanitary booths and not in books.

Therefore, my plan is simple. Before assigning dirty books, the teachers can tear out the pages containing the filth and paste these pages on the walls of the restrooms. Students could then go there to read them.

My plan has several obvious advantages. First, students would not have to waste this time since they have to go there anyway. Second, since students always read what is on restroom walls, teachers will not have to give check quizzes over this material. Third, freed from the necessity of visiting principals and writing the editor, these morally aware and education-minded parents could aid teachers by reading the rest of the books they have complained of to check for dirty pages the teachers might have missed.

I wish no plaudits, tributes, or monetary rewards for giving my plan to humanity. I feel it is my duty.

BOSTON PUBLIC SCHOOLS
School Committee
15 Beacon Street, Boston 8, Massachusetts

Attorney
Thomas S. Eisenstadt
Member

A careful investigation of the facts pertaining to the discharge of Mr. Jonathan Kozol reveal that the administration of the Boston Public Schools were fully justified in terminating his service.

Contrary to publicized reports, I have found that the poem incident was not the sole reason for Mr. Kozol's discharge. Rather, this particular incident was merely the climax to a series of incidents involving this teacher. On numerous occasions during his six months of service . . . Mr. Kozol was advised and counseled by his Principal, Miss ——, and his Supervisor, Mr. ——, to restrict his reading and reference materials to the list of approved publications. These admonitions were brought about by Mr. Kozol's continual deviation from the 4th grade course of study.

It has been established as a fact that Mr. Kozol taught the poem, "Ballad of the Landlord" to his class and later distributed mimeographed copies of it to his pupils for home memorization. It is also true that a parent of one of the pupils registered a strong objection to the poem to the school principal. Miss ——, properly carrying out her responsibility to all of the pupils and to their parents, admonished the neophyte teacher for his persistent deviation from the course of study. She further suggested that the poem "Ballad of the Landlord" was unsuitable for 4th graders since it could be interpreted as advocating defiance of authority. At this point Mr. Kozol became rude and told Miss —— that he was a better judge of good literature than she.

The confirmation of the above facts is adequate justification for the discharge of a temporary teacher hired on a day-to-day trial basis. It has been stated quite adequately that the curriculum of this particular school, which is saturated with compensatory programs in an effort to specially assist disadvantaged pupils, does allow for innovation and creative teaching. However, this flexibility does not and should not allow for a teacher to implant in the minds of young children any and all ideas. Obviously, a measure of control over the course of study is essential to protect the 94,000 Boston school children from ideologies and concepts not acceptable to our way of life. Without any restrictions, what guarantees would parents have that their children were not being taught that Adolf Hitler and Nazism were right for Germany and beneficial to mankind?

It should be understood that the fact of the poem's author [sic] happened to be a Negro had no bearing on this matter whatsoever. As a matter of fact, Mr. Kozol was asked by the school principal why other works of Langston Hughes, non-controversial in nature, were not selected for study. In fact, a reference source suggested in the course of study recommends use of the book entitled, "Time for Poetry," published by Foresman which contains six of Langston Hughes' poems; and the Administrative Library contains the book, "More Silver Pennies," by MacMillian [sic] which includes more of Langston Hughes' poems, and also poems by the Negro poet Countee Cullen.

When Miss —— reported the incident to Deputy Superintendent Sullivan and requested Mr. Kozol's removal from the teaching staff of the —— School, it climaxed a series of complaints made to Miss Sullivan's office concerning this particular teacher. Superintendent Ohrenberger's decision after carefully weighing the facts of the case was to relieve Mr. Kozol from further service in the Boston Public Schools.

It should be understood that many temporary teachers are released from service every year by the administration of the Boston Public Schools. They are released for a variety of reasons. The overwhelming majority of such cases are discharged because in the opinion of the administrators and supervisors the certain temporary teachers are found unsuitable in training, personality, or character. Mr. Kozol, or anyone else who lacks the personal discipline to abide by rules and regulations, as we all must in our civilized society, is obviously unsuited for the highly responsible profession of teaching.

In conclusion, I must add that Mr. Kozol did bring to his pupils an enthusiastic spirit, a high degree of initiative, and other fine qualities found in the best teachers. It is my hope that Mr. Kozol will develop his latent talents and concomitantly develop an understanding and respect for the value of working within the acceptable codes of behavior.

TEXTBOOKS HAILED ON VIEW OF NEGRO

Study Says Role of Blacks Is Being Treated Fairly

By PHILIP SHABECOFF

Special to The New York Times

WASHINGTON, Oct. 10 — For the first time, the role of the Negro in American history is being fairly and adequately treated in school textbooks in this country, according to a study commissioned by the American Federation of Teachers.

The study, called "The Negro in Modern American History Textbooks," was prepared by Irving Sloan, a teacher at Scarsdale Junior High School in Scarsdale, N.Y. The publication, released today, was the fourth edition of a study originally prepared by Mr. Sloan in 1966.

The three previous editions supported criticism that junior and senior high school history texts either generally ignored or presented a distorted view of the American Negro.

In his present study, Mr. Sloan concluded, "The time has come, however, to praise what the American history textbooks have at this point of time achieved in their treatment of black Americans."

At a news conference at the headquarters of the teachers federation here, Mr. Sloan said that when he was preparing his first study in the mid-nineteen-sixties "there was no question that in our schools the fourth 'R —along with reading, 'riting and 'rithmetic—was racism."

The treatment of blacks in textbooks, he said, was the root of much of the racist problems of the schools.

In his new study. he found "that in this particular decade of the nineteen-seventies, this particular disgrace or failure of American history texts has been eliminated. Much of what is now available ranges from adequate to plentiful. Some of it is superb. All of it is acceptable; a finding which no evaluation of the texts, including our own earlier editons, ever made."

Mr. Sloan's study examined 19 recently published history texts. While it found room for improvement in most of them in their treatment of blacks, it also asserted that in terms of historical scholarship, "the texts meet the highest standards, almost without exception."

THE DOWNHOME GUIDE TO POWER!

HOW TO FILL IN THE BLANKS....

Decide who is responsible for each kind of decision listed in the sections below. Then, find the score assigned to that person or group and write it in the appropriate blank.

Scores:

```
student(s)...............................10
teacher(s).............................. 9
department chairman/team leader(s)...... 8
counselor(s)............................ 7
vice principal.......................... 6
principal............................... 5
administrators at the district level..... 4
superintendent or school board.......... 3
negotiated contract..................... 2
state law............................... 1
```

After you finish each section, add up the scores and put the total in the blank provided. Then divide the total by the number of questions to get the Power Quotient for that section. Interpretations of the average scores is below (but not upside down).

WHAT YOU TEACH

_____ 1. Who decides what grade or grade level you teach?
_____ 2. Who decides what subject(s) you teach?
_____ 3. Who decides what books you may use?
_____ 4. Who decides the curriculum--the topics, the order of the topics, and the approach?
_____ 5. Who decides if the class or individual students may deviate from the curriculum?
_____ 6. Who decides if you may teach a new unit not included in the curriculum?
_____ 7. Who decides if you may teach a new course?
_____ 8. Who decides if you may teach outside of your field of certification?
_____ 9. Who decides if you may use new (and perhaps unapproved) books?
_____ 10. Who decides if you are teaching what you're "spozed" to teach?

_____ TOTAL ⟶ 10⟌‾‾‾‾‾↘ _____ P.Q.

WHOM YOU TEACH

_____ 1. Who decides what individual class size minimums are to be?

_____ 2. Who decides how many students will be in your class(es)?

_____ 3. Who controls transfer of students from class to class?

_____ 4. If you want a student temporarily removed from your class for some reason, who makes the final decision about it?

_____ 5. If you want a student permanently removed from your class for some reason, who makes the final decision about it?

_____ 6. If students are tracked by ability in your school, who decides which track they are assigned to?

_____ 7. If there is ability tracking in your school, who decides whether a student may move from one track to another?

_____ 8. Who decides how many classes you teach?

_____ 9. Who decides whether you have responsibility for a study hall?

_____ 10. Who decides how many students may be assigned to you for any given time period?

_____ TOTAL $\longrightarrow$ $10\overline{)}$ $\downarrow$ _____ P.Q.

WHERE YOU TEACH

_____ 1. Who decides in which school you teach?

_____ 2. Who decides in which room you teach?

_____ 3. Who decides if you teach in more than one room?

_____ 4. If you want to transfer to another school, who decides if you may?

_____ 5. Who decides how much and what kind of furniture you may have in your room?

_____ 6. Who decides if the equipment in your room is adequate and in good repair?

_____ 7. Who decides if you may paint your room?

_____ 8. Who decides if you may make alterations in your room other than painting?

_____ 9. Who decides if you may hold your classes <u>outside</u> of your classroom (and perhaps outside the school)?

_____ 10. Who decides if you may go on field trips?

17 _____ TOTAL $\longrightarrow$ $10\overline{)}$ $\downarrow$ _____ P.Q.

WHEN YOU TEACH

_____ 1. Who decides when your working day begins and ends?
_____ 2. Who decides how long each class lasts?
_____ 3. Who decides which method is used to end classes (bells, music, buzzers, nothing, etc.)?
_____ 4. Who decides if you may dismiss students early?
_____ 5. Who decides what your teaching schedule is?
_____ 6. Who decides how much time you have between class periods?
_____ 7. Who decides how much time you have for lunch?
_____ 8. Who decides how much time you have (if any) for preparation?
_____ 9. Who decides how much time you have (if any) for student conferences, conferring with other teachers, informal conversations, etc.?
_____ 10. Who decides when students may have breaks, recesses, free time, etc.?

_____ TOTAL ⟶ 10⟌‾‾‾‾‾‾‾↳_____ P.Q.

HOW YOU TEACH

_____ 1. Who decides if you may/should run a rigidly controlled classroom?
_____ 2. Who decides if you may/should run an open classroom?
_____ 3. Who decides if you have to prepare lesson plans?
_____ 4. Who decides if you have to structure your class(es) around behavioral objectives?
_____ 5. Who decides how much money you have to spend on supplies and materials for your class(es)?
_____ 6. Who decides if your students may do unstructured or independent study?
_____ 7. Who decides if you may teach or plan with a team or group of teachers of your choice?
_____ 8. Who decides if students are involved in planning your class(es)?
_____ 9. Who decides what kind of supplementary materials and resources you may use--books, films, speakers, trips, etc.?
_____ 10. Who decides if you are teaching the way you're "spozed" to teach?

_____ TOTAL ⟶ 10⟌‾‾‾‾‾‾‾↳_____ P.Q.

OTHER GOOD QUESTIONS

_____ 1. Who decides how many students will attend your school?

_____ 2. Who decides how many teachers will be assigned to your school?

_____ 3. Who decides how those teachers are assigned <u>within</u> your school?

_____ 4. Who decides how much money your school gets for materials, supplies, equipment, etc.?

_____ 5. Who decides how much money your department or grade level gets out of the total school budget?

_____ 6. Who decides how much money you get out of the total school budget?

_____ 7. Who decides on what criteria teachers are evaluated?

_____ 8. Who is responsible for writing your evaluation?

_____ 9. Who decides on what criteria students are evaluated?

_____ 10. Who decides on the grading system and how it operates in your school?

_____ 11. Who decides what information is released to the public about your school district?

_____ 12. Who decides what information is released to the public about your school?

_____ 13. Who decides that students should be given a standardized test?

_____ 14. Who decides when and where standardized tests are to be given?

_____ 15. Who decides how the information from standardized tests is to be used?

_____ 16. Who decides on the rules and regulations (code of conduct, etc.) for students to follow in your school?

_____ 17. Who decides on the punishment in case any of the rules are broken?

_____ 18. Who decides how much freedom of movement students have in your school?

_____ 19. Who has the final decision in any teacher grievance?

_____ 20. Who decides whether a teacher's absence is "legitimate"?

_____ TOTAL ⟶ 20⟌ ↳_____ P.Q.

INTERPRETATION OF THE AVERAGE SCORES (POWER QUOTIENTS):

If the average score for each category or for the entire set is:

9 - 10.....tell us where you are, 'cuz we want to teach there, too!

7 - 8......middle management has gotcha, but it could be lots worse.

5 - 6......listen closely to see if your principal whistles "Under My Thumb."

3 - 4......what's your employee number again?!?

1 - 2......what's the superintendent's employee number again?!?

FROM "ROOM 222"

ACT TWO

"THE LINCOLN STORY"

PETE'S CLASSROOM – DAY – now emptied of students.

MR. KAUFMAN There's a citizen in my office in an apoplectic rage, Pete, so something must've happened!

PETE He got up and ran out of the classroom.

MR. KAUFMAN And now he wants to call the newspapers.

PETE He's the hysterical type.

MR. KAUFMAN What about Victoria Langley? Is she hysterical too? She agrees that one of your students called Abraham Lincoln a "hustling honky racist."

PETE I think the expression was a "hustling honky politician."

MR. KAUFMAN Oh, that's much better. Mr. Stiles is upset because he claims you did nothing about it.

PETE It was an open discussion. Everybody's entitled to their point of view. . . . even Mr. Stiles.

Liz comes hurrying IN, followed by Alice.

LIZ What happened?

PETE Nothing serious.

MR. KAUFMAN Someone called Abraham Lincoln dirty names. Mr. Stiles is in an uproar.

LIZ Who was it? Jason?

PETE Ignited by Esther Avedon.

MR. KAUFMAN I have to figure out what I'm going to tell this guy.

ALICE Pete won't get the award?

His expression at the mention of the award.

MR. KAUFMAN Award! Mr. Stiles wants him shipped to Siberia.

PETE You wouldn't want me to muzzle the kids.

MR. KAUFMAN You know I'm all for academic freedom, but it's just a shame that this once your discussion wasn't kept at room temperature.

(muttering on exit)

Now, what am I supposed to say to the man?

To the Editor:

As a taxpayer, I want to let this town know how I feel about the way our high school is run — how our property taxes are wasted on programs that seem to turn out the opposite of the kinds of people I went to school with.

My main complaint is about the behavior of high schoolers — especially after athletic events. My home is close to the school, and I never saw such goings on — yelling, pushing, and all kinds of horseplay that wouldn't be tolerated when I went to school.

If the school were doing what it was supposed to do, we wouldn't have such problems. We would have discipline and respect both in and out of school. I have it on good authority that the kids do anything they want to in school, and the teachers are afraid to do anything about it — or maybe with all this permissiveness — they just don't want to do anything. Student choice, independent study, electives all contribute to the breakdown of discipline, and we ought to look into the possibility of getting rid of them and going back to some of the old no-nonsense ways. And if those teachers won't go along, let's get others who will. We can show them how we feel when the school budget comes up for a vote next month.

Walter Sheridan
Warrentown, Maryland

SCIENCE TEACHING AT ISSUE ON COAST

Biblical Version of Creation Is Urged for Textbooks

By EVERETT R. HOLLES

Special to The New York Times

SAN DIEGO, Oct. 21—A long-standing dispute within the State Board of Education over what California schoolchildren are to be taught about man's origin headed this week toward a public hearing reminiscent of the Scopes "monkey trial" of 47 years ago.

The issue in California, however, is not a clear-cut one of the Book of Genesis v. Charles Darwin, as debated by William Jennings Bryan and Clarence Darrow in their 1925 encounter in Dayton, Tenn.

Instead, it revolves around a demand by several members of the board that new science textbooks to be used by more than a million children in the state's eight elementary grades reflect the Biblical version of "creation by design" as a counterbalance to what the dissidents called "the still unresolved scientific theories of evolution."

Warning on Theory

The National Academy of Sciences, in what it conceded to be an unprecedented action, intervened in the California controversy this week with a warning against including religious theory in public school science teaching because of "national implications" that could adversely affect science study for a generation to come.

In a resolution adopted in Washington, the academy said religion and science were "separate and mutually exclusive realms of human thought" incompatible in their explanations of the origin of life.

To include the concept of divine creation in a science textbook, it added, "would almost certainly impair the proper segregation of the teaching and understanding of both science and religion nationwide," largely because of its effect on the publishers of textbooks for the national market.

An assortment of proposed science textbooks, both scientifically based and Biblically oriented, went on public display for parents throughout the state this week, preparatory to a public hearing that the Board of Education will hold in Sacramento on Nov. 9.

With scientists, educators and spokesmen for fundamentalist religious groups taking sides in the dispute, one member of the state board predicted that the hearing would be "a more sophisticated, modern-day version of the Scopes trial."

Prof. Melvin Calvin, University of California at Berkeley biochemist and Nobel laureate who helped prepare the National Academy of Sciences resolution, said the theory of divine creation "is not science, and I know of no scientific evidence that supports it."

Dr. John R. Ford, a San Diego physician who is vice president of the State Board of Education and its only black member, is leading the fight to have the Biblical concept taught parallel with scientific theory. He is supported by several other board members, including Dr. David Hubbard, president of Fuller Theological Seminary in Pasadena.

Dr. Ford called the National Academy of Sciences resolution "not only shortsighted but extremely biased and showing a lack of true scientific thinking." He said ample scientific evidence existed for the theory that the universe was "created by design and not by chance."

The board's argument over the new science textbooks, which are normally revised or replaced every six years, has been developing for three years since a panel of scientific advisers resigned in a body in 1969 when the board attempted to dictate changes in the panel's proposals.

The scientific advisers, appointed by a curriculum commission established under state law, objected particularly to two insertions demanded by the board that it called "intellectually dishonest." The curriculum commission upheld the scientists.

A new ruling this week by Thomas Griffin, chief counsel for the State Department of Education, held that the board could adopt any textbook previously reviewed by the commission whether or not it had been approved or rejected. This opened the way for two pro-religious textbooks, turned down by the commission, to be included in the books placed on statewide display as a preliminary to the Nov. 9 public hearing.

ACADEMIC FREEDOM
in the secondary schools

AMERICAN CIVIL LIBERTIES UNION

Curriculum

The professional staff, by virtue of its training and experience, has the right and responsibility to establish the curriculum, subject to the approval of boards of education and state departments of education. It is expected that members of the staff will be guided at all times by the highest professional standards of scholarship and methodology, applied with an appropriate sensitivity to the community's educational needs and the expressed views of its citizens. Their professional preparation, however, qualifies them to establish what shall be included in the curriculum and when and how it shall be taught, free from dictation by community groups or individual citizens.

Although the professional staff must develop through general agreement the objectives, content and methods of the curriculum, the individual classroom teacher should be given reasonable scope in their implementation. The teacher's professional integrity requires that he not present unorthodox views in such a manner as to imply that they are generally accepted. It is his responsibility to maintain a free interchange of ideas in the classroom.

Selection of texts and supplementary instructional resources

Selection of textbooks should be on an "open list" basis, allowing supervisors and teachers in schools a wide choice of materials to meet particular needs. Listing of acceptable texts should be the function of a selection committee composed of supervisors and teachers. Textbooks should be appraised on the basis of accuracy and adequacy of scholarship, promotion of the curricular objectives, and freedom from unfounded or prejudiced opinions on racial, cultural, religious, or political matters.

The use of supplementary matter other than text should be left to the judgment of the individual teacher. The classroom should be open to outside speakers, whose special competence the teacher may want to use in the development of subjects relevant to the curriculum.

When an issue is controversial, the objective should be to offer varied points of view. It is not essential that any single work present all sides of a question; other resources may be counted upon to maintain a balance so long as they are freely available. Where parents as

189

individuals, or parent or other community groups, raise the question of suitability of any material out of concern for maturity level, morality, patriotism, literary merit, etc., the decision as to its acceptability should be vested in a representative professional committee.

Freedom to teach controversial issues

"Democracy is a way of life that prizes alternatives. Alternatives mean that people must make choices. Wisdom with which to make choices can come only if there are freedom of speech, of press, of assembly, and of teaching. They protect the people in their right to hear, to read, to discuss, and to reach judgments according to individual conscience. Without the possession and the exercise of these rights, self-government is impossible. In defending freedom to learn and freedom to teach we are defending the democratic process itself." (1952 Committee on Academic Freedom, National Council for the Social Studies). The freedom to teach controversial issues is a critical test of the teacher's freedom in the classroom. Our democratic culture, committed to freedom and to respect for the individual, is not monolithic in its values. By discussion of controversial issues, teachers can help students to analyze issues, to investigate and consider various positions, to keep an open mind and weigh alternatives, to organize and present arguments, to draw intelligent conclusions and thus contribute to the development of effective democratic citizenship.

When a controversial issue is studied, conflicting points of view should be explored. The teacher has the right to identify and express his own point of view in the classroom as long as he indicates clearly that it is his own.

Freedom of discussion of school policies

At faculty conferences and meetings teachers have the right to express opinions on school policies and conditions, make declarations and vote on issues. They should feel free to dissent from the views of the administration and the majority of teachers, if they are so inclined. Teachers should be granted the opportunity to explain their positions. There should at no time be any reprisals such as dismissal, the withholding of salary increases or the assignment of undesirable programs.

Faculty conferences and teachers' meetings should ordinarily be preceeded by a distribution of the agenda and teachers should have an opportunity to place items on the agenda.

Teachers have the right to meet privately, to meet without the presence of the administrative staff, and to disseminate their views either as individuals or groups.

Teachers and organizational activities

With a view to the maintenance of professional standards and academic rights, teachers should be completely free to create and maintain within individual schools, committees or councils to represent them in relationships with the school administration. These committees or councils should be accorded every facility to make possible the determination of teacher opinion and for its presentation to the administration.

Like other occupational groups in an industrial society concerned with the maintenance of living standards, teachers should be free to join unions of their own choosing, whether locally organized or part of a nationwide federation. The right to participate in union activity should include the right to strike. A teachers' strike cannot ordinarily be interpreted as endangering the public health, safety, or welfare. Since they are professionals performing a public service it is assumed that teachers will resort to strikes only when other legitimate means of redress have failed.

Teachers and Political Activity

A teacher is free to participate as an

individual in political activities. He should be free to fulfill his duties and responsibilities as a citizen by participating actively in the affairs of the political party of his choice, by attending party functions, contributing to support of the party, campaigning in the community for its candidates, serving as an official in the party, becoming a candidate of the party for public office and holding such office.

His political activity, however, must not compromise his professional integrity. He must not misuse his professional position to pervert the academic process in the interests of his own political ambitions or those of a political group.

Teachers' Individual and Personal Rights

The teacher's individual and personal rights and freedoms outside the academic setting are no less than those of other citizens. Generally, he should enjoy freedom to go where he will, to associate with whomever he chooses, to dress as he pleases, to engage in whatever sports, recreations, pastimes, or supplementary lawful gainful employment he favors, to affiliate with whatever groups he finds a common purpose, to join whatever religious group his conscience dictates, or to refrain from any or all religious practices, and to espouse whatever cause or idea appeals to him. In sum, a teacher should be free to conduct himself as he sees fit unless it can be shown that his behavior is affecting his professional performance in a demonstrably deleterious manner.

The rights of administrators

If a climate of freedom is to be maintained in the schools, those who administer, direct and advise, must enjoy essentially the same liberties which are vouchsafed to the teachers who function directly in the classrooms. The rights here outlined apply to all members of the professional educational staff, including those in supervisory and administrative positions. However, insofar as a school board has the right to expect its top administrators to carry out its designated policy and the right to dismiss them if they fail to do so, these rights do not apply to the administrative official or officials who are appointed by and directly responsible to the school board. These administrators, however, are entitled to retain their teaching positions, if they serve in both capacities.

In 1872, a New York City principal posted these rules for teachers. Men teachers were allowed one evening each week "for courting purposes" or two evenings a week if they went to church regularly. Women teachers who married or engaged in "unseemly conduct" were to be dismissed.

✸✸✸✸✸✸✸✸✸✸✸✸✸✸✸✸✸✸✸✸✸✸✸✸✸✸✸✸✸✸

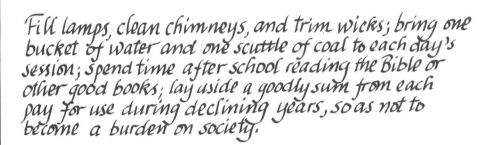

Fill lamps, clean chimneys, and trim wicks; bring one bucket of water and one scuttle of coal to each day's session; spend time after school reading the Bible or other good books; lay aside a goodly sum from each pay for use during declining years, so as not to become a burden on society.

Any teacher who smokes, uses liquor in any form, frequents pool or public halls or gets shaved in barber shops will give good reason to suspect his worth, intentions, integrity, and honesty.

The teacher who performs his labors faithfully and without fault for five years will be given an increase of 25 cents per week in his pay, providing the Board of Education approves.

The Teacher's Lot
Is Not A Happy One

Teachers have always been more or less the butt of youthful jest and abuse; it is only in our day that everyone joins in the fun of kicking the teacher around. Some deserve it, for the teaching profession, like others, has its share of incompetents, indeed more than its share if we are to judge by many of the products of the schools. A good deal of the criticism of teachers is simply evidence of consumer revolt. Unfortunately, the good teacher shares the public buffeting with the teacher who looks on what he is doing as a mere job. And by "good" we mean the teacher who is competent, likes and respects young people, believes in the importance of teaching and the importance of his subject.

This good teacher is assaulted and pressured from all sides. To begin with, he has to survive a training period that is often marked by banality and mediocrity. Although critics have wearied of pointing out deficiencies in teacher training and the public seems to have wearied of hearing them, these deficiencies still exist. Despite many years of threats and promises of reform, the situation remains much as it was ten years ago when criticism was at its most intense: many trainers of teachers lack intellectual distinction and scholarly attainment; there is a paucity of academic content in training programs; and the monopolistic practices of the educationists in such matters as certification still obtain.

The young idealist who is fortunate enough to emerge from his training spiritually and intellectually unscathed enters hopefully on his teaching career. He soon discovers that a lot of people have definite ideas of how he should do his job. Most immediately he feels the influence of the local bureaucracy, which wants to make sure he fits neatly into the institutional pattern, that he does everything through channels, and does not disturb the status quo. This establishment, however, is probably not the strongest influence he has to contend with: most intelligent people learn to outwit and circumvent the system. The greatest pressures on the teacher come from current intellectual and social fashions, fads, and dogmas, and from the general climate of the community and of his particular school.

What are some of these pressures? What are some of the demands current fashion makes on the teacher? One such demand, that he be an individualist and a nonconformist, has a fine ring to it until one realizes that those who make the demand are primarily interested in directing the nonconformity against the distant "establishment." Let the teacher assert his individuality by refusing to join the local teachers' association or local union and see how much praise he gets for his nonconformity. Or let him express unorthodox views — let him cast a vote for accountability or merit pay or anything else the teachers' lobby opposes — and most of his colleagues will consider him a traitor.

Another demand that seems on the face of it to be reasonable is that he be innovative. But innovation in education today does not mean simple human ingenuity in devising ways to interest and motivate students, which is something good teachers have always sought to do. Innovation now means group effort, administrative arrangements, machines, elaborate "programs." There may be virtue in some of these but they tend to leave the teacher who operates best on an individual basis out in the cold. A lone teacher may have discovered new insights to apply to old problems but his practice doesn't become genuine "innovation"

until it has been funded and made into a research project.

The romantics are now demanding that the teacher "love" his students. We doubt very much that love can be packaged for the classroom, or that it should be. Love suggests emotional involvement and personal attachment but are these appropriate in the teacher-student relationship? Yes, say the therapists; but most students, we suspect, would settle for respect, humane treatment, and justice, and be willing to find affection elsewhere.

Demands are also now coming from educational philosophers that the teacher be informal, shun the expression of authority, and not structure or organize subject matter. (Subject matter, indeed, has become a dirty phrase in many quarters.) In that mysterious way that cant phrases become fashionable, we now hear on every hand that in the educational process it is learning, not teaching, that is important, just as if students didn't learn by being taught by somebody or by something. Learning is not a free-floating process in which the teacher's role is only that of tractable attendant or monitor. Undoubtedly some teachers can teach with a modicum of structure and with the assertion of little authority, but this is no excuse for condemning all other styles of teaching.

It is ironic that while teachers are being urged to abandon subject matter, to dismantle knowledge, and to shun the fusty old lessons of history, they are encouraged to make instant judgments, á la Cronkite or Brinkley, about practically any contemporary problem. They are encouraged to propagandize among their students, too — as long as they do so on behalf of the proper Leftish views. Teachers are not only expected to solve or ameliorate all social ills; they are also to become cut-rate Freuds, ministering to the psychological ills of their students.

Still another popular demand is that the student not be put in a subordinate position. The "democracy of the classroom" maintains that teacher and taught are on an equal footing, even though common sense would suggest that the student is by definition subordinate, being not yet an adult, inexperienced, and presumably not yet possessed of the knowledge he is in school to obtain.

The teacher, as has always been the case, is subject to the demands, just and unjust, of parents. At the moment, especially in city schools, parents are demanding that teachers teach their children something, especially how to read, and this is good. But other parents continue to make unreasonable and often irrational demands. This is especially true in regard to discipline. Many parents who cannot, or will not, control their children, are stern in their demands that the teacher do so. There are the parents who have always wanted to foist their own responsibilities onto the schools, the sort of parents who have done much to make the school the catch-all institution it is today.

And so it goes, if you are a teacher. These are but a few of the pressures and demands that confront today's teacher, making his lot indeed like the policeman's, an unhappy one. Isn't it about time that communities did some rethinking about the role of the teacher, attempting to set some reasonable limits to what we can expect of those we put in charge of our youngsters? We would settle for some simple guidelines: all we would ask is that teachers like and respect young people, that they exercise authority with justice and humaneness, that they respect learning, and that they prove their effectiveness by their students' accomplishments. Beyond these simple requirements, we don't care what the teacher's style is, or what he believes, or whose drumbeat he chooses to follow.

Would you want this man to teach YOUR children?

These are the facts.

The teacher is Paul J. Richer, twenty-one-year-old son of a Mason City, Iowa, car dealer. He was graduated from the State University of Iowa with a B.A. degree in speech, completing the usual four-year course in three years.

Husky and looking like an athlete, Richer is a member of Phi Beta Kappa, and was SUI's leading orator. Last year he was a winner in a national collegiate oratorical contest at Cleveland, Ohio. He always had an irrepressible, enthusiastic desire to teach.

Last fall he got his first teaching job in the junior high school in Riceville, Iowa, a village of 962 people. He was assigned to 50 seventh and eighth graders (between twelve and fourteen years old.) He was to teach English, reading, spelling, and social studies.

From the first day there was an astonishing informality about his classes which admittedly were the noisiest in the building. His kids called him Paul, and as one mother put it, "followed him around as if he were the Pied Piper." So many children crowded around him at lunch time that he used the hour to instruct them in Spanish, which wasn't in the curriculum.

Within a few weeks it seemed that if Paul Richer had deliberately planned it that way he couldn't have offended more people in Riceville; he had antagonized the American Legion, the clergy, the members of the school board, some of the other teachers, and most of the parents. It appeared that only the kids loved him.

For one thing, he added four social study units to the course of study: mental health, crime, war, and communism. The two-and one-half week course on communism was an objective, historical study, but most of the parents rose up in arms over exposing their children to the subject at all. One of the most vociferous was the Rev. Wm. Bohi, minister of the 150-member Congregational church. He denounced Richer to his face, and when Richer asked him if he suspected him of being a Communist, the Rev. Bohi, according to his own statement, told Richer, "I do suspect you of being a Communist." With the Rev. Bohi, others also objected to the school's mandatory released-time religious period. Parents joined them in protest, particularly after Richer used the book "How the Great Religions Began" in class, and discussed Buddhism with his kids. They said he was encroaching on the clergy's territory.

When Richer introduced a study of Shakespeare's plays, most of the people in this agricultural community agreed with one farmer who complained: "What does my boy need to know Shakespeare for? It won't help him plow a field."

He read excerpts from "Of Mice and Men," so he said, "the kids could learn this lesson, that everybody in this world needs somebody else," and to show changes in writing patterns, he read parts of "Catcher in the Rye." Most of the parents heartily agreed with Dr. Thomas G. Walker, Jr., president of the school board, who said, "Literature is a fine thing, but first things come first. The kids should learn how to spell. . . . The kids need work in basic English rather than advanced work." Richer countered that his pupil's spelling ability was "about average" and added that instead of neglecting spelling he devoted "more time to that than I should have."

He assigned some odd themes, such as this one from *Green Pastures*: "Even bein' God ain't no bed of roses."

The local American Legion post howled when a play was scheduled that Richer and some of his pupils had adapted from the book *The Blackboard Jungle.* As in the book, a flagpole was used to stab one of the characters. The Riceville Legion viewed this as disrespectful to the flag. Richer refused to substitute another weapon, and the play was abandoned.

Finally, after 27 weeks of teaching, Richer wrote the school board a letter saying he did not wish to teach in Riceville school the next year. (This letter will be quoted in full later.) Studded with accusations of "ignorance," "bigotry," and "intellectual narrowness," it amounted to a total denunciation of Riceville and completely incensed the members of the board.

At a closed meeting the board ordered Richer's immediate discharge in these words: "Your obvious disrespect of administrative authority manifested by your unwillingness to cooperate . . . and your defiant attitude toward the school board and the community as a whole makes it mandatory . . . to terminate your services."

Richer demanded an open hearing but didn't get it. Said the board's president, Dr. Walker, "There was very little point in having an open hearing merely to satisfy him and to drive still more wedges in this community conflict . . . I've got to live here. I can't see myself stirring up a lot more difficulty. Richer is a brilliant chap, very intelligent. But he is a crusader, a reformer. I don't believe Richer had any intent to do harm. He is quite enthusiastic about his work."

Richer's kids wanted to strike to force the board to let him complete the year, but he convinced them that they should go to their classes. Then 21-year-old Richer went back to Mason City to ponder over the past 27 weeks of his first year as a teacher. It was from there that he wrote us the following letter.

DEAR EDITOR:

Thank you for giving me the opportunity of presenting through your widely-read magazine my view of what happened at Riceville Junior High.

Living as we do in a time of awkward anger, it is difficult for a young man to view the world with a dispassionate eye. In spite of this, it is my hope to relate to you reasonably, honestly, and free from emotional involvement how I came to be dismissed as a teacher from the Riceville public school system for such stated reasons as: lack of cooperation, rebellious attitude, and radical point of view.

I have no regrets. This, instinctively, must come first. The stated reasons for my dismissal concerned my attitudes, my abilities, my methods, or more simply, Richer and what he is. The real reason, in a world not prone to see or wanting to see reality, is this: in the dusty, quiet village of Riceville where 962 people had grown into the Main Street pattern, characterized by an intense respect for yesterday, a complete disdain for today, and a rigid denial of tomorrow — in this atmosphere of complacent intellects and over-zealous consciences, 50 youngsters in the seventh and eighth grades began to think for themselves. This was my crime and because of this I was fired, and for this I have no regrets.

The sequence of events leading to my discharge is confusingly complex, as is almost always the case when the human element is involved. The following is an illustration of how, by merely adding the ingredient of a misinformed person to the learning recipe, we can endanger the success of the educational cake and run the risk of poisoning the student-eater and/or destroying the teacher-cook.

Shortly after the start of the school year, we began the comparative study of capitalism, using America as an example, and communism from its philosophical beginnings with Engels and Marx down through Lenin and Stalin and what it is and what it pretends to be today. The unit taught objectively, and we were not afraid to discover and examine the advantages of communism. And just as intelligently we carefully scrutinized its weaknesses. At the end of this survey the students decided that in spite of its efficiencies and rapid economic progress, communism is undesirable because it destroys human inquiry.

The important fact here, however, is not so much the decision, heartening as it is to many of us. The importance lies in the fact that the students decided for themselves.

They not only asked the questions, they also found the answers. This is education, at least from the point of view of one twenty-one year old.

So to this educationally healthy situation, we add the misinformed human element and the Riceville "red scare" is on. A week after the unit was started, the Rev. William Bohi invaded my room and denounced the unit as dangerous and myself as a witting or unwitting aid to the Communist cause. He was further loudly convinced that my Bible reading was a front for my Communist activities and he demanded to know my reasons for introducing the study into the school and thereby contaminating the student's minds with this atheistic dogma.

Stunned into silence, I heard a voice angrily rise from the back of the room. It was thirteen-year-old Willie, confident of his claim to this truth in spite of his 80 I.Q. And with Willy's answer, the defense rests on the issue of communism: "Ain't we gotta know about them if we gotta live with 'em or fight 'em?"

Allow me to quote the Rev. Bohi from the Des Moines *Register* of March 18.

This Richer was interested in a lot of fool things. He talked to them about mental health. He had them write essays on "my outlook on life." Imagine asking seventh and eighth graders that. Then he went into communism. I didn't want my daughter bothered with those things.

Perhaps a very brief theme by Sharon, one of my pupils, might show you the kind of "outlook on life" essays my kids turned out:

Thinking is like loving and dying; each of us must do it for himself. Thinking must be done by you, yourself, no one can do your thinking for you. You may think different than anyone else in the room but do not change what you think so you will not be the odd person; it is the way that you, yourself, think that is important. No one else can do your loving for you, they do not know how you feel toward certain people and would not know how to express your feeling of love. It is surely obvious that no one can die for you. A person's thinking, loving and dying must be done by himself.

The situation involving the course on communism and the Rev. Bohi vividly and accurately paints a picture of the collective mind of an extremely vocal minority which, because of an intense devotion to the cause of open books and closed minds, succeeded in removing me from the Riceville scene. Unless the silent, sleeping majority has awakened, these militant few still play puppeteer to the individual teachers and administrators in the Riceville school system.

I should make one point clear. These people I am discussing and apparently condemning are basically good people motivated by only one consideration: to do what is best for their children. This desire manifests itself in the widely accepted theory that the child who is most protected is best prepared. Agree as I may with them that we must do everything possible for the kids, I cannot agree with their cure: to limit the kids' vision to the good and pure and clean.

Rather, I did my very best to show my 50 kids that nothing is 100 per cent black or white; that we live in a world of twilight gray, and that what we judge as good probably is only 51 per cent good.

These ideas gave rise to many incidents which tended to create discontent in the community. For here were 50 young people who began asking questions: about slums, and juvenile delinquency, and race hatred, and religious intolerance . . . the questions are limitless. And with my youngsters the most important question was "why is it wrong," and then in a grand, proud way, "what can we do about it."

Another point raised for my dismissal was apparent lack of discipline in my classes. I plead guilty to the accusation that Richer's classes were the noisiest in the building. Enthusiasm ran at fever level. We kept busy, not workbook busy but practical project busy. There were days when almost every student was on his feet wanting to be heard. More and more the students were left on their own. Singly or in two's and three's they studied, created and, of course, on some occasions merely chatted. But school, tough as it was, became a challenge and was seldom boring.

Closely allied to the supposed discipline problem was the fact that I became very close friends with the kids. And strangely this angered a great many people. Like good friends, we kidded and insulted each other and together we learned.

Only one fact separated me from my students: I knew more than they did, so I played teacher. But not always. On the day we discussed the farm problem I was the dumbest one in the room and I admitted it. I never played God with the kids as so many teachers tend to do.

I remembered well the advice of one of my University education teachers who said, "Never get too friendly with your students. Always keep the desk between you and them. This is the only way they'll respect you." So on my first day of teaching I walked around that desk to the student's side and stayed there all year. I didn't have their artificial respect as a teacher but their sincere respect as a friend.

Another point of divergence was the stand I took on released time for religious instruction. Riceville released students for two hours a week to go to the church of their choice for study. We teachers were instructed to recruit students for the program through issuing permission blanks to be signed by the parents. I objected.

Not only did this strike me as direct conflict with the doctrine of separation of church and state, but it was apparent to me that we in the schools just did not have enough time to adequately do our job. And so I objected to my principal and my superintendent and to various ministers and priests. For this I was branded in various quarters as an enemy of religion, a co-worker with the devil, and even an atheist. I still object.

There were many other cases in which I sinned in the eyes of the noisy few. Among them: I read excerpts from some "modern" books to my classes; I commented on religion in my class; I produced a school play in which a flagpole is used to stab a character, thus offending some members of the American Legion; I introduced a unit on Shakespeare. And so on.

These were the small camouflages for the real complaint: they just didn't like what I was attempting to accomplish. You see, I had only one thing in mind all year: to give everything I had to the kids. I had grown up in a school system which had had every modern advantage, a big library, science labs with modern equipment, special materials for research and study. In Riceville we had none of these. And as a teacher I was faced with a choice that must surely confront every teacher: to take the easy road of textbook assignment and little else, or to follow the path of true creative teaching. To the best of my ability, I did the latter.

I base my philosophy of teaching on one premise: every student had the right to whatever it takes to enable him to fulfill himself completely. Thus, the individual student is at the center of education, and the teacher and the subject matter are secondary.

It becomes the task of the teacher who truly wants to create out of the raw materials of the human compound to take the wishes, needs and abilities of the student and within that framework create a course of study. It is obvious that this course will be valid for only one student. And so, in Riceville, I never drew up a formal course of study for my class, but evolved a plan of attack for each of my 50 students, separately and as individuals. And as individuals I watched them grow — each at his own rate, each in his own direction, each by the one method most valid for himself. And I exulted with them over their accomplishments, lamented with them over their defeats and, at the moment of this writing, I find, perhaps, I do have one regret: I miss the kids.

For the beauties of creative teaching are an infection. The kids get under your skin and, at the risk of sounding overly sentimental, they get into your heart. Here were 50 very real people preparing to meet a world of contradiction, dishonesty and hypocrisy. Sensitive and sensible as only the young can be, they had questions they wanted answered. Once again the easy way was evasion or the half-truths of generalities, but a kid can spot a liar. I was trying to fashion youngsters with an instinct for the truth into thinking, reasoning individuals. Somehow, in Riceville, this was not wanted.

During my last weeks there, when I had been stripped of every bit of intellectual integrity, when I was no longer able to carry out my responsibilities to my students in a manner acceptable to myself, when I had been reduced to a mere "giver of assignments," I was torn between the desire to stay with the kids no matter what, and the desire to leave this place of sleeping souls. Human fraility being what it is, I wrote this letter to the president of the school board:

Because I have discovered that teaching, at least in the Riceville public schools is not a creative process but a task to be performed by a mental puppet,

Because I have further discovered that within Riceville the puppeteer is not my principal nor my superintendent nor my school board,

Because I have discovered also that the puppeteer within Riceville is that noisy, mis-informed, intellectually corrupt, intolerant segment of a lethargic public,

Because this noisy, narrow few wields such tremendous power and insidious influence that those in position of authority (principal, school board, superintendent) bow to their wishes,

Because these wishes are a compound of ignorance and arrogance and bigotry and intellectual narrowness,

For these reasons, I request that my name not be considered for a position of employment in the Riceville public schools commencing in the Fall of 1956.

My contacts with the students in my grades have been pleasant, challenging and rewarding. This year has proved to be one of great enlightenment, for me as well as, I am sure, for my students.

My decision to leave Riceville is based on one fact — one discovery: that in the middle of the twentieth century, in the middle of the United States of America, there exists a group of people whose chief motivations are cowardice and fear. I cannot, I will not, teach in a mental straitjacket. Thank God, I am not afraid.

In this note, arrogantly intemperate, I gave voice to the illustrations and ideals that are instinctive in a young man like myself. And in closing I should like to re-assert my dreams for those with a spirit young enough to care.

In 1923, Elmer Rice in his strange, dramatic experiment, *The Adding Machine*, commented on American education:

... you'll learn all the wrong things and learn them all in the wrong way. You'll learn to be a liar and a bully and a braggart and a coward and a sneak. You'll learn to fear the sunlight and to hate beauty. They'll tell you the truth about a great many things you don't give a damn about and they'll tell you lies about all the things you ought to know — and about all the things you want to know they'll tell you nothing at all.

Extreme? Certainly. But there are those times — times of moral and mental decay — when the extreme is needed to wake the slumbering masses: a word spoken in the wrong way, a shot fired in the wrong place, a teacher fired at the wrong time.

But my final message is to my kids. To Beverly, in her poetic sweetness; and Dale, in his rapid flight into manhood; and Tommy with his laugh of honest delight at the world; and Mary, with her prayers for a little better world; and Willy, the greatest of them all... Yes, to these and all 50 of my kids and every kid in every corner of this awful, awesome world — know this: you never have to be afraid. Just seek the sunlight and pursue the truth. And when you find that truth, live by it, no matter what.

Help Wanted—Male-Female—2600 | Help Wanted—Male-Female—2600 | Help Wanted—Male-Female—2600

TEACHING OPPORTUNITY

Small town needs junior high school teacher who has strong convictions about value of traditional education and can maintain firm discipline at all times. Must have no-nonsense approach to religious and patriotic values and must teach parental, school, and social authority. Strong background in academic subjects and demonstrated ability to control pupils required. If interested, write Supt. of Schools.

Now that we *know* how positive reinforcement works and why negative doesn't . . . we can be more deliberate, and hence more successful, in our cultural design. We can achieve a sort of control under which the controlled, even though they are following a code much more scrupulously than was ever the case under the old system, nevertheless *feel free*. They are doing what they want to do, not what they are forced to do. That's the source of the tremendous power of positive reinforcement — there's no restraint and no revolt. By a careful cultural design, we control not the final behavior, but the *inclination* to behave — the motives, the desires, the wishes.

The curious thing is that in that case *the question of freedom never arises*. — B. F. Skinner

The older dictators fell because they never could supply their subjects with enough bread, enough circuses, enough miracles and mysteries. Nor did they possess a really effective system of mind-manipulation. . . . Under a scientific dictator, education will really work — with the result that most men and women will grow up to love their servitude and will never dream of revolution. There seems to be no good reason why a thoroughly scientific dictatorship should ever be overthrown. — Aldous Huxley

"I understand you have an ulcer, Smith. I appreciate that expression of loyalty to our system!"

WAYNE BARHAM

two piftfiéré̀ worlds

My name is Fred Smith. I am a teacher. I recently surprised my wife when I announced that we were going to attend the Charity Ball on Saturday night.

"Are they giving us the money it raises?" she asked.

"Of course not. I paid ten dollars for these tickets. We'll just have to take the ten from some unnecessary part of the budget."

"You mean like food, clothing, and house payments."

I ignored her sarcasm. Dorothy is a good

wife and mother, but she doesn't understand high finance. Handling huge sums of money, like my monthly paycheck, overwhelms her.

"As a matter of fact," I continued, "there is a rumor floating around that the school board is going to hand out merit pay next year. All the board members will be at the Charity Ball. I figure I can visit with them, so they won't forget I'm on their staff."

"Sounds like plain old politics to me. What happened to all your scruples?"

"It's just . . . I get tired of all our friends and relatives offering to loan us money. I'm the only one that went to college. I have two degrees, but they are all better paid than I am. They get commissions, bonus money, and all kinds of incentive pay. Perhaps now with a crack at merit pay. . . . Anyway, you have to blow your own horn. The squeaky wheel gets the grease. It isn't what you know, it's who you. . . ."

"Oh knock it off, will you?"

Saturday night arrived and our little Nash Rambler was humming along like a sewing machine. The sound of music was floating from the gym as I turned into the parking lot. What luck! Two school board members were parking their cars, and there was room between them for my own. Driving expertly, I wheeled in between the green Cadillac and blue Lincoln. Mud and water flew into the air.

"Good show!" Dorothy cried. "You got both cars. It isn't easy to splash two at the same time."

Doctor X seemed quite upset about the whole thing. I hurried to get out of the car. When I opened my door, the wind banged it against the side of Doctor Y's car.

"I'm sorry," I apologized.

"Sorry for what?" he growled. "For not breaking the window too?"

Never missing an opportunity to encourage her husband, my wife whispered, "Attaboy,

sport. That's letting 'em know who you are."

Inside the gym, a few smiling ladies had coerced their escorts onto the dance floor. The remaining non-combatants had formed small groups to shout small talk above the din. The decorating committee had adopted the theme of a Paris sidewalk cafe, but the decor came off more like Ed's Carry-out Pizza.

I spied Doctor X conversing with Doctor Y. I moved in on them. Doctor X was saying that he had just given his 16-year-old son a Jaguar, an airplane and karate lessons for which he flies to Minneapolis.

I boasted, "My son has a Honda 90 trailbike."

He answered, "How nice." I kissed his hand.

Doctor Y casually mentioned that he had recently bought a 30-foot houseboat to use strictly on the river. He also had bought a red upholstered Cris-Craft complete with bar for walleye fishing on the lakes.

I blurted, "I have a plywood duckboat. It fits right on top of my car."

Having impressed Doctors X and Y, I glanced around for other school board members. Aha! There was Doctor Z in the middle of a large gathering. I melted quietly into the group. The topic of conversation was travel. Apparently everyone had just returned from Hawaii or the Bahamas, or was leaving for Europe or Sun Valley. Doctor Z was saying, "We certainly enjoy the slopes at Aspen this time of year."

I interjected, "My superintendent let me go 30 miles to Springview for an ACT workshop. Of course, I had to take two nuns from the parochial high school along with me. The school paid me seven cents a mile and bought my lunch too. Golly, that was really living."

Doctor Z peered intently at me. "I like your attitude, Son. What's your name?"

"Fred Smith, sir, and this is my wife, Dorothy." We bowed and curtsied and backed onto the dance floor, disappearing among the mass calisthenics. It was a grand exit. Only Spencer Tracy and Katherine Hepburn could have pulled it off better.

I led Dort off the other side of the dance floor and into the spectators. "That was a quick dance," she complained. But I had other board members to stalk.

Jackpot! There sat Mr. Davis, with his wife, at a corner table. He was the richest man in town. He was also the biggest bore. We accidentally strode directly to their table. They invited us to join them. He was eager to relate his success story to anyone who would listen. He began by informing me of his financial wizardry, then gave me a thump on the back and said, "I started out as a teacher just like you."

"I didn't know that," I encouraged.

"I've wished a thousand times I had never quit teaching," he lied. "It's a noble profession. But I quit teaching and started to peddle books to schools. It was tough, but I clawed and scratched my way to the vice-presidency of the company." (Married the president's daughter and retired, a millionaire, at 54.) He let me know that, even though retired, he still managed to turn a shrewd deal or two.

I looked him straight in the eye and said "I had a $100 war bond once, but I cashed it in when I got married."

Mrs. Davis turned to Dorothy and said, "That's a very pretty dress."

Dort smiled, "Thank you."

I pressed on, "She made it herself. And she bakes bread and makes homemade sauerkraut in a real crock."

"My," Mrs. Davis answered, "that sounds delicious. Our present cook has been a disappointment. We have had dreadful luck with servants lately. It is so difficult to get competent help these days."

I could see she was green with envy. My parting shot was, "Dorothy knows more than 50 different ways to use hamburger in recipes.

And she cans pickles!"

"How quaint," she gasped.

The band's vocalist was singing, "Two different worlds, We live in two different worlds. . . ."

Dort tugged at my arm and dragged me away to the punch bowl. I could see she was miffed. "What's the matter with you?" I asked.

She answered through clenched teeth. "Where is your pride? What happened to the man I married? It's not like you to grovel. Is merit pay that important to you?"

"I've gone this far and I'm not going to blow it now. I only have three more board members to butter up. All three of them right over there. I can get the whole covey with one shot. Trust me."

The covey included Harry Jones, the local banker, Lars Johnson, president of the Savings and Loan, and Ole Olson of Olson's Insurance. The banker was relating his favorite golf story. Last summer he had played in a foursome including Olson, Johnson, and Doctor X. As Jones leaned over his ball for an eight-foot putt, Doctor X said, "Five hundred dollars says you miss, Harry."

The banker didn't hesitate, "You're on, sport."

I gulped at the thought of my entire month's salary riding on a single putt. As the story continued, Harry missed the putt. He paid off the $500 over a martini in the clubhouse bar. I recalled borrowing $150 from this same man's bank to pay for my son's tonsillectomy (by Doctor X).

Several people were still laughing and joshing Jones about dropping the $500 when I heard my own voice saying, "When I was a small boy I was a caddy. I still remember that the richest men invariably owned the heaviest golf bags and tipped the least." I was rambling. "I won the World Series pool once. They held it in the barber shop and it was worth five bucks. I was so happy and excited I nearly wet my pants."

A deafening silence followed. Ole Olson broke it by clearing his throat. He ventured, "Uh, I took a trip up North recently and bagged a polar bear. My guide spotted him from the air. He couldn't escape, because there was no place to hide. We chased him around in circles until he was exhausted. Then we landed the plane, and I walked right up to him. It only took one shot. Let me tell you, it was great sport."

"I'll bet the bear loved it." I muttered.

Ignoring me, he continued. I learned that his trip, including the outfitter's fee, cost more than my entire yearly salary. He looked at me and said, "I've heard that you really love the outdoors. Why haven't you gone after a polar bear, Fred?"

"In the first place, shooting an animal under the conditions you just described makes me sick to my stomach. And secondly, my old man couldn't afford to set me up in the insurance business," I snarled.

Mr. Johnson intervened, "Look here, Son. You're implying that you might be underpaid? I want you to know that we are raising the base pay of our teachers all the way up to $6,400 for the next year. Now I feel that this is most generous. As we see it, a family of four should live quite comfortably on $6,400, if they are careful. Money is scarce. Even the president says we must tighten our belts. We simply have to draw the line somewhere."

"Maybe we have been reckless with our money and haven't budgeted wisely. Why, just recently the president himself was raised a paltry $100,000. And the senators limited their increases to a mere $12,000 per year. Now that's what I call self-sacrifice. I guess it is my patriotic duty to fight inflation too."

My sarcasm was wasted. Mr. Johnson beamed. "That's the spirit, young man. Now then, did I tell you fellows that my wife and I plan to camp in Europe this summer? No guided tours and rushing around for us! We are buying a new camper, one of those self-propelled jobs. Man, it's a regular home on wheels. I got a few drinks into old Ed over at Smith Motors and he finally pushed that pencil down to 13,000 bucks. We're going to take our sweet old time and spend the whole summer camping in Europe. That's the only way to go, right? Where would you suggest we go first?"

I savored each word and I spoke slowly and distinctly. "You can go straight to hell, and take the other six philanthropists on this school board with you."

I had just committed professional hara-kiri. It felt great.

Upon my arrival at school on Monday morning I was summoned to the superintendent's office. I had never visited the inner sanctum before. I should have known that a man making $25,000 would have an impressive office, but this took my breath away. I felt an urge to take off my shoes and feel the plush carpet with my bare feet. He was putting across the floor into an electric ball-return. I mentally compared his office with my classroom. Would it be poor timing to ask if the crack in my chalkboard could be repaired?

He leaned his putter against the wall and stared at me in obvious disbelief before mumbling, "Australia is accepting applications from American teachers. Have you ever thought of...?"

I climbed the stairs and entered my classroom just as the last bell was ringing. The principal's voice was droning the usual announcements via the squawk-box. He ended on a personal note to the faculty. "You are reminded that next year's requisitions for supplies are due in my office today. The school board has suggested that you cut your lists to a bare minimum in order to save money. Paper clips, chalk, and thumb tacks must be used with discretion. I trust you will cooperate in this matter. Please remember to turn off your classroom lights when you leave for your lunch break."

the establishment

6

Public schools are the nurseries of all vice and immorality. — *Henry Fielding* (1707-54)

Public schools are becoming a nuisance, a pest, an abomination; and it is fit that the eyes and noses of mankind should, if possible, be open to receive it.

— *William Cowper* (1731-1800)

There is nothing on earth intended for innocent people so horrible as a school.

— *George Bernard Shaw*

"That's the reason they're called lessons," the Gryphon remarked; "because they lessen from day to day." — *Lewis Caroll*

I never let my schoolin' interfere with my education. — *Mark Twain*

Who so would be a man must be a nonconformist. — *Ralph Waldo Emerson*

and the alternatives

It is the property of true genius to disturb all settled ideas. — *Goethe*

One of the hardest things to realize, specially for a young man, is that our forefathers were living men who really knew something. — *Kipling*

Every revolution evaporates and leaves behind only the slime of a new bureaucracy.

— *Franz Kafka*

Today children who enter school quickly find themselves part of a standard and basically unvarying organizational structure: a teacher-led class. — *Alvin Toffler*

The average Ph.D. thesis is nothing but a transference of bones from one graveyard to another. — *J. Frank Dobie*

If a man does not keep pace with his companions, perhaps it is because he hears a different drummer. Let him step to the music which he hears, however measured or far away. — *Thoreau*

THE MAJOR PROBLEMS

What do you think are the biggest problems with which the *public* schools in this community must deal?

	National totals	No. children in schools	Public school parents	Private school parents	Profes- sional educators
N=	1,790	996	698	144	270
	%	%	%	%	%
Discipline	23	23	23	26	20
Integration/ segregation	18	20	14	17	23
Finances	19	17	22	16	35
Teachers	14	14	14	16	13
Facilities	5	4	7	4	11
Curriculum	5	4	5	4	12
Parents' lack of interest	6	6	6	3	18
Large school, large classes	10	9	10	15	5
Dope, drugs	4	4	4	3	11
There are no problems	2	3	2	2	8
Miscellaneous	9	8	11	12	12
Don't know/ no answer	12	13	12	9	4

naming

1,000

educational innovations

DIRECTIONS

1. Choose any three-digit number.
2. Find the word in each column that corresponds with each digit.
3. The three words should indicate a potential innovation in education.

Column 1	Column 2	Column 3
1. computer	1. oriented	1. instruction
2. input	2. articulated	2. simulation
3. concept	3. structured	3. teaching
4. field	4. correlated	4. program
5. behavior	5. modulated	5. guidance
6. output	6. directed	6. school
7. resource	7. based	7. process
8. reality	8. integrated	8. system
9. value	9. compensated	9. curriculum
10. discovery	10. centered	10. learning

EXAMPLE

The number 007 produces the title "Discovery Centered Process." With no reference to James Bond, this title should suggest an educational innovation. If it doesn't, try another number. If after three trials you don't succeed; give up. You're no innovator!

Copia Verborum: A Cliché Expert Speaks

Rozanne Knudson

Q. — Mr. Counsel, you claim to be an expert in the clichés of education?

A. — That's right. I'm not just role-playing here today. I speak with certified expertise on the cliché-centered school of education.

Q. — Well, then, sir, let us begin with goals. Tell us first of the current goals of education.

A. — A dramatic breakthrough has been made in the goal-setting process. Rigorous new educational objectives replace child-centered togetherness. The recent trend is toward student mastery of carefully structured concepts and constructs.

Q. — I see. Then the change is. . . ?

A. — Definitely away from open-ended life adjustment. But we still aim to meet the needs of the whole child — the rigorously oriented whole child.

Q. — And the curriculum?

A. — The curriculum is always a total-team effort directed toward obtaining a well articulated sequence of meaningful experiences and situations.

Q. — Is the curriculum added to occasionally?

A. — We seldom add. We enrich. And broaden.

Q. — And?

A. — Structure. And lately spiral.

A. — What is the makeup of this total team you speak of?

A. — Well, naturally we try to maintain rapport with the community by including representatives from the various socio-economic levels. And we never exclude the out-groups. But recently the challeng-ing curricular issues are increasingly being turned over to key scholars in the several disciplines.

Q. — And the results?

A. — New frontiers of learning. Blue-sky situations emerging.

Q. — Now as to methods, sir.

A. — It would seem that methodology is frequently implicit in the material, inherent in the classroom climate, and tailored to the needs of readiness of the individual learner.

Q. — More specifically you recommend?

A. — Firstly, involvement of the learner in the problem-solving process. Then channel his mental activity toward the inductive and creative, always striving for an atmosphere of critical thinking.

Q. — All this in order to?

A. — Maximize excellence, yet never minimize adjustment.

Q. — And these methods produce?

A. — Optimum learning conditions.

Q. — You begin with?

A. — Springboard techniques and motivational activities.

Q. — And end?

A. — With stimulating culminating activities involving the total group.

Q. — Consider now the students.

A. — The student-oriented teacher grows increasingly cognizant of individual differences. On the one hand are the gifted.

Q. — Are these students who will attend college?

212

A. — Not only the college-bound. Many of the gifted, being culturally deprived, are unable to attend college.

Q. — And on the other hand?

A. — Are the slow learners. We try to take these students from where they are, meeting their needs by fostering their interest in timeless moral and spiritual values.

Q. — Now as for certain problem students.

A. — We are engaged in making a searching reevaluation of the data on over-achievers. We are studying the effect of peer pressure on the creatively oriented. In addition, the issues and challenges of the school dropout are being met with advanced theoretical models.

Q. — And the others?

A. — We stimulate the underachiever, encourage the exceptional, and challenge the average.

Q. — Would you care to make a summary statement, Mr. Counsel?

A. — Yes. Today, without question, the entire range of human resources and the totality of human experience must be harnessed to produce the maintainence of current rigorous standards of education. Decision-making theory must focus on the reinforcement of national goals, and patient, careful research must aim at a totally balanced program in order to bring about broader horizons of learning.

inutes of Meeting of Faculty-Student Planning Committee

The first meeting of the Planning Committee was held on Wednesday, October 6, in Slater B. Chairman Jean Carnaghan called the meeting to order at 2:45 P.M. Faculty and Student Representatives were in attendance.
The following topics were discussed:

I *MINI-COURSES*

Implementation of the minicourse concept (suggested last spring) has not taken place primarily because of scheduling problems. It was hoped that the Senior Lounge would free both teachers and rooms for this project, but to date complications are preventing this. Both faculty and student enthusiasm for the project was displayed. A study of other schools' approaches to mini-courses will be made to determine which alternative is most suitable to our situation. Joe Levanto was asked to present to the committee the present status of mini-courses but was unable to attend due to prior commitment.

II *STUDENT READING PROBLEMS*

Careen Jennings related her experience of finding that several of her students were found to have reading difficulties so acute that they can be considered "functional illiterates." The situation is further complicated by the termination of "core" programs after the Lower year, especially in English and social studies. No provision seems to exist for the hard-core reading problem especially at the Upper and Senior level. The possibility of having a reading specialist on the faculty was introduced. A study will be made to discover the magnitude of the problem before specific recommendations are made. Anna Payne and Art Jerbert will handle the investigation.

III   *FOREIGN STUDENTS*

The problem of foreign students at the Academy with no basic communicative ability in English was presented. Several teachers have noted that no provision seems to be made for these people. Guidance notes that options for such students are minimal. It was agreed that special tutoring is essential in this situation either through faculty, students, the community, or the Norwich school system. The committee agreed that the administration be made aware of the existing problem, and that a coordinator for foreign student scheduling be formally appointed. The committee's recommendations will be forwarded to the Steering Committee.

IV   *NEW BUSINESS*

Student representatives Sandy Zeitz and Bob Levine informed the committee that student desire for a smoking area is still being sought. Less than half the faculty responded to a questionnaire last spring seeking comments on smoking-related topics. A more pointed questionnaire was suggested to obtain a more accurate faculty reaction. Les Hartson proposed that a poll of parents seems significant under the circumstances. Student leaders will continue their efforts in the direction of acquiring student smoking privileges.

The meeting was adjourned at 4:05 P.M.

Submitted by,

Bill Brokowski
For the Planning Committee

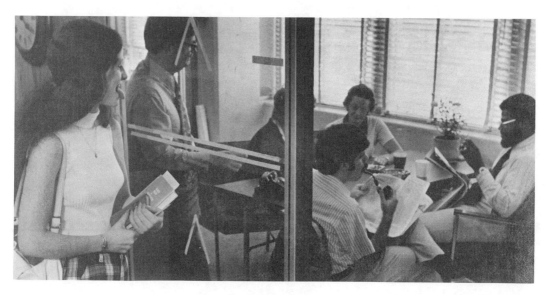

why n☺t?

Ray Scofield

Why not say that school is for kids
rather than teachers or janitors
or secretaries or cooks
or architects or even principals?
Why not say it and believe it.
Why not abandon required homework
and put a few kids on the streets
or reading books or watching tv
or talking with a friend
or waiting for a sunset
or picking pimples
or just sitting?

Why not throw out
mandatory homework
and find another way
to intimidate kids?
Why not bite your tongue hard
and justify all the busywork you've pawned off on kids
under the guise of "excellence in education."
Why not eliminate homework
and find a better way to teach
cooperative cheating?
And if all else fails
Why not try to excite, stimulate, energize, or inflame a kid
and let the homework take care of itself?

Why not build a humanities cafeteria
With an *a la carte* line loaded with goodies.
Perhaps a student will learn to serve himself occasionally
without always waiting sheep-patiently for the waitress
to push the well-cooked curriculum *du jour*
into his hands into his head
                              into his heart
the leftovers into his intellectual garbage can.
Why not advertise the delectable and diverse dishes
from language and lit and composition
and LIFE and maybe
just maybe
MR will be better known as Motivational Research
than as Mentally Retarded.

Why not stop drawing and re-drawing the floor plans
of our homemade curriculum prisons
with every fetter in place
anchored securely with the cement of whatever's current
from the past?

Why not (indeed) stop drawing fresh plans of old prisons
and start tunneling or scaling or vaulting
or even scratching a little.

Why not try to find relevance
between what goes on in class and something else
anything else?
Why not ask a parent for help or a teacher
or a curriculum consultant
or the United States Commissioner of Education?
Why not ask a life guard
                         or a truckdriver
                                          or a poet?

Why not retire the miniature federal reserve board
in every school
that controls the banking practices in classrooms?
A kid earns a credit and puts it into the bank
and once it is safely deposited
he throws away all of his notes and admits
original innocence
just another virgin brain
with thirteen credits in the bank.
Earn another credit and put it in the bank
earn still another credit and put IT in the bank
earn them, bank them, forget them
earn 'em, bank 'em, forget 'em
findem, earnem, bankem, forgetem
Why not claim language as our rightful stock-in-trade
our raw material
and also our finished product
Why not help a kid take pride
in the power of language personal and social

Why not help a kid use language to communicate
with an editor a draft board
                         a girl
or to discover the nobility of man?

Why not dissolve the red ink communion
(the grades that DEgrade)
Why produce self-satisfaction grade mongers
judging their worth by OUR standards
that make credit bankers out of philosophers
that make us teach multiplechoice knowledge
and that convince kids
that the dung beetle
who collects the biggest cognitive ball is best.

Why not try to evaluate kids honestly
individually
Why not try to find what a kid learns from you
rather than what he hasn't learned from his past teachers.
The difference between a student and a teacher
should be something more than a grade book

                                        or an answer book.

Why not make attendance optional?
If the multi-mediated McLuhan is right
and going to school interrupts education
Why not entice with connections to life
not plague with demands for inconsequence.

Why not take our eyes off the rearview mirror long enough
to think September 6, 1999
What will IT be?

                    pain?

                        vitamin-enriched soma??

                                    darkness???
Why not look into a crystal book or ball and find out
and at the same time find out how our classes can
let a student want to learn throughout life
or make him mankind-sensitive
or let him see his choices and decide
or show him how to love himself
or prepare him for more leisure time AND for cybernation
one cyber Nation, under IBM
indivisible
with conformity and structure for all.
Maybe.

WASHINGTON HIGH SCHOOL

NOTICES

There will be a special 7 period schedule.
Order of periods: 1, 2, 3, 4, 5, 6, Activity Period.

Students

1. Federal Forms are to be completed and returned as soon
    as possible. Any students who have not yet received
    their forms should obtain a set from their homeroom
    teacher today.
2. Today is the day for the Cheerleaders "bake sale" –
    see you in the cafeteria A & B lunch periods!

Activity Period

1. Extra help and makeup work with subject teachers, as
    scheduled.
2. Yearbook pictures will be taken of homerooms 143A, 143B,
    203, 204, 205, and 206 in the gym.
3. The Student Council meeting scheduled for today, will
    be held tomorrow, Thursday, after school in the Lecture
    Hall, to avoid a conflict with the S.A.T. review class
    today.
4. Review sessions in Mathematics with Mr. Crowe in Room
    121.
5. Aviation Club meeting in Room 137.
6. Radio Club meeting in Room 135.
7. Meeting of Spanish-speaking males (Selective Service)
    in the Conference Room – 102.
8. Science Club meeting in Room 127.
9. Rifle practice will be held in the Rifle Range during
    Activity Period and after school.
10. Theatre Workshop will meet in the auditorium – 1:45 to
    3:30 p.m. Students with priority engagements may join
    the group at 2:30 p.m.
11. There will be a meeting of the Photography Club in the
    Audio Visual Room (231). Club officers will be elected.
12. Intramurals, games and "Happy Hour" in the gym.
13. The Library will be open for research and quiet study.

14. The Senior Lounge and Cafeteria may be used as waiting areas for bus students who are not participating in any activities.

Guidance Notices

1. Applications for the State Scholarship Program are available in the Guidance Office. Seniors are encouraged to apply.
2. Application forms for the 1974-1975 Elks Youth Leadership Contest are available in the Guidance Office. Seniors are encouraged to enter this contest. For further information see your guidance counselor.
3. CONNTAC application forms are available in the Guidance Office.
4. ALL Juniors planning to attend college are urged to take the Preliminary Scholastic Aptitude Test on October 28. Please sign up in the Guidance Office.
5. Mr. Dane has three scholarship forms from the Society of Professional Engineers. Students in the upper quarter of the graduating class who seriously plan to major in engineering are asked to contact Mr. Dane for further information.
6. Students interested in attending the Campus Day next Monday, October 9th, are urged to sign up in the Guidance Office.

Teachers

1. Senior Homeroom Teachers: Please distribute the "Graduation Forms" you received this morning to all students in your homeroom.
2. The United Fund Drive begins October 6. Please support this noteworthy campaign.

HEL**P**!

The New School Workshop, 10 State Street, Portland, Me. is taking applications from teachers who are experienced with ages 8 to 12. Male teachers, or couples are preferred. The New School will begin its second year as the only non-graded free school in the Greater Portland area. It draws from all economic levels and is housed in a model city neighborhood. Study units are based on the ecology of the area, and many crafts are available. Please send resume and brief description of teaching philosophy.

Mort Guiney, 402 Star Rd., Albany, N.Y. I'm trying to locate a school for my brother. My brother will be going into the 9th grade in September and is 14 years old. Unfortunately, the schools should be accredited as this is important to my parents. My brother is really a good person and is very "aware" for his age. I'd hate to see him stifled by a rigid private school or military school which are the kind of schools my parents are thinking about. I think my brother and I can convince them to let him go to a freer "student-centered" school.

HEL**P**!

help!

Central State College, Chairman of General Studies, Fairlain, N.J. My division needs innovative, creative teachers interested in crossing traditional organizational lines into interdisciplinary, radical and area studies programs. I would like to hear from young teachers who are not afraid to fail, to state questions which haven't been asked lately, to fearlessly confront themselves and their students at close range. The single vice we are stalwartly against is that of being usual. A yet-to-be-built college on 1584 primitive and forested acres with a 60 acres lake; 10 miles from the Atlantic, 50 from Philadelphia, 100 from NYC. Send vita.

Michael Shea, 24 Pinewood Dr., Sarasota, Fla. I am a 17 year old boy who, though reasonably intelligent, was unable to complete high school because of failure to adhere to certain political and social ideas of the Florida State school boards. In other words, I am a drop-out. I have spent the last 6 months traveling and working around the country looking for a meaning in life. I believe I have found it. Now I am looking for a school in a free, progressive, but studious environment in which I can finish high school and enter college. Perhaps you can help me.

help!

Peoples Community School, RFD 2, Halleck, Va. We have openings for a few students ages: 10, 14, & 15. We also want children 9 years old and up with talented parents, to be an integral part of our newly forming multi-purpose community. Our present projects: 1 — To constitute a co-operative community; 2 — To design a school for our children; 3 — To develop an experimental village for inner-city poor. School starts in September. We anticipate a minimum of 6 children, a maximum of 30. We will live within walking or biking distance of each other in this lovely country abutting Shenandoah National Park. Facilities will be crude, the curriculum improvised. Community members will serve as teachers. We hope to differ from public school by offering greater leeway, higher quality, and more focus on the arts. Above all we will share the adventure of creating our own tailor-made school.

help!

Ruth Glenn, 31 Oakdale Ave., Westburg, N.Y. I'm sort of particularly interested in schools with focus on the arts, but I'm also interested in millions of other things which I wouldn't like left out. I will be 16 in September, I flunked 10th grade.

BOARD OF EDUCATION

Regular Meeting

The regular meeting of the Board of Education convened on Monday, May 22, in the Board Room of the Administration Building.

A. CALL TO ORDER
The meeting was called to order at 8:08 p.m., by Chairman Hanson.

B. RECOMMENDED ACTIONS
A motion was made (1 – Smyth, 2 – Walker) and passed unanimously to accept the minutes of the regular and executive sessions of the meeting of May 8.

Correspondence
1. Letter to Mr. Hanson from Carl Worth, representing parents of students who will be double-sessioned. The letter was an invitation to the Board and Mrs. Hastedt and Mr. Chapman to attend a meeting to be held at Fitch Senior High School on May 31 at 8:00 p.m. Also enclosed was a flier which is being mailed to these parents on the east side of town.
2. Dr. Smyth presented a proclamation received from the Governor naming June 14 as Flag Day.
3. An invitation from Jean Bailey from the Town Hall to the Board and Administration to a Dutch Treat dinner on May 25 with the Representative Town Meeting.
4. Mr. Chapman informed Board that a hearing was held with the wage board and the State Association re retroactive pay for teachers. No action taken. The association carrying issue to next level. Board not invited to hearing as letter was mislaid and not received in time. Referred to New Business.

Citizen's Requests
1. Mrs. Cassandra Burnett representing GRO, requested permission to attend all executive sessions of the Board to represent minority groups in area. Dr. Smyth explained purpose of executive sessions and why they are private. Mrs. Gloria Manning also spoke on this issue.

2. Elace Comrie spoke re retaining elementary art program in budget.
3. Ambrose Burfoot, teacher at Mary Morrison, spoke presenting petition asking for reinstatement of vice principals in the new budget.
4. Mrs. Sidney Hall spoke re reinstatement of music, art and sports in the elementary schools. Suggested via a proposal that a teacher now employed in the program who is qualified, could handle all three subjects.
5. Ronald Ross, Principal at Fitch Senior High School, spoke in favor of retaining the athletic program at the senior high level and why it is a vital and necessary part of the curriculum.

C. NEW BUSINESS
1. John M. Wilson, President of AGA, along with Barksdale Macbeth, Jerome Fitzgerald, Russell Leonard, Harrison Day, all principals in the town school system, spoke to Board requesting Vice Principals be reinstated in the budget and giving various reasons why this move is an absolute necessity. Also speaking was Florence Crowley, teacher at Mary Morrison School.

   Brief recess called at 9:30. Reconvened at 9:52 p.m. Mr. Bishop made a motion that meeting be adjourned at 11:30. Seconded by Dr. Smyth. Passed unanimously.

General Characteristics of New Formal Educational Institutions.

Ivan Illich

A good educational system should have three purposes: it should provide all who want to learn with access to available resources at any time in their lives; empower all who want to share what they know to find those who want to learn it from them; and finally, furnish all who want to present an issue to the public with the opportunity to make their challenge known. Such a system would require the application of constitutional guarantees to education. Learners should not be forced to submit to an obligatory curriculum, or to discrimination based on whether they possess a certificate or a diploma. Nor should the public be forced to support, through a regressive taxation, a huge professional apparatus of educators and buildings which in fact restricts the public's chances for learning to the services the profession is willing to put on the market. It should use modern technology to make free speech, free assembly, and a free press truly universal and, therefore, fully educational.

Schools are designed on the assumption that there is a secret to everything in life; that the quality of life depends on knowing that secret; that secrets can be known only in orderly successions; and that only teachers can properly reveal these secrets. An individual with a schooled mind conceives of the world as a pyramid of classified packages accessible only to those who carry the proper tags. New educational institutions would break apart this pyramid. Their purpose must be to facilitate access for the learner: to allow him to look into the windows of the control room or the parliament, if he cannot get in by the door. Moreover, such new institutions should be channels to which the learner would have access without credentials or pedigree – public spaces in which peers and elders outside his immediate horizon would become available.

I believe that no more than four – possibly even three – distinct "channels" or learning exchanges could contain all the resources needed for real learning. The child grows up in a world of things, surrounded by people who serve as models for skills and values. He finds peers who challenge him to argue, to compete, to cooperate, and to understand; and if the child is lucky, he is exposed to confrontation or criticism by an experienced elder who really cares. Things, models, peers, and elders are four resources each of which requires a different type of arrangement to ensure that everybody has ample access to it.

Vouchers Reshape a School District

Special to The New York Times

SAN JOSE, Calif., Sept. 24—The voucher financing system, being tried here for the first time in the nation, has caused a major restructuring of education in the Alum Rock Union School District.

Under the voucher system, a local school district issues "tickets" to parents of school-age children, one for each child in the family. The parent can choose to send his child to any school in the district. Upon enrollment, the parent presents the "ticket," or voucher, to the school, which then forwards it to the district and receives, in return, the money with which it will operate for the year.

In Alum Rock, a voucher is worth $680 for a child in elementary school and $970 for a seventh- or eighth-grade pupil.

In this way, the school that draws the most pupils gets the most operating money.

Choice of Curriculum

Instead of being forced to accept one basic course of study, parents in the Alum Rock district are free to choose from a wide range of curriculums offered by 22 minischools.

Because the amount of money that each program has depends on the number of students it attracts, the teachers have designed interesting courses of study.

Although parents have the option to enroll their children in a minischool stressing traditional education, 60 per cent of the 3,800 participating pupils are in such programs as a minischool oriented toward the future, a half-work and half-study program for seventh graders, a fine arts program that uses sheet music to help to teach mathematics and a daily living minischool that emphasizes "learning by doing" for such things as baking a cake, mathematics and art.

Joel Levin, the project director, said:

"Traditional education is socialism, very stable and very secure and very little upside potential. Vouchers are a free enterprise system, where you have a choice. It's almost classic Adam Smith economics."

O.E.O. Awards Grant

The voucher system is financed with a two-year grant from the Office of Economic Opportunity totaling $1,845,240. Only six of the 24 campuses in the racially and economically mixed Alum Rock district are involved in the project now, but Mr. Levin hopes to double that number next year.

Each of the participating schools last year had a student body that was roughly half Chicano, 40 per cent white and 10 per cent black. There was no significant shift in the racial mixture this year, Mr. Levin said.

Many critics of voucher financing systems have maintained that they will be used to segregate students racially, with parents using their vouchers at schools where children of one race predominate.

"Vouchers have been perceived from the outset by the liberal establishment as a covert way of segregating schools," Mr. Levin said.

The project here is not a full voucher system, because parents cannot use their vouchers to send their children to private schools, and therefore the project may not represent a full test of whether racial segregation would result from voucher financing.

Despite this, it seems to have achieved the two major goals of voucher systems: reforms in education and a variety of choices in educational style.

Printed in Two Languages

The vouchers are green cards printed in both English and Spanish. Regular district income provides funds for the vouchers, which are worth $680 for children in kindergarten through sixth grade and $970 for seventh and eighth-grade pupils.

In addition, the grant from the poverty agency provides compensatory vouchers to one-half of the students. These are worth one-third more than the basic voucher. These pupils all qualify for free school lunches under an unrealted Federal program and are classified, for purposes of the voucher experiment, as poor.

"The idea behind the compensatory voucher is to change poor kids from being the least desirable to perhaps the most desirable students because they bring more money than other students," Mr. Levin said. "This creates incentives for the educators to develop programs for poor kids."

Springtime Study Hall Blues

It isn't easy,
this sitting inside when it's springtime.
You get restless
and feel like jumping up
and running out the door
into the world
— without a corridor pass.
The Whisperers shrill
back and forth
across the rows of desks.
You can't sleep.
You listen to the noises of monotony:
pencils scratching
fingers drumming
pages idly turning
pens tapping. . . .
You watch the clouds move
or stare at the ripples of heat
rising from the radiators
past the open windows.
Your eyes feel heavy
and your leadweighted feet ache
to be barefoot and pounding against the
packed sands
of a hot windy beach.
Outside, a truck roars past
and everything vibrates for a brief
instant.
Floors, desks, students —
everything comes wavering to life
and nods back into death.
You glance at the clock on the front wall
and sigh.

                              — *S. Danny Riemer*

Søren Hansen, Jesper Johnson,
Wallace Roberts

the little red schoolbook

About learning

If you're bored, you learn only how to be bored, whether the schedule says math, geography or whatever.

If you have to do as you're told all the time, all you learn is to be obedient and not to question things. You learn not to think.

If you're forced to learn, you learn that learning is unpleasant. It's no help that the teacher says it will come in useful later in life.

If you're not given any responsibility or allowed to choose or decide anything for yourself, you learn to be irresponsible and to depend on others, even if your work gets straight "A"s.

If you're always taught to do things the same way, you learn only one way of doing things, and it becomes harder to cope with all the new things you'll have to face later on.

To learn anything useful it's important
that you should want to;
that you find the subject interesting;
that you understand why you have to learn it;
that you get a chance to say something yourself;
that you are allowed to work on the subject in your own way;
that you are allowed to cooperate with your friends.

If you think a particular teacher isn't very good at teaching, you should try to work with him to make his teaching better.

You yourself know best when you are bored. Or when you feel you're never allowed to say anything. Tell the teacher. He wants you to learn. Most teachers also want you to enjoy classes. Because then they enjoy them more, too. Talk to your teacher and see if you can't persuade him to make his teaching more interesting.

The Alternative

David Morse

A child is fastening words into a sculpture ... a poem-tree. Others are constructing an inflatable. Another group lounging on sofa cushions argues the merits of adding tadpoles or watercress to the aquarium. At the potter's wheel the potter's silent hands teach a child how to form the shoulder of a vase: silence even while *Jesus Christ Superstar* issues from the next room. "Shut the fucking door," one of the tadpole people yells, and in a moment stalks over and slams it himself. Silence of the boxwood stick pressing against the whirling clay, then the wet sponge: dull to shiny, back to dull. The vase is severed neatly from the wheel, and the small hands take over.

This is a "free school," or "alternative school." Alternative to the monolith of public instruction. Springing up by the hundreds all over the country. Where before only a handful existed, patterned mainly after Summerhill, the number has doubled every year for the past three years, until now free schools total roughly 1000 and the trend gives every indication of continuing its phenomenal growth.

The rise of the free school closely parallels the proliferation of "underground" media, chiefly in the form of magazines, newspapers and films during the 'sixties, and now including local small-scale "block" radio broadcasting and shoestring productions in "free" video aimed at breaking the monopoly of public broadcasting — until now it is accurate to speak of "alternative media."

Not only do many of the observations offered in the following pages, concerned mainly with alternative schools, have clear application to alternative media, but finally the two movements can be seen evolving in a special dynamic relationship, which is central to the Alternative Culture growing piece-by-piece about our ears.

The free school is unique in the history of American education. For one thing it is not simply one more large-scale innovation sweeping the country (Progressive Education, tracking, flexible scheduling, etc.) but a complete turnabout from the whole trend of Bigness. These are small do-it-yourself *non*-institutions, brought into being by teachers and parents and sometimes by students themselves out of antipathy for the public schools and the hope of creating for themselves a meaningful learning-environment on a people scale. Teachers are often dropouts from the straight system, working for subsistence salaries, with parents and college students volunteering. Classrooms are housed sometimes in storefronts, geodesic domes, or churches, or sometimes float "underground" from one meeting to another; or embark in fleets of VW buses. Sometimes students build their own schools.

"Curriculum" ranges vastly, from cybernetics to hassles with building inspectors, to organizing food co-ops. Junk cars, Zen gardens, goats and occasional VTR portapacks, serve as audio-visual aids. But "audiovisual" is too delimiting a term in this multi-sensory, "soft" environment. Words like "audio-visual" and "curriculum" imply the alienation which is parcel to the public schools and which the new schools are doing their best to tear out of.

This concern with wholeness and with the senses, along with the absence generally of "classes," places a different stress on media, if we consider that one of the chief uses of educational media traditionally has been to project a message to relatively large groups of people; also when we consider that Bigness in the marketing domain has produced software aimed toward passive children of conservative parents. But before examining these implications, a closer look at free schools is in order.

What is a free school?

Within a movement characterized by mind-boggling diversity there can be no really "typical" model. The term "free school" or "alternative school" has been used to refer to experiments as diverse as schools-without-walls, apprenticeship programs (such as Riverun, which describes itself as "a network of information and contacts with individuals, groups, organizations, and other less essential resources such as space and money"), to ethnic consciousness-raising trips for Blacks and Chicanos, and store-front drop-in centers such as Troutfishing in America, in Cambridge.

Despite this variety, a few characteristics are shared by most free schools. The point of listing them here is not to stereotype the movement but to acquaint the newcomer with some of its rough contours.

Generally, free schools are
- nonauthoritarian, libertarian, even democratic;
- "unstructured" in the sense of imposing minimal formal requirements, and in valuing non-directive behavior;
- concerned with unity of life; aesthetic, ethical, sensory experiences viewed as elements inseparable from the whole learning/life experience;
- politically radical, in the context of the dominant culture.

All the above characteristics are themselves interlocking parts of a whole — one quality implying or leading inevitably to the next. For example at the Sudbury Valley School in Framingham, Massachusetts, all students and staff get one vote each in the School Assembly, and award diplomas after a candidate has defended himself satisfactorily against attack in an open meeting. Presently the school is seeking accreditation to grant B.A. and Ph.D. degrees. Obviously this sort of continuum could not exist except in a nonauthoritarian context; nor can learning be nonauthoritarian where formal requirements are exacted and final judgments are imposed by the few. This commitment to democracy in turn, is radical compared to those public schools which take pride in their nonauthoritarian "atmosphere."

Other characteristics are more peripheral, but should be added. Free schools tend to be
- oriented toward ethical, social aesthetic and various non-rationalistic concerns (not to be confused here with the "Humanities"), often at the expense of science, foreign languages and mathematics;
- attuned to the Earth — in the sense of land, ecology, cottage crafts, and also in the sense of the global concerns expressed by Buckminister Fuller and Marshall McLuhan and reflected in *The Whole Earth Catalog.*

The list could go on. It could include for instance the growing resolve within the movement to transcend the barriers separating school and community (See Jerry Friedberg's "Beyond Free Schools: Community," which has been reprinted widely); it could include the altruism which is no small part of free school thinking and which translated into cash, means tuitions are typically low and often assigned on a sliding scale according to ability to pay. (Tuitions range from $0-$1000; anything above that is generally considered a rip-off.) An inevitable postscript is that almost every one of these schools is struggling for its economic existence.

How much impact can we expect free schools to have on public education?

The numerical strength of the movement is difficult to assess, given the present ferment. *New Schools Exchange Newsletter* can speak with some authority, having served for nearly two years as the central clearing house for information on alternative schools. Its founder, Harvey Haber, last year estimated the number at 2000. But whether or not a school is "free" leaves obvious room for interpretation. Mike Rossman, also writing for the *Newsletter* (No. 52, "Projections on the New Schools Movement"), last January estimated the number of schools he considered to be "truly free, with no qualifications," at 500. Free schools defined in the broadest sense, including "those schools which would be rated 'progressive and liberative' through those which are radical," Rossman placed at 1,600. He estimates that by 1975 the rate of growth will have leveled off and there will exist some 25-30,000 free schools, comprised of 1,400,000 students.

Rossman's prediction is based, soberly enough, on the straight-line growth of the past 2-3 years. However, two factors could boost the gain even higher. One is the cumulative effect inherent in introducing choice, where before there was monopoly. The other is the effect of alternative media. Whether or not the actual numbers accelerate beyond the *Newsletter* projection, the leverage is such that the impact on public schools can be expected to exceed by far the numerical growth of the movement.

Implied in this leverage is a tenet which is central to the broader aims of the generation of 30-year-olds engaged in transforming the old culture – a point which is not always obvious to those outside the Movement – that the intent is not to produce an experimental model for an educational elite to consider but to provide working "grassroots" alternatives to the existing institutions for individuals to resort to. The principle is profoundly egalitarian, even while favoring the middle class, because it takes responsibility out of the hands of professors and bureaucrats and places it in the hands of people functioning *as people.*

For this reason the alternative school concept can be threatening to those who have predicated their existence on paper. In his proposal to the Borough President of Manhattan, for instituting "Mini-Schools," Paul Goodman cites the objections to be encountered in any plan for decentralizing the schools.

First, the Public School administration does not intend to go largely out of business. Given its mentality, it must see any radical decentralization as impossible to administer and dangerous, for everything cannot be controlled. Some child is bound to break a leg and the insurance companies will not cover; some teen-ager is bound to be indiscreet and the *Daily News* will explode in headlines.

The United Federation of Teachers will find the proposal to be anathema because it devalues professional prerequisites and floods the schools with the unlicensed. Being mainly broken to the public school harness, most experienced teachers consider free and inventive teaching to be impossible.

Choice implies risk; and choice is the heart of the free school. As Ibsen's characters become real through their choices, so too does the student in the alternative school who is free to come up against his own limits – limits which George Dennison calls "the true edge of necessity," as opposed to the arbitrary rules imposed by an authority-figure. Student and teacher become real, when learning is seen as a continuum involving constant choice and in which "teacher" and "learner" are used to describe often momentary relationships between people, instead of rigid roles which must be filled at the cost of their mutual humanity.

The odds are against widespread public acceptance of an alternative which requires risk-taking on the one hand, and on the other faith in the fundamental goodness of people.

Our present society tends to reject both, and nowhere is that rejection more blatant than in the public schools.

Nevertheless, a few responsive chords have been sounded recently within the public systems — in places where one would least expect it. In North Dakota, a large number of the public schools have been revamped along the Leicestershire model. In Vermont, the "Vermont Design for Education" sets forth a student-centered philosophy worthy of any free school. In Philadelphia, a running dialectic between public and private alternatives has generated a renaissance; now Connecticut is borrowing Philadelphia's Parkway program for application in Hartford, while Board of Ed funded "free schools" are springing up in Philadelphia.

The idea of public funds being used to support alternative schools was given impetus last fall at the White House Conference on Children, which entertained the recommendation that school systems hand over some of the schools and some of their budget to groups that want to run competing schools. At present one of the plans being considered at various levels is the so-called "Voucher System," which would allow parents to apply tax money in the form of a voucher toward tuition in a private school of their choice. Yet the racial and religious ramifications of such a plan will take time to be worked out.

Despite these hopeful overtures from the public sector, the preponderance of delays, the hassles of red tape, the dangers of co-option, have kept most founders of free schools clear of the funding arms of Government and foundations alike. (In order to have as little as possible to do with the restrictions laid on nonprofit corporations and schools, Troutfishing in America chose to incorporate as a store.) The strategy remains not to count on solutions from "higher up"; to go it alone.

Independence, however, is purchased only at great cost. Money remains an enormous problem.

Thus when we turn to educational media available commercially, we find severe strictures on what alternative schools can afford. This enforced frugality — in an affluent marketplace — imposes a special clarity in assigning needs, which on one level are simply the needs of schools at large: competently designed individual programs, especially in math and foreign languages; portable language labs with a pricetag people can afford; in Science and Social Studies, materials which make the invisible world visible; accurate overviews. Most important, materials that respect the learner. This last point deserves special comment.

Too many audiovisual materials betray an underlying contempt for the audience. Too many films profane their topic, treating Ecology, for example, as a catchword and in their hard-sell arrogance fail to comprehend the possiblity that the learner already might feel a mystical connection with the Earth, or that the viewer of a Science film might tolerate the inclusion of political considerations, or might be aware of beauty *for its own sake* (and untrammeled by some imperious narrator delivering a half-megaton rap about the Beauty of Nature). Too many Black Histories, however good some of them may be, conceal the paucity of People Histories which acknowledge the contributions of all peoples in the world continuum and not merely the rise of the technocratic Caucasian. The same film catalogs that are blind to Fascism in Spain and South Africa treat Shakespeare externally, so that what you remember is the beard and the funny pantaloons. Why not a film of snippets of actors simply saying his lines fantastically well? Why not spaces for thought — silences/visuals/ music — interspaced with the harder data?

Why not — in the manufacture of software — a little more love?

Other requirements of the new schools cannot be generalized. Because on another level, the alternative school uses media differently, both internally, as a direct learning-aid, and externally to link individual schools with the free school movement at large. This second function, too, differs radically from its counterpart — the traditional dialogue between pedagogues contained in scholarly journals and annual professional conferences. The new communications are speeded up, "cooled" down. Conferences are called around a communal pot, often on a couple of months notice, and anybody is welcome. Written communications have seen the quarterly journals, with their one or two-year lag, give way to fast-breaking newsletters which combine the overview of Buckminster Fuller with the pragmatism and verbal alacrity of a floating crap game. Not only has the tempo quickened, but the direction has changed, becoming more reciprocal; a looping information-exchange.

Thus, shut out of the commercial market on economic grounds and at the same time searching for more authentic materials which reflect this faster, cooler, feedback-geared massage, the alternative schools have chosen to grow their own. Basically, this means tape: audio and video. In fact, the one hardware item which will tempt the most backwoods communal school into the cash economy is a portable videotape-recorder. Not only are the portapack VTRs adaptable to the varied terrain of a "soft" environment, but they provide access to the growing number of underground tape banks, and the chance to "loop" into the larger system.

Gene Youngblood, writing in a new magazine called *Print Project Amerika*, describes the excitement which has soared among video freaks during the past year:

In what is being called the Alternate Television Movement, an increasing number of young people around the world are doing just that, teaching themselves television: in Amsterdam, the Video Workshop; in London, TVX Video Co-op; in San Francisco, Ant Farm, Homeskin,

the National Center for Experiments in Television, New People's Media Project; in Los Angeles, Nam June Paik's video lab at California Institute of the Arts. The largest concentration of alternate television groups is in New York City. Recently the New York State Council on the Arts allocated $263,000 to the Jewish Museum to establish a Center for Decentralized Television — with enormous implications for the future of the movement. The funds were to be available to everyone working in alternate video in New York; a substantial portion, however, would be divided amongst the four major groups which constitute practically the whole movement — Raindance Corporation, Videofreex, People's Video Theatre, and Global Village.

Each group approaches decentralized alternate television in its own way, but all share a common technical base — portable half-inch videotape recording systems, of which Sony's AVC-3400 Videorecorder popular. [*sic*] For $1500 — that is, for less than a Volkswagen — one can purchase a complete audio-visual information system that is autonomous within itself, unlike film, which is dependent on expensive processing labs. Because of its dependability and versatility, the Sony is preferred over other half-inch systems as produced by, say, Panasonic or Shibaden. With the flick of a switch, the shoulder-slung battery pack becomes a playback deck, and the camera's viewfinder becomes a monitor. Instant replay in the middle of the forest. Or, with an RF adapter, the playback deck plugs into any TV set. Or, for $2500 — easily afforded by, say, a group of ten persons — one can purchase a complete "theatrical" information system including camera, 23-inch monitor, shoulder pack, studio playback deck with editing capability, omnidirectional microphone and extension speakers. Put it in your VW bus and you've got a mobile TV station. Tape costs as little as $15 for 30 minutes or $30 for an hour, may be erased and reused dozens of times, and may be played as many as 400 times.

The alternate television groups, cropping up almost wholly in the past year and a half, have not yet tied together in a network for distribution. But even without a broadcast capability as yet, they are moving in that direction. Plans for Videofreex and Raindance Corporation to set up a video counterpart to the already highly successful Underground Press Service are still in the "very early formation stages," according to Ann, of Videofreex. The grant from the New York State Council on the Arts will permit the nine people who comprise Videofreex to outfit a mobile media system and wheel into communities all over the state, turning people on to the human uses of television and to the possiblities of local cable TV as a community "information and problem-solving tool."

Cable TV, of course, could make it possible to hook up nothing less than an alternative broadcast grid.

In the meantime, the strategy is clear: to eliminate the existing state of monopoly in broadcasting, by providing people with visible alternatives. This has meant bringing audiences into television theatres, as the People's Video Theatre has done in New York City. And taking televison into the street, projecting from within giant inflatables — in effect, creating giant soft television sets — as the Ant Farm and Video-freex have done. Also banking tapes and distributing them by mail. Producing and distributing video magazines, as *Broadside — the Free Video Press* has done on the East Coast, and as *West Coast Video Magazine* is starting to do from San Francisco.

Two print magazines have appeared suddenly, both of them nonlinear in format and exuberant proselytisers of alternative video: *Print Project Amerika* and *Radical Software.* Two others — *Edcentric* and *Media Mix* — keep an exceptionally keen eye posted for media, while being devoted to radical educational reform.

Print media has played an extraordinary role in the rise of the alternative school network. *Vocations for Social Change* was the first of the new generation of newsletters, and still offers access to apprenticeships. *New Schools Exchange Newsletter*, according to Harvey Haber, was "the first grass-roots national educational reform tool."

. . . An old hand-crank mimeograph and a type-writer and the New Schools Movement was defined. We were quick to discover that all that is necessary to have a movement is to declare it as such, which we did. So, a couple of dozen new schools with pretensions no greater than wanting to save a couple of hundred kids from the death of public schools found themselves part of a national movement. . . .

Today the *Exchange*, like *Whole Earth Catalog*, channels tremendous energies.

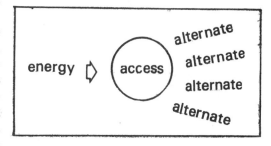

Energy. Access. Alternatives. *Whole Earth Catalog* provides "access to tools." Media Ithaca speaks of "accessing the public broadcast waves." The principle underlying today's radical reform is that — quite simply — information is energy. If people can be provided with access to the alternative media, then the Global Village can *become real.* Once access to cable TV can be obtained, once the alternative educational system can plug into a wealth of programming — so, too, can the public schools — So can we all, plug into the media-sphere.

If this "soft revolution" succeeds, then a lot of flimflam disguised presently as educational media will be consigned quietly to oblivion. But to the manufacturers will fall important new priorities: the production of "hard" instructional materials for video broadcast; development of computerized multi-sensory and reciprocating learning-aids, including trans-sensory programs for the blind and the hearing-impaired; tactile learning kits, on the order of the "soft boxes" developed by Anthony Barton and David Stansfield, and like the Match Units put together by the imaginative people at the Children's Museum in Boston which permit a child to experience a culture through its artifacts by role-playing, actually drilling soapstone with a Nesilik Eskimo bow drill.

What the alternative schools and the alternative media are teaching us is what we have known all along; that education is concerned with providing individuals with access to the world.

Photo Courtesy of NASA

HANSEL & GRETEL

ARTHUR PEARL

ansel and Gretel lived with their father, Fred, and stepmother, Mary, in a neat little suburb where houses looked much like each other and lawns were well manicured and dogs were big, friendly, and obedient — which was more than could be said of the children! Hansel and Gretel's father wasn't poor, he had a good job that required his presence five days a week for eight hours a day, and he worked very hard, and he had his own secretary and a key to the men's room and was on a cordial first-name relationship with the vice-president.

Unfortunately, however, he owed everybody money. The nice, neat, manicured house he lived in would be paid for after 303 more easy payments. His first wife agreed to be warm, friendly, and cordial; in exchange she received a sizable portion of his monthly check. The new car he drove would be his in thirty-one more payments; the old car his wife drove would be his in seven more payments (but it was getting pretty run-down and would probably run out before he could claim it). But money wasn't his biggest problem — Hansel and Gretel were. They did not like school. It was dull, irrelevant, dreary, and dumb. Hansel's

teacher was "icky"; Gretel's was downright mean. As a result, the children grew distant, hostile, moody, unhappy, and even got into trouble. But Hansel and Gretel's stepmother was young, together, and hip. She was not caught up in "things" — she wasn't trapped by middle-class values.

So one day she came home with some terrific news. She had discovered an alternative school — a school deep in the woods where exciting things occurred. There were ecological projects in the wilderness; there were art and music and theater and rap sessions; it was a place where children made things and went on field trips. She asked the children, would they like to go there? Hansel and Gretel were insistent, and they promised everything — they even promised to be good if they were allowed to go to the new, exciting alternative school. That night, after Hansel and Gretel went to bed, Fred and Mary talked about the new school. Fred protested, and the more Fred protested, the more Mary insisted. Fred said it cost too much money and, second, it seemed like giving in to the children and, third, he was afraid of such a loose, permissive place. But Mary was persuasive and pointed out that the children were not doing well in traditional school and if they kept it up they were going to get into serious trouble, and Fred finally agreed.

So early the very next morning Mary, Hansel, and Gretel drove to the new school. It was exciting! "Wow!" said Hansel; "Far out!" said Gretel. The school was tucked into a lovely little setting of woods surrounded by wild flowers, and while it was made of redwood, it looked like it was made of gingerbread, cake, and sugar. Children were running inside and outside, and teachers were running with them, and everybody looked like they were happy. Above the door of the new school was inscribed the motto: "Man was born free, and everywhere he is in chains." "Wow!" said Hansel; "Far out!" said Gretel. The children walked into the office of the headmaster, whose name was Thomas Superwitch, who welcomed the children by saying that he was "Tom," and he told the children, as he sat on the corner of his desk and puffed on his pipe, about the philosophy of the school. "This school is for you to have fun, and all your teachers are here to be your friends and help you have fun. There are no tests, no grades, no lectures — students can do almost anything they want." "Far out!" said Hansel; "Wow!" said Gretel. Hansel and Gretel were then introduced to one of their teachers, John Holtwitch — who told them to call him "John," and they did. And John said, "What would you like to do? The one thing we want you to know here is that there is no way you can fail — there is no way anybody can fail — so what do you want to do?" So Hansel and Gretel said that they would like to go out there and play with the sheep and milk the yak and do all the wonderful things that other kids were doing out in the yard. And John said, "Fine." He said, "Anything you want to do is fine with me as long as you don't hurt yourself and don't hurt others." And they promised they wouldn't hurt anybody, and off they ran to join the others.

Hansel and Gretel thought they were in paradise. They thought the desks they sat in were just like soft, feathery beds to sleep in and the classes every morning to every afternoon were just like having creamy milk to drink and rosy apples and honey cake to eat. And John Holtwitch seemed to want them to eat and think and do good things, and he would never accept any thanks. He said, "You please me best if you do as much of what you like and as much of what you want to do. There is nothing I like better than to see happy little boys and happy little girls."

And Hansel and Gretel would go home and tell their parents about the great school, and they would bring back various little things that they had made and they would talk about the rap sessions they had had about Vietnam and racism and things like that. And they would talk about the plays they had been in, and even Fred had to admit that the school seemed like a good thing, and everything seemed to be going well, and the fact that he had found a peculiar little wrinkled, brown cigarette-looking thing in Hansel's room didn't bother him too much, and the fact that Gretel seemed to be a little bit more distant and a little bit all wrapped up in herself more than she used to be didn't bother him too much because they weren't getting into trouble. And the fact that the school was maybe a little expensive didn't bother him too much because they weren't getting into trouble.

John was not the only teacher they had. *All* of the teachers turned them on — which was their sole criterion for teaching excellence (more and more in their own eyes Hansel and Gretel became electrical appliances). They talked about the other teachers — Neal Postwitch, who pointed out they didn't have to read. He was a "heavy dude," said Hansel. "For sure," said Gretel. There was George Denniwitch, who said that they didn't have to think about the future. He was a "heavy dude," said Gretel. "Really," said Hansel. There was yet another "heavy dude" — Bill Glasswitch, who turned them on because he said, "Humans are role-oriented, not goal-oriented," and had them sit in circles and discuss "heavy" things. And finally there was Ivan Illwitch, who said that there should be no schools at all, and he was a "very heavy dude," said Hansel and Gretel. "For sure," said Mary. And Fred said, "I have a headache," and went to bed — but it was worth it because the children didn't get in trouble.

f inally, the time came for graduation — what excitement, what joy, what a different kind of graduation! — students wore what they liked, and you never saw such an array of color and variety of clothes. The stage, where the children were garlanded with flowers, mostly wild, plucked from their natural origins near and not far from the school itself — and the smell of the flowers blended neatly with the aroma of those funny, brown cigarettes that most of the children smoked more openly now (and that made them somewhat different from kids in regular schools, who still did those kinds of things clandestinely). And although they were aware that they were violating the law, they didn't care because unjust laws did not need to be obeyed — and that was only one thing that they had learned at school.

Then came the final moment, and Tom Superwitch turned them on for the very last time — he recounted the great times that they had had together; he rode on excitedly with nostalgic metaphor, and they encouraged him in choruses of "ride on," and Hansel and Gretel rode on to attack the real world — of work, politics, leisure, culture, and personal encounters.

But they didn't go to work — work was dull, work was wrapped up with a "Protestant ethic" and middle-class values, work was a "rat race of bureaucracy," and, besides, work just helped the wealthy get wealthier. They didn't mind work, you understand, and if a good job came along, which turned them on and fulfilled them, they would take it in a minute. In the meantime they needed very little money, except for records and a subscription to *Rolling Stone* and organic foods and leather things and, of course, tickets to flicks and concerts. (Fred's headaches seemed to be getting worse, and even Mary's patience was wearing thin.)

Hansel and Gretel were political — make no mistake about that; they marched, they baited policemen, they chanted slogans and demonstrated (although, in truth, there were not too many demonstrations any more). They were too sophisticated for traditional politics — they weren't going to be sucked into supporting "bourgeois" liberals — and while they were as pure and uncorrupted as the organic food they ate, Presidents continued to preside, governors to govern, and legislators to legislate. And thus it was that even more hundreds of billions of dollars were appropriated for defense, taxes were paid by the poor to support the profit-making activities of the rich, the nonwhites (with whom Hansel and Gretel identified through concerned inactivity) continued to receive less than their fair share at home and abroad, and the environment that Hansel and Gretel loved continued to deteriorate.

In culture and leisure Hansel and Gretel, for all their school involvement, found little to enjoy. They strummed their guitars less and less; they dabbled with paints almost never at all. They never learned that hard work was important if one were ever to master anything.

They weren't good company either. They didn't like many people, and not very many people liked them. They tended to be dull, self-centered, remote, and ill-tempered. They didn't belong to anything; they didn't contribute to anything.

And so it was that when Hansel and Gretel entered the real world, they were eaten up.

here is, however, something more to be said. Hansel and Gretel's counterparts — the children who stayed in regular schools — didn't fare too well either: they, too, found work adjustment difficult; they, too, were politically impotent; they, too, failed to contribute to cultural activities; they, too, had difficulty in belonging, contributing, and feeling competent.

And the parents of Hansel and Gretel and the parents of the children who went to regular schools — they, too, weren't doing too well. They, too, found work adjustment difficult; they, too, were politically impotent; they, too failed to contribute culturally; and they, too, had difficulty belonging, contributing, and feeling competent.

So there you have it. Children educated in both traditional and open schools, and their parents, end up much the same. There must be a moral there someplace.

MORAL: . . . .
. . . .
. . . .
. . . .

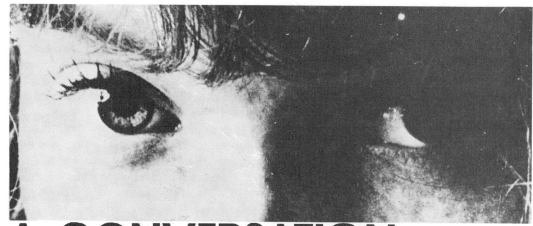

A CONVERSATION WITH a.s. neill

Herbert C. Rudman

RUDMAN Do you feel, as you look back over the years, that you have accomplished what you hoped to accomplish with these youngsters?

NEILL Oh yes. I've no doubt about that. It's difficult to prove, of course, but for fifty years I've never regretted a moment or felt I was doing things the wrong way. As I asked one of my old pupils, whose field is history, "Can you imagine some of the old Summerhill people, who grew up in freedom, performing in a play with fornication on the stage?" He said, "No." And I said, "Neither can I." That sums up what I think is the success of Summerhill. The kids have a balanced view of life and a balanced view of sex. I don't care whether they're professors or dustmen. It's a question of balance; it's this tolerance thing I have here at Summerhill. Some parents have complained to

me that Summerhill made the children far too tolerant, which is rather a compliment.

So that's about it. And looking at the education scene, I find John Holt, for example, whom I like very much – a bright lad. But I think John is more concerned with the learning process. And I am concerned with the *living* process.

I don't care a damn whether the children learn or not. We have eight teachers for sixty-four children – Americans, Germans, French, Danes; we run an international school here. And the lessons are there if you want them. The lessons have to be there because of this exam system outside. You can't get into a university without passing O and A level exams. So you have to have the teachers. But that's unimportant from my point of view. I don't care if a child doesn't go to lessons for years.

I have two boys who never went to a lesson in ten years. One of them has an engineering business; he's in charge of 600 men. The other boy works — making do. Mind you, these boys, as students, were always in the workshop. They learned nothing about English and German and history and things like that. So I've never bothered with a child who doesn't go to lessons. I know that if they've got the ability and the guts to use it, that's all they need. I've no doubts about that.

RUDMAN One of my students gave me Ivan Illich's new book, *Deschooling Society*. Do you know of him? It's a fascinating book. He never once mentions Summerhill or even that there is a school like Summerhill. It's almost as if he has a tendency to rediscover the world all by himself.

But his concept is one I think you'd adhere to — that the trouble with society is that all of the institutions have become so formal. Hospitals don't really cure; they contribute to illness. He maintains that schools don't educate; they contribute to illiteracy. He argues that what we need to do is deinstitutionalize the schools — get rid of school as a formal institution. And in its place he talks about four webs of learning. One web has to do with learning from your peers; another has to do with learning from your elders; another with learning from things around you, and a fourth with learning from professionals.

Is that the kind of approach that you're shooting for in Summerhill — to try to deinstitutionalize the notion of the school as a school?

NEILL I expect it is. But my view is conventional in some ways. We have classes and bells. The bell rings and the children go to various classes. Of course, they are free to stay away.

My old friend, Wilhelm Reich, thirty years ago in his *Mass Psychology of Facism*, pointed out that the function of the school is not to teach history and geography. It's to castrate children, to make them obey authority, be guilty about sex, be guilty about religion — to be sheep, so to speak, so that when they grow up, they haven't the guts to challenge anything. Hence Hitler's Germany was a nation that, against all its own interests, followed a madman. Hence Britain at the moment — where the majority of people are working class — puts in a Tory government, and the government goes against them. It's this mass psychology of obedience and following that I'm up against.

Summerhill children wouldn't follow anybody. They won't follow me. I can't remember anyone coming to me for advice about anything. They're not sheep.

It's appalling to me to see a TV film of China, with thousands of children marching in fours, holding up the little red books, and shouting, "Mao!" All castrated, as it were, in their cradles, and no longer individuals; they're just a mass following of sheep.

You get it everywhere. You get it in America. You get it here. In a way Summerhill is an unconscious attempt to break down mass psychology and mass following and get more individuals.

Unfortunately, as you know, very few people in life challenge anything. The *New Statesman* said some time ago that 85 percent of English teachers wanted to retain the cane. Obviously people who want to keep the cane are violent. That sort of thing makes me pessimistic.

But I get optimistic about the revolt of youth — even though the revolt is often about nothing. So many hippies, for example, rebel against the length of hair or the color of a jacket, but not enough of them are rebelling against stupid schools or religious indoctrination or politics. But that, too, is beginning to come. There's a passage in Reich that says the majority knows it has right on its side. I suspect it believes it has; I suspect he was right. So if Summerhill became a majority, it would be wrong. . . .

RUDMAN I'd like to return to the purpose

of Summerhill and the education the youngsters get. I'm using education not in a schooling sense. I am using it in a broader sense than that.

Do you have much contact with the children when they leave? Do you know what happens to them as they go back into a world that is really more restrictive than Summerhill?

NEILL   Well, I see quite a lot of them. On the third of January, we had a big party in honor of our fiftieth anniversary. And we had a number of alumni there. I'm not having a celebration this year. I'll be eighty-eight next week, and I've got a bad heart, so I'm not going up to London any more.

My graduates aren't rebels. They don't go marching around with flags and things like that. It's difficult to describe. An American woman asked me not long ago, "Why aren't your alumni striving to cure the world of its sickness?" And I said, "That's an interesting question, and it's difficult to answer. But let me give you one or two instances. One former student is a professor of history, one's a professor of mathematics, one's an assistant professor of physics, and others are lawyers and doctors. Well, take those three professors. They've got their jobs to do. If they stand on a box in Hyde Park on Sunday morning and talk about freedom, they're wasting their breath and their time. What can they do?"

I got an answer to that question from the mathematics professor. He said, "All I can do is bring up my children in freedom, hoping that they'll carry on with their children and that other people might be influenced." And I think that's about all one can do.

RUDMAN   Have your former students sent their children to Summerhill?

NEILL   Ten percent, no more. But a lot of them can't afford it, you see. They don't go in for money; they're not built for business.

RUDMAN   How are they represented in the professions, arts, and so forth?

NEILL   They run to the arts and professions.

Quite a few are doctors, and one or two lawyers. One person is making a name for himself illustrating children's books. Two girls are artists, and they have exhibitions in London. Some of the boys are engineers.

One parent said a very interesting thing to me. She said, "You know, Summerhill doesn't come out until the second generation. We were brought up the wrong way, and Summerhill saved us from the authority of the family. But we bring up our kids free." I think there's something in that. I think it's the second generation that tells.

RUDMAN   What happens with the third generation?

NEILL   I won't live to see that.

RUDMAN   It would be interesting, though, wouldn't it, to see the extent to which the kids react against — or react to — the freedom that the parents have given them?

NEILL   I don't think they react against freedom. Not really. As a matter of fact somebody asked me how anybody could improve on Summerhill in the future. "Well, I don't know," I said.

We go as far as we can with freedom. We're limited in certain ways. I believe in sexual freedom. But you can't have it in the present circumstance. That's the only advance I can think of in the future — to allow sexual life for adolescents in a free school. But I don't see how freedom can go any further than Summerhill. As I've often defined it, freedom in Summerhill is doing exactly what you like as long as you don't interfere with somebody else.

RUDMAN   You mentioned the rule about visitors, pointing out that some people who come here to visit have confused freedom with license. They allow children to play with their cameras and do all sorts of things that you probably would not agree with. On the door there's a large sign with a list of about eight rules. This implies to me that freedom does not mean lack of rules, so far as you're concerned.

NEILL   No, of course not.

RUDMAN   It doesn't mean anarchy or license in that sense?

NEILL   No.

RUDMAN   What are the parameters, then, of freedom? What are the limits of freedom? Are they just simply that you don't interfere with the rights of others?

NEILL   That's about it. We recently had an American girl bullying a smaller girl. It's a matter for the community to tell her off, because you can't do that sort of thing. And that's as near to democracy as we can get, you see.

RUDMAN   How many youngsters do you have at Summerhill right now?

NEILL   I never know. Sixty-four, I think. I've got twenty-eight Americans, ten Germans, and two Swiss, I think. The Germans are being a bit of a nuisance at the moment. I've got a bit of a problem with them, because they speak German to each other and become isolated. And I don't want racial antagonism developing.

It never has. We've had black children here. The kids don't notice, of course. But we are open to such antagonism. On television we've watched the hateful faces of white kids throwing rocks at black children. It just shows you how easily you can indoctrinate hate. But children have no natural feeling about color. They don't know what it is. They don't know what a Jew is. They don't understand that. There are a lot of Jews here. I don't know which is which. Nobody knows or cares.

We're very tolerant with these children and with each other. But there are limits to democracy, there are limits. I mean certain things don't enter into government. For example, my wife doesn't ask the children what food to prepare. Mind you, if there was a meeting and they said, "We object to so and so," she'd go along with them.

I don't ask them to help me select a teacher of mathematics. They haven't the

knowledge to do things of that type. And they don't want to. They know the limits. Their democracy is living together and jumping on the people who upset the community.

RUDMAN   That's interesting, because today in the United States — and it seems to be taking place in many parts of the world — students are demanding a larger and larger say in the running of the institution, not just in those matters that affect their own lives, but in other matters like hiring and firing faculty and having a voice in their promotion. The youngsters here at Summerhill don't have, or don't care to exercise, that kind of power?

NEILL   That's right.

RUDMAN   Would you be in favor of granting them that power if that's what they wanted?

NEILL   No, because they haven't the knowledge to back it up. I appointed a man not long ago to teach art, without consulting anybody. But the kids came to me and said, "He's no good. He's a bad teacher. We won't go to his lessons." So I had to say to the poor chap, "Look here, you'll have to clear out because the kids say your lessons are no good." They have the power that way in a secondary way, although they haven't the power to appoint the chap to begin with.

RUDMAN   What were some of the reasons that they gave you for saying he wasn't a good teacher?

NEILL   He had no imagination. Every lesson he gave was dull. He interfered with their pictures and put his brush on them, which of course was appalling. A teacher should never put his brush on a child's painting. That kills the painting of the child.

So the students had a general meeting. Somebody called him a bloody fool or something, and he complained to me. "My dear chap," I said, "why the hell did you come here if you've got any dignity? Haven't you noticed the kids following me about all day shouting, 'Neill, Neill, orange peel,' expecting me to get angry with them?" Incidentally, the title of my autobiography is *Neill! Neill! Orange Peel!*

You see, the teachers at Summerhill do not expect any deference because they are adults. The whole staff are treated by the children as pals and playmates. But so many teachers want to be little gods protected by dignity. They're so afraid that if they act human, their authority will disappear and their classrooms will become bedlam. They fear to abolish fear, and innumerable children fear their teachers. Of course, it's discipline that creates the fear.

But getting back to the idea of students exercising power. It's difficult because students are a floating population. If they had a say in the hiring of professors, then a new group of students would come in each year and want to hire other professors.

I had two visitors here not long ago. One was taking his B.A. at Harvard or Yale in psychology. I asked both of them what a teacher should do with a kid who is stealing. And I got the same answer. "Good God, they don't mention things like that at the university. They only tell us what happens to Skinner rats when you condition them." It looks as if you can get a B.A. in psychology and know nothing about human nature. . . .

RUDMAN   What about the parents' attitudes? Obviously the reason students are here is because the parents are supportive of Summerhill. Or at least I'm assuming that.

NEILL   That's the ideal solution. But it isn't always true. A few years ago we had half a dozen boys from America, little boys eight, nine, and ten. And they all had problems. One of the boys, for example, was nine. His father wrote that he was a normal boy but he hated lessons. When he came here, his face was filled with hate. He was a bully and a thief. Obviously the father dumped him on us. We get a lot of that.

We've got one now, a European boy. At eleven he's in bad trouble. The parents didn't

tell us, and we don't like sending people home.

I sent one boy home to America. He told me, "I hate this damn school!" He was one of those broken home people who would be unhappy anywhere. "I want to go home," he said. "I'm going to break windows so Neill will send me home." Well, when his number of broken windows came to thirty-two, I told his parents to take him home.

RUDMAN   What about the other youngsters who come from America? What about the boy who came here with hate in his face? Did he stay? Were you able to do something for him? Were the other kids able to do something with this youngster?

NEILL   No. We couldn't do very much for him. He went back to America after thirty months, and his parents sent him to a school in New York state modeled after Summerhill. He was eleven, and he was a failure. And he didn't want to be that.

When you get a boy like that from a broken home, you can't do much with him. Nearly all homesick children, I've discovered, are from unhappy homes. Kids from unhappy homes are lost; they've got no anchor. One little American boy said, "I want to go home." And he kept saying that. I asked him why. He said, "Because I want to protect mother from daddy always hitting her." That's an extreme case, but it precisely sums up the situation of the homesick kid who wants to go back to a broken home.

RUDMAN   Are the balance of the children from warm, loving, supportive homes — normal homes? Or do you agree with my assumption that a normal home is loving and warm and supportive?

NEILL   The best and happiest kids we've ever had were from homes where there was love. But there's one case you can't do much with. When the child is abandoned as a baby, he never compensates for it. You can never give him back what he has lost. I've had it again and again in Summerhill — especially with adopted children, children with ersatz parents. I'm tired of pulling parental chestnuts out of the fire.

RUDMAN Can you ever avoid that if the school is going to do more than just teach cognitive material to children?

NEILL You can avoid it if you have enlightened parents.

RUDMAN But then you don't have to pull those chestnuts out of the fire.

NEILL Yes, that's true. Mind you, we can do a lot for a child ourselves because we are a family, so to speak. If you have a big school of 1200 children in large classes, the teacher can't do anything to save the souls of those kids.

RUDMAN How many children do you have with each teacher? Do you have grades or forms?

NEILL We have classes, and we get up a list of them each term. If Johnny is in class three and he thinks he ought to be in class four, he automatically goes there; he chooses for himself. The list of classes is put up merely as a guide, you see.

RUDMAN How many teachers do you have on your staff?

NEILL Eight, and sixty-four children.

RUDMAN If a youngster who you've suggested should go into the third class goes to the fourth class, and in the teacher's estimation he's not doing the work that he should be doing, does the teacher then have the power to veto the child's choice and put him back in third class?

NEILL No. They don't do that. That situation doesn't really crop up. And if it did, you'd take the kid and teach him individually.

RUDMAN Neill, I've taken so much of your time. And I appreciate having you do this.

NEILL I don't mind talking to a man like you, but I get tired of some of the questions people ask me. I was talking with a group of people last term about the stupidity of school subjects that have no connection at all with life outside. I said that in the Leiston Grammar School children are taught to read Shakespeare, Tennyson, and Thomas Hardy. And I said I'd like to go to a football match with 100,000 people and ask how many would come to hear Shakespeare or Tennyson. I said I'd be surprised if I found two. An American woman got up and said, "I don't believe it. I'm very glad that I was forced to do things in school I'd never have done on my own, like mathematics." So I asked her, "Can you do a quadratic equation?" And she said, "No." I said, "Let's have a show of hands." Well, only two hands went up. I said, "You're mathematics teachers?" And they were, which proved my point.

At the university, I had to take English history as a compulsory subject. I got 95 percent; I liked history. But today I don't know a thing about history. I don't even know who won the War of the Roses. I know that Henry VIII had six wives, but that's about all. We're always teaching children things like that. Those subjects will have to go sometime. If people want history and geography, then we'll have to dig them up.

If I were minister of education, I'd abolish the teaching of history and geography, and possibly English. You'd have to keep mathematics. You have to learn mathematics from books. You'd have to keep science. But all the rest of the things, I think, can go by the board....

RUDMAN Can one make judgments about his life, himself, or his future, if we don't give him some basis that we, in a sense, inculcate?

For example, George Counts, the educational philosopher, once asked me if I believed in inculcating democratic values. And I asked him, "What do you mean, 'inculcate'?" He said, "I mean indoctrinate." And I asked, "Isn't that an inconsistency in the whole concept of democracy?" But to him it wasn't inconsistent. George's notion was that we start with a blank board, and we write on that blank board. If we're going to make intelligent choices between political systems or between philosophies, we have to have some base from which to start. And we get that base from indoctrination and inculcation.

I suppose George might argue — and I have no business putting words in his mouth — that the very life that children lead at Summerhill is a form of indoctrination.

NEILL   You can call it that. It's a matter of semantics. It is indoctrination, if you like: indoctrination of our community spirit. I don't know what it means, really. I can't think in philosophical terms. I never understood philosophy. I said to Bertrand Russell one day, "Russell, I love your conversation, but I can't read your bloody books and understand them."

Indoctrination to me involves power. A Hitler can indoctrinate. A Mao can indoctrinate. A headmaster at Eton can indoctrinate, because he's a power person. And it implies inferiority on the part of the people being indoctrinated.

That doesn't happen at Summerhill. Half the proposals I make at meetings are outvoted. I'm not in authority here. If you asked the children at Summerhill, "What's Neill's re-ligion? What does he think of politics?" they wouldn't know. And they wouldn't care.

So indoctrination to me means somebody with a set purpose telling people how to live. We don't tell people here how to live. Telling people how to live is indoctrination, which nobody has the right to do. Nobody's wise enough. Nobody's good enough.

Don't ask me any more philosophical questions because I don't understand them. . . .

One day in April I received a letter from Neill that I will share, in part, with the readers of this article. It wraps up in a few poignant lines the essence of the man.

At eighty-eight and a half I am out of things. . . . I don't fear death; I just hate the idea of the candle's blowing out, never knowing the ultimate result of my work, what will happen to Summerhill, the sick world. . . .
I grieve to see how slowly freedom for kids grows. The National Union of Teachers here has just sanctioned the cane by a great majority. Difficult to be an optimist in a world of war, hate, racialism, killing of infants in their cradles. However, there is a bright side. My heart specialist tells me that whiskey is good for my coronary. All the best, good friend.

Neill

SUMMARY OF THE MONTESSORI METHOD

Maria Montessori (1870-1952), Italy's first woman physician, became interested in applying the scientific method to education while working with retarded children in a psychiatric clinic. What evolved from Dr. Montessori's experience and observations was a whole new philosophy of education — and a method based on her distinctive concepts about children's early learning potential, individualized instruction, programmed teaching materials, and a shift in teacher function.

Dr. Montessori believed that from birth to six, every child is endowed with what she called an "absorbent mind," which allows him to learn more quickly and easily than at any other time in his life.

The years between three and six, according to Dr. Montessori, are unusually "sensitive periods," during which children can benefit profoundly from serious learning. If the school is aware of these "sensitive periods" and provides adequate stimulation for the child, he will *naturally* move himself toward learning.

Related to this view of child development was Montessori's theory about the "prepared environment." She coined the aphorism, "things are the best teachers," and invented a rich array of educational "didactic materials" — like her famous movable alphabet and sandpaper letters — that develop the child's ability to see, touch, feel and discriminate between shapes, sounds, textures, size, quantity and dimension. Utilizing the same principles that programmed learning and teaching machines apply today, Dr. Montessori developed her material to test the child's understanding at each step of his learning experience and to help him correct his own errors.

Within the prepared environment, every available material was designed for educational purpose and, therefore, Dr. Montessori had no qualms about offering children the liberty to move about the room as they wished, as long as they did not infringe upon the rights of others. Furthermore, children must be free, she felt, if there is to be any discipline in the classroom and in learning, since the only real discipline is self-discipline — which children need the opportunity to develop.

With the didactic materials carrying the burden of the instruction, Montessori moved the teacher or "directress" from center stage in the classroom to the background, where she functions primarily as a diagnostician, a link between the child and the materials, and a guide to helping each child pursue his own individual learning interests. — K. A.

free   schools

JONATHAN   KOZOL

I know that I will antagonize many people by the tenor of these statements; yet I believe them deeply and cannot keep faith with the people I respect, and who show loyalty to me, if I put forward a piece of writing of this kind and do not say these things. In my belief, an isolated upper-class Free School for the children of the white and rich within a land like the United Sates and in a time of torment such as 1972 is a great deal too much like a sandbox for the children of the S.S. guards at Auschwitz. If today in our history books, or in our common conversation, we were to hear of a network of exquisite, idealistic little country schools operated with a large degree of personal freedom, but within the bounds of ideological isolation, in the beautiful sloping woodlands outside of Munich and Berlin in 1939 or 1940, and if we were to read or to be told that those who ran these schools were operating by all innovative methods and enlightened notions and that they had above their desks or on their walls large poster-photographs of people like Maria Montessori and Tolstoi and Gandhi, and that they somehow kept beyond the notice of the Nazi government and of the military and of the police and S.S. guards, but kept right on

somehow throughout the war with no experience of rage or need for intervention in the lives of those defined by the German press and media as less than human, but kept right on with water play and "innovative" games while smoke rose over Dachau . . . I think that we would look upon those people now as some very fine and terrifying breed of alienated human beings.

It is not a handsome or a comfortable parallel; yet, in my judgment it is not entirely different from the situation of a number of the country communes and the segregated Summerhills that we now see in certain sections of this nation. At best, these schools are obviating pain and etherizing evil; at worst, they constitute a registered escape valve for political rebellion. Least conscionable is when the people who are laboring and living in these schools describe themselves as revolutionaries. If this is revolution, then the men who have elected Richard Nixon do not have a lot to fear. They would do well in fact to subsidize these schools and to covertly channel resources to their benefactors and supporters, for they are an ideal drain on activism and the perfect way to sidetrack ethical men from dangerous behavior.

MEDIA & METHODS

Interviews
John Bremer, Director
of the Parkway Program

M&M   Do you feel, John, that the program at this point is a teaching and learning success, or have your problems become so complex and numerous that they are beginning to weigh you down?

Bremer   I think that the principal difficulty we faced at the beginning was, on the one hand, that we were trying to create a new organizational and administrative model and, at the same time, were trying to use that new organizational model for running the program. Now, I think you can separate the two — at least analytically. First, I'm fairly confident that the question of the new organizational model has been successfully completed; that is, we now understand fairly well what the best administrative model is. We understand much better than we did at the beginning how the faculty, parents, students and community people generally can participate in decision-making procedures. The second thing is, if we have successfully created a model, is it now being successfull used by the people who are in it? I thing the answer to that is, "Yes, it is."

M&M   Now that you have determined that it is successful — on both counts — what is it, exactly, that you have called successful?

Bremer   That is rather hard to answer, for the simple reason that since it is a new model, there is no vocabulary for it. I have to say what it isn't. For example, I think it is fairly clear that in most educational organizations that we know, the administrative model is very clearly a patriarchal, or perhaps, matriarchal, one. It is a kind of triangle or pyramid in which the administrator sits at the top, and the power to do things is vested in him and, on the whole, in him alone. As a result there is not much opportunity for students to participate in management. We have tried to get away from that, so that everyone who is connected with the program has an opportunity to participate in decision-making.

M&M   From your point of view, John, is the important variable from one educational model to another this question of power, or "Who makes the decisions?"

Bremer   There is a great deal of confusion about the relationship between power and learning. As far as I'm concerned, if I have power over someone, it makes it impossible for me to help them learn anything because they are never in a position to see whether they have really learned something or whether they are merely being obedient in the face of a superior power. So I would have to say that, yes, this is what is most characteristic about the model. But I wouldn't say "power." It is rather a question of sharing in a common enterprise. We are here as a learning institution. The trouble with a triangular or pyramidical is that the highest office in the school or the system — the principal or superintendent or whatever — is essentially a non-learning role. You have, then, set up a system in which the ultimate office is a non-learning one. It is not surprising, then, that the students at the bottom of the triangle don't learn a great deal. Now, here I think it is very important that we all share in the common enterprise of learning and I learn. The trouble with my job, and the painful part of it, is that I have to do most of my learning in public. So that if I decide I want to face a particular problem and try to deal in it a certain way and I go to the community they may say, "You can't do that because we feel that there are other factors you're not taking into consideration; you're going to have to change your mind." I have to learn. So it's not a question of simply sharing the power; I think it's the question of sharing in the common enterprise of learning, which can only take place if we have mutual respect for one another. That is I'm un-hesitating in telling students that they should go to class. I say that because I have respect for them, not because I don't have respect for them. They came here to learn and I think it would be a disservice to them to allow them to think they can do anything they like. This is not a program in which they do as they like. Similarly they tell me in no uncertain terms when they feel I'm letting them down that I'm letting them down. They do this, you see, in a context which enables us to keep mutual respect. They have a stake in the situation; they are not here to serve my ends and I'm not here to serve their ends either. We are here together to serve each other's ends.

M&M   To what extent do students participate in decision-making. To what extent are they contributors to curriculum, for example?

Bremer   I'm not sure that's not the old vocabulary, which, of course, reflects the old taxonomy. I'm not sure that's relevant to education any longer. Of course, I know what curriculum is. But it has to be redefined. If you

look at the way a school operates there is no doubt the only thing that is really being learned by students in that school is the social organization of the school. The so-called subject matters — normally thought of as subject matter — are nothing other than machines, engines, tools, for accomplishing that end. Well, now there is no doubt that one of the most important parts of what students and faculty learn here is how to cooperate and work together. That is the curriculum in one sense of the word. Now, it is also true that since we are a public school in the middle of a large urban area, the boundaries of our cooperation extend beyond our own community; so therefore, we have to learn how to live in the city. That means, then, that the city is our curriculum. The creation of the curriculum in a more academic sense is up to the students and faculty working together.

M&M   Do you really mean working together "equally"? The faculty must have some prerogatives here.

Bremer   We obviously had the initiative as a faculty because we were, in a sense, here first; we just took upon ourselves the inevitable arrogance of educators and made some proposals. But I do not think we made the mistake of supposing this was somehow like God's word. We just put this out as a proposal. Students added and subtracted. Since, with the exception of the basic skills handled in the tutorials, the courses are all elective courses anyway, students by not choosing a course do it out of existence. This is now becoming a continuing process and I look forward to the day when the initial prerogative of the faculty will be completely lost.

M&M   You are saying then, that whatever is taught is decided on in this managerial process in which everyone shares.

Bremer   I don't want to disagree with that but I think that you put it in a rather one-sided way. I think that we're very clear about what is to be learned, but I don't think that we are uniformly agreed and never will be, or shouldn't be, as to how you learn. Now, for example, I think everybody should learn how to cooperate. Because this is what our future survival depends upon. That was not always true but that is true now. Now, if you make that, as it were, an essential part of the curriculum and students know this by choosing to come, then I think no matter what you do, you're learning. So, the question becomes, "Do you want to learn to cooperate by talking about novels?" "Do you want to learn how to cooperate by being a member of an athletic team?" "Do you want to learn how to cooperate by building a model with some other people?" There are millions of ways of learning how to do this. And in one sense what we normally call a subject matter or public school courses only become the vehicles for other things — first of all, learning social attitude, activity and skills, secondly, to learn the true basic skills.

M&M As an educational institution granting high school diplomas, you have to satisfy the requirements of the state of Pennsylvania for that certificate — in foreign language, English, history, mathematics, etc. Aren't you setting yourselves up for all manner of problems in allowing students to collaborate in curriculum? Don't you, in effect, have to require that students take certain courses?

Bremer That has not turned out to be a problem. All subject matters, at best, are conventional ways of dividing up the universe. Furthermore, the subject matters we have now were mostly devised in the 19th century and they reflect the structure of a society that is no longer extant. If you want to think about going to the moon, television — anything that is important today, you can't classify it into one subject matter; in fact, you need six or seven.

I got a catalogue from our third unit (Gamma) last night which states the problem of satisfying state requirements and how we go about solving it. What the faculty and students, working together, come up with must be converted into conventional subject matter for credit purposes. Here is a course in the Gamma catalogue: "What is Creativity?" We say that course can be taken for credit in English. But, depending on the needs of the student, the credit might apply elsewhere. Here are some of the other courses: "Poems of Protest," "The Short Story" — that's conventional enough — "Scenery Design and Construction," "Newspaper Writing," "Contemporary Literature About Education." These can be classified but, really, what difference does it make? Here are more: "Alienated Man" — Where does that go? Here's one called "Man and Events" . . .

M&M The point would be that these courses reflect whatever discussion is current between students and faculty at the new unit. The fact that they fall within traditionally defined content areas is beside the point.

Bremer They don't fall in; they are put there. One of our principles in creating curriculum is simply to ask faculty what they would like to teach. For example I'm very interested in clipperships.

M&M In what?

Bremer In clipperships. Particularly those built by Donald McKay in Boston and even more particularly one built in 1854, called the Lightman. Now I feel perfectly confident that students learn some damn important things working with me in clipperships — their history, design, influence on the economy and all the rest of it. If I teach clipperships, I can do a better job because I'm enthused and excited about it. If you ask me to teach a course in geography or commerce, about which I know less than I do about clipperships, the result would differ. Similarly every faculty member has the right to say that this is what he wants to teach. Because there is no list of things to teach which is sacrosanct and beyond question, there are a million ways of getting the educational job done, therefore, it just makes good sense to let teachers do what they want.

M&M Do your kids understand and accept the overall goals for the program?

Bremer I don't think they understand them, at least not in the way the faculty does and not in the way in which I do.

M&M Isn't that a kind of tyranny?

Bremer Certainly not, because there's no great big secret about them. Now you can want to learn something without understanding it before you begin. And I don't think that there is anything tyrannical about it. It would be tyrannical if the students were assigned here. But what we really do here is to exhibit ourselves very publicly and say, "Look, this is the kind of program this is. Do you want to join us? If you want to join us we're delighted to have you." Now you cannot know, and no student can ever know in advance whether he wants to learn what he will learn in the program. That's impossible, because if he knew that he wouldn't need to take the program. So this is not tyrannical because it is being done perfectly publicly and nobody is assigned here.

M&M How about evaluation, John? In light of what you've previously said, it doesn't seem likely that Parkway would dispense A's & B's.

Bremer I think it's about time in education we forgot this judgmental business and got on with the problems of helping people to learn, so that we are not judges but teachers. It is a pity that those two things have become confused. My job is to help people to learn and not to tell them they're stupid or they're brilliant or whatever else it is.

M&M But you have to agree that if your job is to help people learn you must find some way of finding out whether that learning has actually taken place or not.

Bremer Why?

M&M Because if you don't you can't be sure people have learned anything.

Bremer I can't be sure anyway. The people who are sure are the students themselves. We always assume in education that the only way you find out if anybody ever learned anything is by testing them. This is just like a little process I used to go through in secondary school. I would wait until the end of the term for the results of the examinations to come out to discover whether I learned anything.

M&M Aren't you oversimplifying, John? There are other ways of evaluating. Culminating activities which would reflect whether the kids had in actuality learned a particular process are non-judgmental.

Bremer There is a much more simple way, which is ask them, and this is what we do. Let me try to outline what our procedure has been up to now. We may discover that this has not worked satisfactorily, but I would like to be very clear that the evaluation itself has to be a part of the educational process. This is not a post mortem that takes place after the patient has died. What we try to do is in the openness of our relationship build in what I would call a process of continuous self-assessment, which goes on all the time as part of the learning process. At the end of each term we want to take a look at the program. What we do is first of all ask our faculty to give a written evaluation which may be two sentences or a page on every student in every course that they have; we ask the students to evaluate, first of all, the course, and then the actual teaching. Then there are conferences held for all faculty and all students involved. Now obviously in that kind of situation you begin to take in account what has actually been done. If you are evaluating a photography course, you can't just sit and talk about how good or how bad the course may have been, independent of the actual photographs that you have taken developed and printed. One of the things we are very anxious about in this program is that there should be as much as possible of what I would call "reality testing."

M&M   The secondary school in this country, at least the urban school, is becoming more and more custodial — if that's possible. I imagine that the kids who come here come from high school situations have long been conditioned to schooling that is repressive. They obviously can't make a quick transition to a liberated, non-structured unrepressive situation such as this. What kinds of problems have you had in terms of control or in terms of student's inability to take responsibility to themselves or share in decision making?

Bremer   You may find it hard to believe this, but we don't have any control problems at all.

M&M   Because really there are no limits to violate, in a sense.

Bremer   No, I think that puts it unfairly; there certainly are limits that can be violated. But our students learn in something less than three weeks, that we mean what we say to them, that our attitude is genuine. They do not try just to cause trouble for us, or for themselves. They see that this is a genuine cooperative enterprise. Every school, of course, in its little statement of philosophy, says that student-teacher relationships are an important part of the school. But that is so much guff. Here, students come and see that it's real. If they start breaking the laws, the customs, the mores whatever you want to call them — they discover they are harming themselves. Quite honestly this is not such a difficult piece of learning for the students who wish to apply and to come here. Now I'm not saying that you can do this kind of thing with all students. I don't believe that at all. But you can do this with our kind of student.

M&M   How do you recruit staff?

Bremer   Well, our situation is a little complicated, because we operated with private funds the first term. But basically what we've done so far is what I would like to go on doing. In the first place I don't think any teacher should be assigned to this kind of program. Like the students, they should choose it. We let it be known last May that we were going to be hiring more faculty; we let it be known by sending a notice to all the schools in the city. We got about 300 applications for 15 or so places. The applicants were screened then by a committee made up of an educator, a community person or a parent or a business person, a university student and a high school student. The individuals on the committee were asked to rate the applicant on a five point scale. The selections were then made by the committee.

M&M   Where do you go from here, John?

Bremer   Well, we are trying to start an elementary unit in January. I would like to start a unit that takes students in the middle range, that is grades 5 to 8 so that by the end of the year we would have students from pre-kindergarten to graduate school. We have undergraduate students working as interns with us now, as part of their program. That's the first thing. Secondly I have already proposed that we create what I would call a Parkway Volunteer School District, which would be a programmatic school district, as opposed to a geographical school district. Any student who wants this kind of program could join it and we would offer it all over the city to as many people as wanted it. I want to do this for a number of reasons. One is simply that we know that the educational problems that ensue from geographical school districts are insoluble. There is no way in which we can solve those problems. Recreating the structure to get rid of the problem is, in a sense, what we are doing at Parkway. So, in the future, I am looking towards setting up a system in which the city would be split up into maybe five or six or seven school districts, all of which would be programmatic districts. So that if you wanted to do this kind of learning in this kind of way, you would join this kind of program.

M&M   Do you feel that you will have to radically alter the model for K through 6, or 5 through 8, compared with 9 through 12?

Bremer   The basic educational principles that we are working from are applicable to learning generally and not to any particular age group. Obviously they will look different when they are embodied in a program for a different age group. In terms of principles, there is no difference. The basic elements of Parkway will apply from kindergarten to octogenarians.

M&M   Thank you, John.

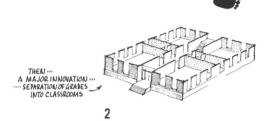

THEN ...
A MAJOR INNOVATION ...
.... SEPARATION OF GRADES
INTO CLASSROOMS

2

THE
ONE-ROOM
SCHOOL
WAS A
HOME BASE
FOR EDUCATION
... WITH EXTENSIONS
OUT THRU FARM AND TOWN

1

AMERICAN SCHOOLHOUSE

... AN HISTORICAL PERSPECTIVE

BY CHAS. WILLIAM BRUBAKER, FAIA
PRESIDENT, PERKINS & WILL ARCHITECTS

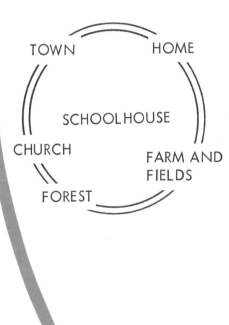

TOWN   HOME

SCHOOLHOUSE

CHURCH   FARM AND
        FIELDS

FOREST

BUSINESS
DISTRICT
        HOME

COMMUNITY   SCHOOL

        CULTURAL
WORKPLACES   FACILITIES

7

NEXT—
THE SCHOOL MAY REACH OUT
WITH SATELLITES IN THE COMMUNITY
.... AND WE'LL HAVE COME FULL CIRCLE!

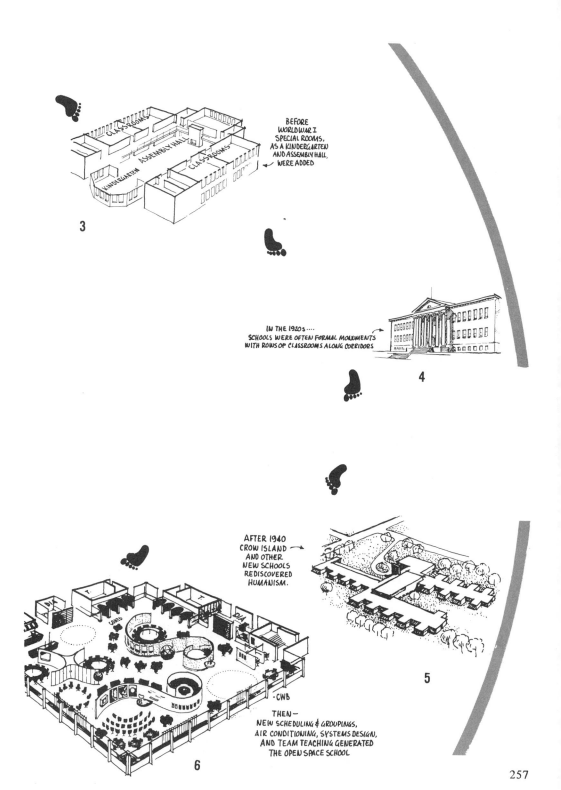

BEFORE
WORLD WAR I
SPECIAL ROOMS,
AS A KINDERGARTEN
AND ASSEMBLY HALL,
WERE ADDED

3

IN THE 1920s....
SCHOOLS WERE OFTEN FORMAL MONUMENTS
WITH ROWS OF CLASSROOMS ALONG CORRIDORS

4

AFTER 1940
CROW ISLAND
AND OTHER
NEW SCHOOLS
REDISCOVERED
HUMANISM.

5

—CWB

THEN—
NEW SCHEDULING & GROUPINGS,
AIR CONDITIONING, SYSTEMS DESIGN,
AND TEAM TEACHING GENERATED
THE OPEN SPACE SCHOOL

6

257

The School Without Walls

In most communities students can learn many things outside the school. Would you approve or disapprove if the schools here reduced the amount of classroom instruction to allow students to make greater use of the educational opportunities outside the school?

	National totals	No. children in schools	Public school parents	Private school parents	Profes- sional educators
N=	1,790	996	698	144	270
	%	%	%	%	%
Approve	56	60	49	63	72
Disapprove	34	29	43	29	26
No opinion	10	11	8	8	2
% totals	100	100	100	100	100

The Nongraded School

Should a student be able to progress through the school system at his own speed and without regard to the usual grade levels? This would mean that he might study seventh-grade math but only fifth-grade English. Would you favor or oppose such a plan in the local schools?

	National totals	No. children in schools	Public school parents	Private school parents	Profes- sional educators
N=	1,790	996	698	144	270
	%	%	%	%	%
Favor	71	69	74	73	87
Oppose	22	22	22	22	11
No opinion	7	9	4	5	2
% totals	100	100	100	100	100

Report Hails Oregon High School's Experiment in Free Study

By WILLIAM K. STEVENS

Special to The New York Times

PORTLAND, Ore.—The clean-lined, futuristic colonnades, courtyards and skylights of Portland's John Adams High School symbolize a fresh view of how teen-agers should be educated.

Opened just over a year ago on a site south of the Columbia River, it houses what may well be the country's "most important experiment in secondary education," according to the recently published report of a three-and-a-half-year study of American schools commissioned by the Carnegie Corporation.

Adams High seeks to determine whether ordinary teen-agers are willing and able to accept day-to-day responsibility for their own education—planning their own studies, sometimes developing their own tailor-made courses and managing their own time.

Thus a black senior, Don Bilbrew, is free to embark on a two-year independent study of black history in Portland that requires him to make use of the disciplines of sociology and economics as well as history. At the same time he can, and does, study such subjects as Shakespeare, drama, biology and journalism.

And Diane Crane, a sophomore, can branch out from her state-required biology course and undertake an independent study of genetics.

Conceived at Harvard

The Adams experiment is attempting to eliminate what the Carnegie study found to be some of the most damaging features of the typical American high schools: Encouragement of docility and conformity; over-regulation of students' lives; and a pallid, uniform curriculum.

The experiment was conceived three years ago by seven young PhD. candidates at the Harvard University Graduate School of Education. One of them, Robert Schwartz, 32 years old, is now the principal of the school.

Similar ventures in "free" or "open" education for teen-agers are going on elsewhere, but in relatively small, especially constituted environments with selected or volunteer students. Adams, by contrast, is a regular district high school operating within political and economic realities. Its student body of 1,600 is drawn from all social strata, with a heavy contingent from white working class families. A quarter of the students are black.

"If the approach works here," says Mr. Schwartz, "it will work anywhere."

Rules Are Few

The Adams approach begins with the proposition that the overall climate of a school may have a stronger effect on student learning than the formal curriculum.

"If you require a kid to have a hall pass you're saying you don't trust him," Mr. Schwartz said. "You then undercut the value of any 40-minute lesson in self-direction."

Except for the fact that students must come to school and participate, and that they must obey civil laws, Adams has few rules and regulations.

Legitimate authority at Adams is held to be rooted in experience and knowledge. Since adults are by and large more experienced than children, it is reasoned, they have a kind of "natural" authority that makes itself felt when an adult deals with a youngster on an equal, respectful footing.

Teachers are viewed as helpmates and colleagues, not dictators. "We try not make decisions for kids," Mr. Schwartz said. "We press the student to confront himself and what he's going to do with his life, and to make responsible choices. We are not permissive."

For many students accustomed to being told what to do, the pressure to choose has been uncomfortable, even painful. Some students have simply refused to act for themselves or to go to class, but Mr. Schwartz said that a large majority of doing adjusted to the new way of doing things.

Curriculum for Generalists

Students at Adams choose as electives many essentially traditional courses—for example, physics, chemistry, electronics and industrial arts. Often students work independently in such courses, checking with the teacher only when help is needed.

But the pride of Adams's effort at curriculum reform is an interdisciplinary "general education" course set up this way: Students and faculty are divided into seven "teams," each of which designs its own learning program that will lead students to explore key concepts in the state-required sub-

jects of English, social studies, mathematics and basic science. Typically, a team will do this by focusing on some real-life problem—race relations, for example—that can be attacked through the application of several disciplines.

Thus, a team headed by teacher David Mesirow has begun a unit called "the psychology of self," designed to enable students to become surer about their own identities and their relationship to the rest of the world. The team will focus in sequence on politics, students' rights and the process of change; values, advertising and the media; the experience of poverty; the black experience; alternative life styles; and the urban environment of Portland.

General education meets for half a day every day, but a student may skip the group sessions in favor of independent study if he wishes. Should general education spark several particular students' interest in some particular subject—say, general philosophy—a six-week "mini-course" is organized.

Each student has two free option periods a day, during which he can do anything he likes, or nothing. Some do nothing.

Students choose whether to be given letter grades or to receive a "credit-no credit" rating.

Parents' reaction to the experiment has been mixed.

A survey of students indicated that they considered Adams a "humanized" school. "At least you feel like a person here," said one student. But the same survey found that many students felt the intellectual content of the curriculum should be strengthened.

 **BULLETIN**

IS COMMON SENSE BREAKING THROUGH?

As we have pointed out before in these pages, there are reformers and reformers in education. One group is concerned with what it believes to be the primary function of schools, skills and knowledge, and concentrates therefore on strengthening the curriculum and on better preparation of teachers. Then there are the radicals of reform who are less concerned with academic accomplishment than with making the school an agency for the reform of society and for producing people who will be humane, loving, and noncompetitive.

The effort to use the schools for social and personal regeneration has resulted in some rather bizarre programs and practices, especially in the high schools. In some "innovative" schools there are only the loosest of requirements and the students may for the most part choose their own courses. It is possible to become the well-rounded man by studying macrame, tie-dying, revolutionary theory, wilderness survival, yoga, or Black Women I and II. In some schools students sit on the floor in the halls, playing cards or strumming on guitars. The "musts" are love and relevance and calling the teacher by his first name. Mass cutting of classes is a commonplace and the truant officer is a quaint historical figure, like the lamplighter.

There are not too many of these freewheeling schools but because conventional schools are often willing to adopt parts of the innovative programs their influence is greater than their numbers. But in the last year or so there have appeared faint intimations of dissatisfaction with the radical reforms. For one thing, that spineless wonder, the average American parent, is beginning to think that the PTA should be something more than a place to discuss Saturday's baked goods sale and uniforms for the band, and so this hitherto bland forum now often rings with demands to know what's-going-on-here. This has happened at the John F. Kennedy High School in Montgomery County, outside Washington, D.C., a school considered to be one of the most innovative and independent in the East. Last fall members of the PTA registered strong protests against the school's lack of structure, its exotic course offerings, and its policy of never entering failure on a student's transcript. Some parents did not think the school could be proud of the fact that the number of students taking National Merit Scholarship exams had dropped in two years from 170 to 40. The parental revolt resulted in the resignation of the principal and present indications are that John F. Kennedy High is headed for more confrontations and further reexaminations of its program. (See "Innovation and Discord at a Model High School" by Peggy Thomson in *Washington*, the weekly magazine published by *The Sunday Star*, August 15.)

Not only parents, but some of the teachers and administrators who have been most enthusiastic about the new programs, are beginning to look soberly at what they have wrought. In this connection we refer our readers to five articles about the John Adams High School in Portland, Oregon, which appeared in the May issue of *Phi Delta Kappan*. Adams has a national reputation as a model innovative school.

The five articles are written by staff members of Adams, including the principal. Naturally the writers are committed to the program but their remarkably candid discussion suggests that they not only see some flaws in practice but may have uneasy philosophical doubts. Before quoting some of these comments, let us state briefly the Adams pedagogical credo. The central experiment at Adams is the General Education program, described in one of the articles as "a means to learn about a society in flux, one in which the only constant is change." General Education is based on the study of contemporary problems such as air and water pollution, slum conditions, urban renewal, etc. (Students may also take electives, such as math, science, and foreign languages.) The planners of the programs are generally sympathetic to the ideas of John Holt, Paul Goodman, and Herbert Kohl. They think learning is best in an unstructured, free setting with the students involved as fully as possible in determining the program. The teacher "tells the student neither what he is to do, what he is to learn, nor how."

Perhaps the frankest of the five articles is the one by Allen L. Dobbins, who heads the instructional division at the school. He points out that not all students are happy with freedom, especially those with "severe kill limitations" (and this includes many who are "very bright"). These students simply cop out by roaming the halls or dancing in the lounge. The staff was pained to discover that these students thought "they weren't learning anything, that teachers didn't make them do any work." The solution was to create a basic skills department, highly structured and with much tighter constraints — that is, the solution was to revive what the program was originally designed to get rid of. Says Mr. Dobbins: "The popularity of basic skills with students has presented all of us with undeniable evidence that many students were not adequately served in these areas elsewhere." He has much to say about the difficulties of reaching any agreement about aims and program. Many parents, teachers, and not a few administrators, he says, would like a return to a more traditional school. A number of teachers "and some of our more radically oriented students" want an even more loosely organized school. He says that the majority of parents, teachers, and students are somewhere between these two poles.

Another staff member at Adams, Patricia A. Wertheimer, agrees that many students feel they are not learning much and that they want more direction from teachers and more organization of class work. She says: "By spring 1970, it appeared to many of us that the school was characterized to far too great an extent by a pervasive restlessness and lack of commitment to the effort required to achieve excellence." She believes Adams needs to offer alternative modes of learning; that is, alternatives to the free, unstructured program which is the heart of the Adams plan.

SCHOOLS FOR CHILDREN

What's Happening in British Classrooms — Joseph Featherstone

My wife and I have just spent a month in England visiting classes in primary schools, talking to children and teachers. Friends told us about good things happening in British classrooms, but we were scarcely prepared for what we found; in recent decades there has been a profound and sweeping revolution in English primary education, involving new ways of thinking about how young children learn, classroom organization, the curriculum and the role of the teacher. We saw schools in some good local educational authorities: Bristol, Nottingham, Leicestershire, Oxfordshire and a few serving immigrant areas in cities like London.

In the first part of what follows, I'm going to be as specific as I can about how classes work in a good English school, how the room is laid out, what sort of things are in it, how the teacher and the children spend the day and, in some detail, how a child learns to read, as an example of the kind of learning that goes on. I know that teachers in this country, particularly good ones, are rightly suspicious of most talk on education, because so little of what they hear ever relates to actual classroom practice. I hope I can be specific enough. The relevance of these classrooms to us is another,

more difficult question which I'll leave for later. I don't have any easy answers.

Primary schools divide into "infant" and "junior" schools. Much of this report will focus on the infant schools, which take children from the age of five to seven, and in some authorities eight. (As in Israel, children begin compulsory schooling at the early age of five in England.) It is in the infant schools that people learn to read and write and to work with numbers. Junior schools take children from seven or eight to 11, when they go on to secondary school. Infant and junior schools sometimes occupy the same building, and some authorities — Oxfordshire, for example — have a policy of putting them together in one unit, like an American elementary school.

It is important to understand that what goes on in the good infant schools is much the same. The approach is similar, though the quality of teaching and children's work varies greatly.

Westfield Infant School is a one-story structure, like any of a thousand American buildings, on a working-class housing estate in Leicestershire. If you arrive early, you find a number of children already inside, reading, writing, painting, playing music, tending to pets. Teachers sift in slowly, and begin working with students. Apart from a religious assembly (required by English law) it's hard to say just when school actually begins, because there is very little organized activity for a whole class to do together. The puzzled visitor sees some small group work in mathematics ("maths") or reading, but mostly children are on their own, moving about and talking quite freely. The teacher sometimes sits at her desk, and the children flock to her for consultations, but more often she moves about the room, advising on projects, listening to children read, asking questions, giving words, talking, sometimes prodding.

The hallways, which are about the size of those in our schools, are filled with busy children, displays of painting and graphs, a play grocery store where children use play money and learn to count, easels, tables for collections of shells and plants, workbenches on which to pound and hammer nails and boards, big wooden boxes full of building blocks.

Classrooms open out onto the playground, which is also much in use. A contingent of children is kneeling on the grass, clocking the speed of a tortoise, which they want to graph against the speeds of other pets and people. Nearby are five-year-olds, finishing an intricate, tall tower of blocks, triumphantly counting as they add the last one, "23, 24." A solitary boy is mixing powders for paint; on a large piece of paper attached to an easel, with very big strokes, he makes an ominous, stylized building that seems largely to consist of black shutters framing deep red windows. "It's the hospital where my brother is," he explains, and pulls the visitor over to the class-library corner, where a picture book discusses hospitals. He can't read it yet (he's five), but says he is trying. And he is; he can make out a number of words, some pretty hard, on different pages, and it is clear that he has been *studying* the book, because he wants badly to know about hospitals. At another end of the hall there is a quieter library nook for the whole school. Here two small boys are reading aloud; the better reader is, with indifferent grace, correcting the grateful slower boy as he stumbles over words.

The rooms are fairly noisy — more noisy than many American teachers or principals would allow — because children can talk freely. Sometimes the teacher has to ask for quiet. With as many as 40 in some classes, rooms are crowded and accidents happen. Paint spills, a tub overflows, there are recriminations. Usually the children mop up and work resumes.

The visitor is dazed by the amount and variety and fluency of the free writing produced: stories, free-verse poems, with intricate images, precise accounts of experiments in "maths" and, finally, looking over a tiny little girl's shoulder, he finds: "Today we had visitors from America. . . ."

After a time, you overcome your confusion at the sheer variety of it all, and you begin making more definite observations. The physical layout of the classrooms is markedly different from ours. American teachers are coming to appreciate the importance of a flexible room, but even in good elementary schools this usually means having movable, rather than fixed, desks. In these classes there are no individual desks, and no assigned places. Around the room (which is about the size of one of ours) there are different tables for different kinds of activities: art, water and sand play, number work. (The number tables have all kinds of number lines — strips of paper with numbers marked on them in sequence on which children learn to count and reason mathematically — beads, buttons and odd things to count; weights and balances; dry and liquid measures; and a rich variety of apparatus for learning basic mathematical concepts, some of it homemade, some ready-made. The best of the commercial materials were familiar: Cuisenaire rods, the Dienes multibase material, Stern rods and attribute or logical blocks. This sort of

266

thing is stressed much more than formal arithmetic.)

Wendy and puppets

Every class has a library alcove, which is separated off by a room divider that also serves as a display shelf for books. Some library corners have a patch of carpet and an old easy chair. Every room has a "Wendy House," a play corner with dolls and furniture for playing house. Often there is a dress-up corner, too, with different kinds of cast-off adult clothes. The small children love the Wendy houses and dress-up corners, but you see older ones using them as well. Some classes have puppet theatres for putting on improvised plays with home-made puppets — although many make do with the legs of one table turned upside down on top of another for a makeshift stage. Often, small children perform dance dramas involving a lot of motion and a minimum of words.

Gradually it becomes clear how the day proceeds in one of these rooms. In many infant and some junior schools the choice of the day's routine is left completely up to the teacher, and the teacher, in turn, leaves options open to the children. Classes for young children, the visitor learns, are reaching a point in many schools where there is no real difference between one subject in the curriculum and another, or even between work and play. A school day run on these lines is called, variously, the "free day," the "integrated curriculum," or the "integrated day." The term scarcely matters.

In a school that operates with a free day, the teacher usually starts in the morning by listing the different activities available. A lot of rich material is needed, according to the teachers, but the best stuff is often homemade; and, in any case, it isn't necessary to have 30 or 40 sets of everything, because most activities are for a limited number of people. "Six children can play in the Wendy House," says a sign in one classroom. The ground rules are that they must clean up when they finish, and they mustn't bother others.

A child might spend the day on his first choice, or he might not. Many teachers confess they get nervous if everybody doesn't do some reading and writing every day; others are committed in principle to letting children choose freely. In practice, a lot of teachers give work when they think it's needed. In this, as in any other way of doing things, teachers tailor their styles to their own temperament and the kind of children they have. But the extent to which children really have a choice and really work purposefully is astonishing.

How they learn reading offers a clear example of the kind of individual learning and teaching going on in these classrooms, even in quite large ones. (The mathematics work shows this even better, but I'll talk of math in another context.) Reading is not particularly emphasized, and my purpose in singling it out is purely illustrative, though the contrast between English classes and most American ones, where reading is a formidable matter, is vivid and depressing.

At first it is hard to say just how they do learn reading, since there are no separate subjects. A part of the answer slowly becomes clear, and it surprises American visitors used to thinking of the teacher as the generating force of education: children learn from each other. They hang around the library corners long before they can read, handling the books, looking at pictures, trying to find words they do know, listening and watching as the teacher hears other children's reading. It is common to see nonreaders studying people as they read, and then imitating them, monkey doing what monkey sees. Nobody makes fun of their grave parodies, and for good reasons.

A very small number of schools in two or three authorities have adopted what they call "family," or "vertical," grouping, which further promotes the idea of children teaching children. In these schools, each class is a cross-section of the whole school's population, all ages mixed together. This seems particularly successful in the early school years, when newcomers are easily absorbed, and older children help teach the young ones to clean up and take first steps in reading. Family grouping needs smaller classes, teachers say, because it requires close supervision to make sure small children don't get overshadowed and big ones are still challenged. Teachers using it swear by the flexibility it provides.

Books in profusion

Teachers use a range of reading schemes, sight reading, phonics, and so forth, whatever seems to work with a child. (Only about five percent of English schools use the Initial Teaching Alphabet, an improved alphabet, not a method of reading, that has proved successful with poor readers and adults both in England and in this country; heads of good schools we visited thought that ITA was unnecessary with a truly flexible reading program, but that in a rigid scheme, it gave the slow reader another chance, and thus a break.) Increasingly in the good infant schools, there are no textbooks and no class readers. There are just books, in profusion. Instead of spending their scanty book money on 40 sets of everything, wise schools have purchased different sets of reading series, as well as a great many single books, at all levels of difficulty. Teachers arrange their classroom libraries so they can direct students of different abilities to appropriate books, but in most classes a child can tackle anything he wants. As a check, cautious teachers ask them to go on their own through a graded reading series — which one doesn't matter.

However a child picks up reading, it will involve learning to write at the same time, and some write before they can read; there is an attempt to break down the mental barrier between the spoken, the written and the printed word. When a child starts school, he gets a large, unlined notebook; this is his book for free writing, and he can put what he wants in it. On his own, he may draw a picture in it with crayon or pencil, discuss the picture with the teacher, and dictate a caption to her, which she then writes down for him: "This is my Dad." He copies the caption, writing just underneath. In this way he learns to memorize the look and sound of his dictated words and phrases, until he reaches a point where, with help, he can write sentences. Often his notebook serves as his own first reading book.

He also gets a smaller notebook, his private dictionary, in which he enters words as he learns them. "I got a new word," a five-year-old brags to the visitor. Children are always running to the teacher for words, as they find they have more and more to write. Good teachers don't give in without a struggle; the children have to guess the first letter and sound the word out before they get it. Thus they pick up phonetic skills informally, although some teachers do use sight cards at the outset with their children. Gradually as a child amasses a reading and writing vocabulary, he reaches a fluent stage and you see six-year-olds writing stories, free-verse poems, accounts of things done in class, for an audience that includes other children as well as the teacher.

As a rule, teachers don't pay much attention to accuracy or neatness until a child is well on in his writing. They introduce grammar and spelling after a time, but not as separate subjects or ends in themselves: they are simply ways to say what you want better and more efficiently. Under these methods, where the children choose the content of their writing, there seems in fact to be more attention paid to content than externals, such as punctuation, spelling and grammar. In the good schools, these are presented as what they are, living ways to get a meaning across, to be understood. Even some unimaginative teachers, who quibble with children about other work, can respect the content of the free writing books and take it seriously. This emphasis on self-chosen content has produced a flowering of young children's literature in schools working with many kinds of teachers and children. There is growing recognition that different people flourish on different kinds of writing; storytellers and poets are not necessarily the same as those who can do elegant and graceful writing about mathematics. Impressive examples of free writing and poetry similar to what we saw are contained in the West Riding Education Committee's anthology, *The Excitement of Writing*. Samples of "maths" writing are included in the Schools Council's *Mathematics in the Primary Schools*, a wonderfully instructive book on many accounts. Books made and illustrated by the children are coming to be a regular part of the curriculum in some schools.

I've focused on reading, although of course children spend their time doing other things, and the teachers in the schools we saw would be annoyed at the manner in which I've singled out one academic subject. The very best often argued that art was the key. Miss Nash, the head of Sea Mills School in Bristol said firmly that if the art is good, all else follows. All else does follow, richly, at Sea Mills, where the infants sat us down and performed a concert of skillful poetry and songs they made up on musical instruments.

But my purpose was to show not reading, but the changed role of the classroom teacher. Formal classroom teaching – the instructor standing up front, talking to the group, or even the first-grade room divided up into reading groups which the teacher listens to separately as she tries desperately to keep order – has disappeared from many infant and a number of junior schools. It has disappeared because it is inflexible, because it imposes a single pattern of learning on a whole group of children – thus forcing the schools to "track," or to group classes by ability – because it ignores the extent to which children teach each other, and because in many workaday schools other methods are working better. Ordinary teachers, trained formally, take to the new role when they can see with their own eyes that the result is not chaos.

Informality is hard work

These methods mean more work for the teacher, not less. In informal conditions, it is essential for the teacher to keep detailed and accurate accounts of what a child is learning, even though at any given moment she might not know what he's up to. Children help by keeping their own records: in some schools, they have private shelves where they store writing books, accounts of experiments and work in "maths," lists of the books they've read, and dates when they checked in with the teacher to read aloud. If American parents could ever see some of the detailed histories kept of each child's separate path, including his art work, they would feel, quite rightly, that a report card is a swindle.

When the class seldom meets as a unit, when children work independently, discipline is less of a problem. It does not disappear as a problem, but it becomes less paramount. The purposeful self-discipline of these children is, we were told, just as surprising to middle-aged Englishmen as it is to Americans. It is a recent development, and by no means the product of luck: much hard work and thought go into the arrangement of these classrooms and their rich materials. When they work at it, teachers find they can make time during the day for children who need it. "I can give all my attention to a child for five minutes, and that's worth more to him than being part of a sea of faces all day," said a teacher in an East London school overlooking the docks. Other teachers say they can watch children as they work and ask them questions; there is a better chance of finding out what children really understand.

What we saw is no statistical sample. The practices of the good schools we visited in different kinds of communities are not universal; but there are reasons for thinking that they are no longer strikingly exceptional. The schools we saw are, for the most part, staffed by ordinary teachers; they are not isolated experiments, run by cranks and geniuses. A government advisory body — the Plowden Committee — published a massive, and to American eyes, a radical report early this year, in which it indicated that about a third of England's 23,000 primary schools have been deeply influenced by the new ideas and methods, that another third are stirring under their impact, and that the remaining third are still teaching along the formal lines of British schools in the thirties, and of American schools now.

The change is most widespread and impressive in the infant schools, and becomes more scattered on the junior level. Junior schools in some authorities are playing stunning variations on the free themes developed by the infant schools; but, in general, change in the junior schools is slower, more diffident and faces more problems.

Many formal schools — English and American — are probably doing a more effective job, in conventional terms, than many of these schools. It doesn't do to dogmatize. For example, by and large, in terms of measurable achievement on conventional tests, children in traditional, formal classes in England do slightly better than children from the freer classes. (The survey is submitted by the Plowden Report.) The difference is greatest in mechanical arithmetic, and least in reading. These are facts, but there are reasons for discounting them, apart from evidence that the differences disappear in later school years. Formal schools teach children to take conventional tests; that is their function, and it would be surprising if all their efforts didn't produce some results. In view of the lack of test training in the freer schools, the students' results seem to me surprisingly high. It is perfectly clear that the mathematics taught in the informal schools — mathematical relationships in which process of thought counts for more than arithmetical skill — and the English — free writing, rather than grammar and so on — put their students at a disadvantage on achievement tests, whose authors would probably be the first to admit this. England and America badly need new kinds of tests. My own very strong impression is that in areas easy to define and probably not hard to test — ability to write, for example, or understanding of the math they were doing — the children in the good schools I saw, including slum schools, were far ahead of students in good schools in this country.

The external motions teachers go through in the schools matter less than what the teachers are and what they think. An organizational change — the free day, for example, or simply rearranging classroom space — is unlikely to make much difference unless teachers really believe that in a rich environment young children can learn a great deal by themselves and that most often their own choices reflect their needs. But when you see schools where teachers do believe in them, it is easy to share the Plowden Report's enthusiasm for informal, individual learning in the early years of school. (The Plowden Committee is in a sense the official voice of the primary school revolution.) The infant schools are a historical accident — nobody years ago gave much thought to why children should begin school at five — but British teachers are now realizing their advantages. With kindergarten and the first few years fused together, children have an extended time in which to learn to read and write and work with numbers. This is especially effective if the pattern of learning is largely individual; if the teacher is important, but she doesn't stand in the way or try to take over the whole job. Many of the difficulties that plague formal first-grade classes disappear; children aren't kept back from learning, nor are they branded as problems if they take their time.

school around the bend

Tomorrow's school will have no rejects: it must guarantee every child a high minimum of accomplishment in fundamental skills.

We no longer can talk of "dumb" or "lazy" children. Almost every child learns, by age three or four, basic skills that are infinitely more complex and more difficult than anything we try to teach in school. Even the least-endowed normal child learns the language, for example. We will expect tomorrow's schools to help each child acquire other, lesser skills, just as we expect every family to enable a child to learn to speak and to walk.

peter drucker

The schools must utilize the individual's own rhythm, his own learning speed, his own pattern. This too we have learned by watching the infant acquire his basic skills. No two children learn to speak the same way. One child experiments for hours with sounds and apparently does not tire. The next child plays with sounds for 10 minutes, then shifts to something else, then 10 minutes later comes back to playing with sounds again, and so on.

The traditional lock step of education once was a necessity when the teacher had 30 or 50 children. He had to impose the same pattern on all of them — or thought he did. Certainly with today's tools, this no longer is so — even in large classes.

The traditional school is labor-intensive; it has neither tools nor capital equipment. We have invested little more than $100 per student — except in medical schools, physics laboratories and such — as against the $30,000 or $40,000 or $50,000 the modern communications company invests per employee. We have relied on labor, which meant that the teacher's convenience had to be imposed on the entire class. Yet teachers were both underpaid and underused. American education tomorrow will require a great deal more by way of tools than we have had.

Today's school is still the school of the scribes. We are beset by verbal arrogance, contemptuous of whatever is not reading, writing, or arithmetic. And yet one look should show us a world in which verbal skills are not the only productive ones. They are necessary — a foundation. But the purely verbal skills are not necessarily the central performance skill when electronic media carry the main information load.

People are endowed differently in different areas, but today's school dismisses three quarters of human endowments as irrelevant. This is inhuman and stupid. It is also incompatible with the realities of our economy and our society. We need craftsmen in thousands of areas; everywhere we need people with excellence in one area — and not necessarily a verbal one. We will expect the school to find the individual's real strength, challenge it, and make it productive.

The school of tomorrow will be neither behavioristic nor cognitive, neither child-centered nor discipline-centered. It will be all of these.

These old controversies have been phonies all along. We need the behaviorist's triad of practice/reinforcement/feedback to lodge learning in memory. We need purpose, decision, values, understanding — the cognitive categories, lest learning be mere behavior, activity rather than action.

The English open classroom, now widely copied in this country, usually is considered cognitive and child-centered. It is. But it also is one of the first rigorous applications of behaviorism to large numbers of human learners. The child does indeed learn his or her way there. He programs himself according to his own pattern, rhythm, speed and sequence. But he programs himself also according to a strict behaviorist scheme. What he is working (or playing) on is determined by the tools, playthings and experiences offered. Reinforcements and rewards are built in at every step. Above all, the school predetermines the norms of achievement as rigorously as a scientist lays them down for a rat in a maze. And the child does not move on to the next level until he attains and retains the norm.

Whatever one may think of performance contracts, focused on the organization of specific skills, they also are both behaviorist and cognitive. Together, teacher and child work out a plan and follow it with a verbal or written contract that commits the child to work toward his own goal. In their methodology, these contracts focus strictly on behavior and discipline. But the main argument for performance contracts is strictly cognitive: what the child needs is self-confidence – the capacity to feel that he is the master of his environment – that is, the human development that comes with achievement and social approbation. The greatest of the cognitivists – Johann Heinrich Pestalozzi or Jean Piaget – could not have put better the case for the child-centered approach.

The traditional issues of educational methodology and philosophy are simply different tools in the same toolbox. Indeed, they may be only the obverse and reverse of the same coin.

While it is moving out of the Middle Ages academically, tomorrow's school also must integrate itself into the community and become an integrator of the community. As the school system exploded in this century it had to become professional. But in the process it ceased to be part of its community.

A great deal can be said against the rigidity of the small college of the mid-19th century with its narrow religious blinkers and its authoritarian structure. But it was part of a denominational community. Today's larger university may be intellectually richer, freer, more rewarding, but it is no community and it has no community. The students of 1870 complained bitterly but they didn't feel alienated.

The same was true of the small school in the rural community; in fact, the teacher often felt smothered and dominated by the community.

I do not advocate a return to what we had a century ago. But we must bring the community back into the school. American education will have to think through who its constituents are and get across to them – students, teachers, taxpayers, parents, alumni and prospective employers – what they can expect from the school, and also what the school can expect of them.

One way or another education will become accountable for performance. I do not know how one measures performance in education. First you have to know what the objectives and goals are. If the first job of an elementary school is to have the children learn to read, one can measure performance easily. But if the school at the same time is also to socialize, to make civilized human beings out of children, to develop the whole person – prepare him for work and life – then no one can measure performance. The school will be expected to think through its goals, get them accepted, and be accountable for them. If it fails to do so, measurement standards will be imposed from the outside, and the educators who protest have only themselves to blame. Schools are too powerful and too important; they must be responsible for performance.

Finally, and most important, American education must acknowledge that learning is lifelong – it does not stop when one starts working. The most important learning, the most important true education, is the continuing education of educated, achieving adults.

The educator has not yet accepted the idea of continuing education. Most schoolmasters believe that one can learn only when one is young and only before five in the afternoon. Most of them still believe that learning is for the immature, that it is not serious enough for adults. The realization that adults continue to learn will have a profound impact on the structure, curriculum, methods and position of traditional education. We will demand much more from it, but we will no longer consider it *the* education.

These changes in tomorrow's education may come to pass first in the continuing education of adults. The restraints are lowest there – no school boards and no teacher associations, no taxpayers, no schools of education, no concerned parents, no headlines. Students

273

control continuing education — it depends on their motivation and achievement. It is decentralized, thus experimentation is easy. It has far fewer problems with budgets, especially when business, Government agencies, or other large employers support or run it. It can spend capital. And, continuing education already practices, though on a narrow, mostly vocational front, most of the basic principles of tomorrow's school. It is a working model, on a small scale, but it is proof of what we can achieve. It is also the most rapidly growing segment of organized education.

Schools are very old. But the identification of *learning* with *school* is very recent — hardly more than a century old. That so far we have not delivered on the promise that the school will be the learning institution is hardly surprising. It is, perhaps, far more surprising that we already know, if only in rough outline, what the school needs to be to live up to its importance, its power, and its responsibility.

WILLIAM C. MILLER

274

The gears of the half-track protested loudly as Richard Bolton down-shifted to prepare for the barricade. He stopped directly in front of the high, barbed wire-topped gate to the compound and waited for the armed and helmeted figure to come from the shelter of the guardhouse. Bolton showed his identification, gave the current password, and received the correct countersign. He waited, tapping the accelerator impatiently, while the guard checked inside and under the vehicle. Finally, after receiving the go-ahead, Richard Bolton prepared himself for the most dangerous part of his day. He always dreaded his vulnerability as he moved from the safety of his armored vehicle to the shelter of the building. There had been talk of a tunnel or covered walkway because snipers had already killed two and inflicted a near-fatal wound on a third predecessor.

The trip into the inner city each day was tedious and time consuming. First it was necessary to reach the assembly point early enough for the convoy to be formed. Then came the slow, grinding journey behind the ponderous, outdated tanks through the "no man's land" which separated the center city from the suburbs. The convoy system was necessary since any individual or group of vehicles not flanked by such protection was almost certain to be firebombed by the Free Revolutionary Army (FRA).

As Bolton reached the safety of the doorway, he stopped to catch his breath. The dash from the compound parking lot was a long and emotional trip. Bolton reflected on how the cities had reached this state. Certainly things had been bad in the early seventies. However, it was Bolton's belief that it was the initiation of the "Neighborhood Protection Doctrine" and the supporting legislation which precipitated the revolution. This questionable legal move raised the voting age to 25, overturned the 1954 desegregation court decision, and mobilized the National Guard in each state on a permanent basis.

Born of fear and frustration when moderate law and order reforms backfired, the doctrine and the accompanying mass internment of revolutionaries and liberals was a last ditch move on the part of the establishment to retain the status quo. What resulted was just the opposite. Outraged citizens stormed the internment camps, freed the political prisoners, and formed the FRA, which now nearly controlled many of the major cities of America.

Breathing more easily now, Bolton turned, knocked for recognition, was scrutinized by the security guard through the peekhole, and was finally admitted. He was greeted briefly by Tom Sloan, head of Security, a bright young fellow who was attracted from the FBI by the lucrative hazard pay his job offered.

Bolton glanced at his watch and realized that before long they would begin to enter. His carefully kept records showed that each day there were fewer who braved the retaliation of the FRA and subjected themselves to the laborious showing of ID cards and the personal and electronic frisking. Although their safety and security required it, Bolton was sure few would continue to show up to spend the day in this oppressive atmosphere. He felt that no matter how greatly the federal and city officials desired to retain a foothold in the inner city, the task was impossible. He knew what a political and psychological blow it would be to close down, but hanging on much longer didn't seem feasible.

Now he could hear their hushed tones as they filed in. No joy in these voices. Then a slight sound of chairs scraping as the group rose. Dr. Bolton could hear clearly some of their words, ". . . one nation, indivisible, with liberty and justice for all," and then a bit of a familiar song, ". . . sweet land of liberty, of thee I sing. . . ." Then a brief scraping of furniture, and another day had begun for Dr. Richard Bolton, principal of Lincoln Compound School.

electronic
security check
system
being tested for schools

Under a grant from the National Aeronautics and Space Administration, the Jet Propulsion Laboratory has developed an electronic security check system for schools, which is now being tested at John F. Kennedy High School in Sacramento, Calif. Each teacher, administrator, and employee, equipped with a pencil-sized ultrasonic transmitter, can light a bulb on a large map of the school, in the principal's office, and sound a small horn, alerting the office. As a result, help can be dispatched to the trouble scene within 30 seconds. Principal Frank Schimandle reported that the system so far has nipped in the bud several potentially major racial incidents.

Reader: See if you can find a picture (or take one yourself) to illustrate this page.

It may take a while.

the
ideal
school

Well I think the ideal school is a school where children can get to know each other and the world around them, a place where children can do any subject they want, and I would have children from all over the U.S.A. Children from many parts of the country. I would put my school in the city and anybody can come. No matter who or what they look like. It would be a huge school with a large library with a great amount of books and about four huge rooms for the class. If I pick teachers they would be willing to teach what the kids and their mother think is good for them. They would have the best books. In this school if the student is willing to work he may, if he doesn't want to work he doesn't have to. But most of all I would teach the children to live with each other.

— Davis

ACKNOWLEDGMENTS (continued from p. ii)

6 Alvin Toffler, "Is Your High School Obsolete?" *Seventeen* (September, 1972). Reprinted by permission from *Seventeen;* copyright © 1972 by Triangle Communications, Inc.; all rights reserved.

11 Mortimer Smith, "Fundamental Differences Do Exist." in *American Education Today,* ed. Paul Woodring (New York: McGraw-Hill, 1963), pp. 28–29. Copyright © Saturday Review.

12 Dean Lobaugh, "Why Do We Have to Learn This?" *Nation's Schools* (April, 1953). Reprinted by permission; all rights reserved.

14 Joey Windham, "A Little Box," *New Voices in Education* (Spring, 1971). Copyright © 1971 by New Voices in Education; reprinted by permission.

15 Jacques Barzun, "The Intellectual Life and the School System," address delivered at the Aspen Institute on Education and the Human Potential, Aspen, Colorado, August 15, 1967 (multigraph); © 1967 by Jacques Barzun; reprinted by permission.

16 J. Abner Peddiwell, *The Saber-Tooth Curriculum* (New York: McGraw-Hill, 1939), Chap. 2, pp. 24–44. Copyright © 1939 by McGraw-Hill, Inc.; used with permission of McGraw-Hill Book Company.

22 "A Vote for the Beatles," letter from R. David Price to the editor of *Time* (25 September 1972). Reprinted by permission of Time, The Weekly Newsmagazine; copyright Time, Inc.

23 Letter from Bernard F. Dick to the editor of *The New York Times* (4 September 1972). Copyright © 1972 by The New York Times Company; reprinted by permission.

24 James Baldwin, "A Talk to Teachers," *Montage* (New York: Macmillan, 1970), p. 135; reprinted by permission of the author.

25 Arthur E. Bestor, *The Restoration of Learning* (New York: Knopf, 1955).

25 N. J. W., "I Taught Them All," *The Clearing House* (November, 1937).

26 Robert L. Ebel, "What Are Schools For?" *Phi Delta Kappan* (September, 1972). Copyright © 1972 by Phi Delta Kappan; reprinted by permission of author and publisher.

27 David Hackett Fischer, *Historians' Fallacies: Toward a Logic of Historical Thoughts* (New York: Harper & Row, 1970).

27 Ann Landers' Advice column, appearing in *The Hartford Courant,* 2 October 1972; reprinted by permission of Ann Landers.

28 Neil Postman and Charles Weingartner, "Pursuing Relevance" from *Teaching as a Subversive Activity* (New York: Delacorte Press, 1969), Chap. 4. Copyright © 1969 by Neil Postman and Charles Weingartner; reprinted by permission of the publisher, Delacorte Press.

30 Tom Paxton, "What Did You Learn in School Today?" Copyright © 1962 by Cherry Lane Music Co.; used by permission; all rights reserved.

31 Jules Feiffer cartoon (New York: Publishers Hall Syndicate). Copyright © 1970 by Jules Feiffer; reprinted by permission of the artist.

32 Charles E. Silberman, *Crisis in the Classroom* (New York: Random House, 1970), p. 237. Copyright 1970 by Random House, Inc.

33 Max Rafferty, *Classroom Countdown: Education at the Crossroads* (New York: Hawthorne Books, 1970), pp. 59–61. Copyright 1970 by Max Rafferty; reprinted by permission of Hawthorne Books, Inc.

35 Haim G. Ginott, *Teacher and Child* (New York: Macmillan, 1972), p. 317. Reprinted by permission of the author.

36 Robert F. Mager, Preface to *Preparing Instructional Objectives* (Palo Alto, Calif.: Fearon, 1962), pp. vii–viii. Copyright 1962 by Fearon; reprinted by permission of Lear Siegler/Fearon Publishers.

37 Roscoe L. Davidson, "Moving Your School from Where It Is to Where It Could Be," *The National Elementary Principal* (1973), p. 53. Copyright 1973 by The National Association of Elementary School Principals; all rights reserved.

38 Marshall McLuhan and Quentin Fiore, "Your Education" from *The Medium Is the Massage* (New York: Bantam Books, 1967), pp. 18, 100–101. Copyright © 1967 by Marshall McLuhan, Quentin Fiore, and Jerome Agel; reprinted by permission of Bantam Books, Inc.

40 Alvin Toffler, *Future Shock* (New York: Random House, 1970), pp. 409, 410, 414. Copyright © 1970 by Alvin Toffler; reprinted by permission of Random House, Inc.

42 Fred M. Hechinger, "Excess is not the Way," *New York Times,* 22 October 1972. Copyright 1972 by The New York Times Company; reprinted by permission.

46 David Mesirow, "Notes for Intern Survival," *The Teacher Paper* (October, 1970). Copyright 1970 by Fred L. Staab; reprinted by permission of The Teacher Paper.

48 "The Beginning Teacher," *Today's Education* (September, 1971). Reprinted by permission of Today's Education: The NEA Journal.

53 Mildred J. Fischle, "The Day They Locked up the Textbooks," *The National Elementary Principal* (November, 1972). Copyright 1972, National Association of Elementary School Principals; all rights reserved.

56 Ann Landers' Advice column reprinted by permission of Ann Landers.

57 "Hy Max," note found in a wastebasket in an eighth grade classroom in a suburban Philadelphia school, from *Media and Methods* (December, 1968).

57 Richard Brautigan, "The Memoirs of Jesse James," from *Rommel Drives on Deep into Egypt* (New York: Delacorte Press, 1970). Copyright © 1970 by Richard Brautigan. A Seymour Lawrence Book/Delacorte Press; reprinted by permission of the publisher.

58 Gregg Shaw, "Factory" poem by high school student in *How Old Will You Be in 1984?* edited by Diane Divoky (New York: Avon Books, 1969). Copyright © 1969 by Avon Books; reprinted by arrangement with Avon Books.

60 Paul Zindel, *My Darling, My Hamburger* (New York: Harper & Row, 1969). Copyright © 1969

by Paul Zindel; reprinted by permission of Harper & Row, Publishers, Inc.

61 Charlotte Leon Mayerson, ed., *Two Blocks Apart* (New York: Holt, Rinehart and Winston, 1965). Copyright © 1965 by Holt, Rinehart and Winston, Inc.; reprinted by permission of Holt, Rinehart and Winston, Inc.

63 Sunny Decker, *An Empty Spoon* (New York: Harper & Row, 1969), pp. 48–50, 11–13. Copyright 1969 by Sunny Decker; reprinted by permission of Harper & Row, Publishers, Inc.

64 Gallup International, "Placing Blame for Poor School Work." poll for CFK, Ltd. (April, 1972).

65 "Opinions on Plan Books," from *Today's Education* (December, 1971). Reprinted by permission of *Today's Education:* The Journal of the National Education Association.

67 Plan and Record of Work, Courtesy of Professor Christine LaConte, University of Connecticut.

68 Teacher Evaluation Form from Groton (Connecticut) Public Schools.

69 John Gauss, "Teacher Evaluation," *Phi Delta Kappan* (January, 1962). Copyright 1962 by Phi Delta Kappan; reprinted by permission of the publisher.

71 Cartoon by RAB in *The Teacher Paper* (October 1972). Copyright 1972 by Fred L. Staab and Robin B. Staab of *The Teacher Paper;* reprinted by permission.

72 "The Real Teacher," from M. Greer and B. Rubinstein, *Will the Real Teacher Please Stand Up?* (Pacific Palisades, Calif.: Goodyear Publishing, 1972), p. 104.

72 Gallup International, "Teaching as a Career." poll for CFK, Ltd. (April, 1972).

73 Haim G. Ginott, *Teacher and Child* (New York: Macmillan, 1972).

76 "The Faculty Lounge," cartoon by Don Allen and Halsey Taylor (John Laney) from *Media and Methods* (March, 1972). Copyright 1972 by Taylor-Allen; reprinted by permission.

78 "Students Evaluate Their Teachers," student evaluations of their English class done in David Kelley's high school class. Reprinted by permission of David Kelley.

79 Photograph reprinted with permission of PLAN* Individualized Learning System Division, Westinghouse Learning Corporation.

80 Bud Church, "Silence Makes the Heart Grow Louder," *Media and Methods* (October, 1970). Reprinted by permission of Bud Church.

84 B. F. Skinner, "The Free and Happy Student," *New York University Education Quarterly* (Winter, 1973), pp. 2–6. Reprinted by permission of the author and New York University Education Quarterly; copyright 1973 by New York University.

92 Bel Kaufman, *Up the Down Staircase* (Englewood Cliffs, N.J.: Prentice-Hall, 1964). Copyright © 1964 by Bel Kaufman.

94 Albert Shanker, "For Many New Teachers, the First Days Are Rough." *New York Times* (10 September 1972). Copyright 1972 by Albert Shanker; reprinted by permission.

96 Cartoon reprinted from *Liberation News Service* by permission; copyright 1972 by Liberation News Service, Inc.

97 Herbert Kohl, *Thirty-Six Children* (New York: New American Library, 1967), pp. 29–31. Copyright © 1967 by Herbert Kohl; reprinted by arrangement with The New American Library, Inc

98 Art Buchwald, "Don't Be a Pal to Your Son." Copyright 1960; reprinted by permission of Art Buchwald.

99 Cartoon by RAB from *The Teacher Paper.* Copyright 1972 by Fred L. Staab and Robin B. Staab of The Teacher Paper; reprinted by permission of The Teacher Paper.

100 Cartoon, "School in the Last Century," reprinted by permission of The Bettman Archive.

100 Fritz Redl, "Aggression in the Classroom," *Today's Education* (September, 1969). Reprinted by permission of *Today's Education: NEA Journal.*

105 From *Can't You Hear Me Talking to You?* by Caroline Mirthes and the Children of P.S. 15. Copyright © 1971 by Bantam Books, Inc.; all rights reserved.

106 Advertisement for Ritalin, courtesy of Ciba Pharmaceutical Company.

108 "High School Vandalized," *The Hartford Courant* (13 February 1973); reprinted by permission of *The Hartford Courant.*

109 Photograph of vandalized classroom, courtesy of World Wide Photos.

110 Lexan window advertisement, courtesy of the General Electric Company.

111 "Work Punishment Asked for Vandals," *The Day* (26 March 1973). Reprinted by permission of *The Day,* New London, Connecticut.

112 Sidney Trubowitz, *A Handbook for Teaching in the Ghetto School* (New York: Quadrangle, 1968), pp. 52–54. Copyright © 1968 by Sidney Trubowitz; reprinted by permission of Quadrangle/The New York Times Book Co.

114 James Herndon, *The Way It Spozed to Be* (New York: Simon & Schuster, 1968), pp. 28–31. Copyright © 1965, 1968 by James Herndon; reprinted by permission of Simon & Schuster, Inc.

116 Disciplinary referral form, courtesy of the Norwich Free Academy, Norwich, Connecticut.

117 Bernard Packin, "Seventeen Precepts for Classroom Control," *Professional Growth for Teachers* 7, no. 1 (January, 1961). Reprinted by permission of Crofts Educational Services.

119 From *Can't You Hear Me Talking to You?* by Caroline Mirthes and the Children of P.S. 15. Copyright © 1971 by Bantam Books, Inc.; all rights reserved.

120 Sunny Decker, *An Empty Spoon* (New York: Harper & Row, 1969), pp. 48–50, 11–13 (hardbound edition). Copyright © 1969 by Sunny Decker; reprinted by permission of Harper & Row, Publishers, Inc.

121 "Opinions Differ: Dropouts Are Losers," *Today's Education* (April, 1972).

122 Charlotte Leon Mayerson, ed., *Two Blocks Apart* (New York: Holt, Rinehart and Winston, 1965). Copyright © 1965 by Holt, Rinehart and Winston, Inc.; reprinted by permission of Holt, Rinehart and Winston, Inc.

123 George Dennison, *The Lives of Children* (New

York: Random House, 1970), pp. 152–53.

126 John Holt, *How Children Fail* (New York: Pitman Publishing Corporation, 1964), p. xiii. Reprinted by permission of the publisher.

127 Excerpts from a CBS News Special entitled, "Sixteen in Webster Groves," broadcast on February 25, 1966; published with the permission of the Columbia Broadcasting System, Inc.

129 Ann Landers' Advice column reprinted by permission of Ann Landers.

130 Nancy Stahl, "Jelly Side Down" (18 March 1971). Copyright 1971, Universal Press Syndicate.

131 Report card form for second and third grades, courtesy of the Waterford Board of Education.

132 Mortimer Smith, "Grades and Report Cards," *Council for Basic Education Bulletin* (June, 1970); reprinted by permission of Mortimer Smith.

134 "Grades, Bah Humbug!!" from *How Old Will You Be in 1984?*, edited by Diane Divoky (New York: Avon Books, 1969). Reprinted by arrangement with Avon Books; copyright © 1969 by Avon Books.

135 Cartoon by Peter Charpentier, *Connecticut Daily Campus* (15 January 1973). Reprinted by permission of the *Connecticut Daily Campus*.

136 "Confidential Reports Prompt Discussion by School Board," *The Day* (2 February 1973). Reprinted by permission of *The Day,* New London, Connecticut.

138 Permanent record form and transcript form, courtesy of the Norwich Free Academy, Norwich, Connecticut.

140 Gordon Parks, *The Learning Tree* (New York: Harper & Row, 1963), pp. 180–85 (hardbound editlon). Copyright © 1963 by Gordon Parks; reprinted by permission of Harper & Row, Publishers, Inc.

144 From "A Report on Racial Imbalance in the Schools of Massachusetts," quoted in *Death at an Early Age* by Jonathan Kozol (Boston: Houghton Mifflin, 1967), pp. 136–37. Copyright © 1967 by Jonathan Kozol; reprinted by permission of the publisher, Houghton Mifflin Company.

145 From *The Autobiography of Malcolm X* (New York: Grove Press, 1964). Copyright © 1964 by Alex Haley and Malcolm X; © 1965 by Alex Haley and Betty Shabazz; reprinted by permission of Grove Press, Inc.

146 Adrian Dove, "The Dove Counterbalance Intelligence Test." Copyright 1968 by Dove/Jet; reprinted by permission of Adrian Dove.

150 "Teachers, like IQ tests . . ." excerpt from *Learning* (November, 1972). Reprinted by permission of *Learning,* The Magazine for Creative Teaching; © November 1972 by Education Today Company, Inc.

151 J. Rymond Gerberich, "How Is Intelligence Tested?" from *Your Child's Intelligence* (Washington, D.C.: National Education Association). Reprinted by permission of National Education Association Publishing.

153 H. J. Eysenck, "Battleground IQ: Race, Intelligence, and Education," from *New Society* (17 June 1971). This article is based on part of the book, *The IQ Argument* published by Library Press, Inc.

157 "A court case in the San Francisco area . . ." *Learning* (November, 1972). Reprinted by permission of Learning: The Magazine for Creative Teaching; © November 1972 by Education Today Company, Inc.

158 John Holt, *How Children Fail* (New York: Pitman Publishing Corporation, 1964), pp. 205–11. Reprinted by permission of the publisher.

161 Søren Hansen and Jesper Jensen with Wallace Roberts, *The Little Red Schoolbook,* trans. Berit Thornberry (New York: Pocket Books, 1971). Copyright © 1971 by Stage 1, London; reprinted by permission of Pocket Books, a division of Simon & Schuster, Inc.

163 "Tests and Evaluations," excerpt from *Learning* (November, 1972). Reprinted by permission of *Learning,* The Magazine for Creative Teaching; © November 1972 by Education Today Company, Inc.

166 Royce Van Norman, "School Administration: Thoughts on Organization and Purpose," *Phi Delta Kappan* 47 (February, 1966), pp. 315–16.

168 Connecticut Civil Liberties Union, "Proposed Student Bill of Rights."

172 Cartoon by RAB in *The Teacher Paper* (February, 1972). Copyright 1972 by Fred L. Staab and Robin B. Staab; reprinted by permission of The Teacher Paper (Portland, Oregon).

175 "Legal Advice to Principals," from "Legal Memoranda," *National Association of Secondary School Principals* (1 September 1971, March 1972, 11 September 1972, 1 October 1971). Reprinted by permission of the National Association of Secondary School Principals; copyright © 1971, 1972 by the NASSP.

176 "How to Appraise a Textbook," *Saturday Review* (19 April 1952). Copyright © 1952 by The Saturday Review Associates, Inc.; used with permission.

177 Citizen's Request for Reconsideration of a Work form, from pamphlet *The Students' Right to Read* (Urbana, Ill.: National Council of Teachers of English, 1972). Copyright © 1972 by NCTE; reprinted by permission of the National Council of Teachers of English.

178 Frederica K. Bartz, "An Immodest Proposal," *English Journal* (January, 1970). Copyright © 1970 by the National Council of Teachers of English; reprinted by permission of the publisher and Frederica K. Bartz.

179 Letter from Boston Public Schools explaining dismissal of Jonathan Kozol, in *Death at an Early Age* (Boston: Houghton Mifflin, 1967). Copyright © 1967 by Jonathan Kozol; reprinted by permission of the publisher, Houghton Mifflin Company.

181 Philip Shabecoff, "Textbooks Hailed on View of Negro," *New York Times* (11 October 1972). © 1972 by The New York Times Company; reprinted by permission.

182 "The Downhome Guide to Power," *The Teacher Paper* (February, 1972). Copyright © 1972 by

Fred L. Staab; reprinted by permission of The Teacher Paper.

186 Bud Freeman, "The Lincoln Story." Copyright © 1970 by Twentieth Century-Fox Film Corporation; reprinted by permission of Twentieth Century-Fox Film Corporation.

188 Everett R. Holles, "Science Teaching at Issue on Coast," New York Times (22 October 1972). © 1972 by The New York Times Company; reprinted by permission.

193 Mortimer Smith, "The Teacher's Lot Is Not a Happy One," Council for Basic Education Bulletin (February, 1971). Reprinted by permission of Mortimer Smith.

196 Editors of Pageant, "Would You Want This Man to Teach Your Children?" September, 1956), pp. 63–71. Reprinted by permission of Pageant Magazine; copyright © 1956 by Pageant Magazine.

203 B. F. Skinner, Walden Two (New York: Macmillan, 1960), p. 262.

203 Aldous Huxley, Brave New World Revisited (New York: Harper & Row, 1958).

204 Cartoon by Ford Button in School Management (December, 1972); reprinted by permission of Ford Button.

204 Wayne Barham, "Two Different Worlds," Phi Delta Kappan (October, 1972). Reprinted by permission of Phi Delta Kappa, Inc. and Wayne Barham; copyright 1972 by Phi Delta Kappan.

210 Gallup International, "The Major Problems," poll for CFK, Ltd. (April, 1972).

211 "Naming 1,000 Educational Innovations," Phi Delta Kappan (September, 1967). Copyright © 1967 by Phi Delta Kappa, Inc.; reprinted by permission of the publisher.

212 Rozanne Knudsen, "Copia Verborum: A Cliche Expert Speaks," Clearing House (March, 1966). Reprinted by permission of The Clearing House.

216 Ray Scofield, "Why Not?" Media and Methods (September, 1968). Copyright 1968 by Media and Methods; reprinted by permission of the author and publisher.

220 "Notices," (4 October 1972); reprinted by permission of New London High School, New London, Connecticut.

225 Photograph reprinted courtesy of General Telephone and Electronics.

226 Ivan Illich, "General Characteristics of New Formal Educational Institutions," from Deschooling Society (New York: Harper & Row, 1970), pp. 75–76. Copyright © 1970, 1971 by Ivan Illich; reprinted by permission of Harper & Row, Publishers, Inc.

227 "Vouchers Reshape a School District," New York Times (25 September 1972). © 1972 by The New York Times Company; reprinted by permission.

228 S. Danny Riemer, "Springtime Study Hall Blues," in How Old Will You Be in 1984?, ed. Diane Divoky (New York: Avon Books, 1969). Reprinted by arrangement with Avon Books; copyright © by Avon Books.

229 Søren Hansen and Jesper Jensen with Wallace Roberts, The Little Red Schoolbook, trans. Berit Thornberry (New York: Pocket Books, 1971). English translation copyright © 1971 by Stage 1, London; reprinted by permission of

Pocket Books, a division of Simon & Schuster.

230 David Morse, "The Alternative," Media and Methods (May, 1971). Copyright © 1971 by Media and Methods; reprinted by permission of the author and Media and Methods.

237 Arthur Pearl, "Hansel and Gretel," Saturday Review (9 December 1972). Copyright © 1972 by Saturday Review, Inc. First appeared in Saturday Review of Education, January, 1973; used with permission.

241 Herbert C. Rudman, "A Conversation with A.S. Neill," The National Elementary Principal (January, 1973). Copyright © 1973, National Association of Elementary School Principals; all rights reserved.

248 Kathy Ahlfeld, "Summary of the Montessori Method," Nation's Schools January, 1970). Reprinted by permission of Nation's Schools; copyright 1970 by McGraw-Hill, Inc.

249 Jonathan Kozol, Free Schools, pp. 11-12. ©1972 by Houghton Mifflin Company; reprinted by permission.

250 Frank McCaughlin, "An Interview with John Bremer, Director of the Parkway Program," Media and Methods (January, 1970). Reprinted by permission of the author and Media and Methods; © 1970 by Media and Methods.

256 Charles William Brubaker, "The American Schoolhouse: An Historical Perspective," Journal of the National Association of Elementary School Principals (September, 1972). Copyright 1972, National Association of Elementary School Principals; all rights reserved.

258 Funky Winkerbean comic strip reprinted courtesy of Publishers-Hall Syndicate.

260 Gallup International, "The School Without Walls," and "The Nongraded School," poll for CFK, Ltd. (April, 1972).

261 William K. Stevens, "Report Hails Oregon High School's Experiment in Free Study," New York Times (19 October 1970). © 1970 by The New York Times Company; reprinted by permission.

263 Mortimer Smith, "Is Common Sense Breaking Through?" Council for Basic Education Bulletin (September, 1971); reprinted by permission.

265 Joseph Featherstone, "Schools for Children," from Schools Where Children Learn (New York: Liveright, 1971). Copyright © 1971 by Joseph Featherstone; reprinted by permission of Liveright, Publishing, New York.

271 Peter Drucker, "School Around the Bend," Psychology Today (June, 1972). Copyright © 1972 Communications/Research/Machines, Inc.; excerpted by permission of CRM, Inc.

274 William C. Miller, "Another Day," Educational Leadership (October, 1972), pp. 63-64. Reprinted with permission of the Association for Supervision and Curriculum Development and William C. Miller; copyright © 1972 by the Association for Supervision and Curriculum Development.

277 "Electronic Security Check System Being Tested for Schools," Councilgrams of the National Council for Teachers of English vol. 33 (November, 1972).

278 From Can't You Hear Me Talking to You? by Caroline Mirthes and the Children of P.S. 15. Copyright © 1971 by Bantam Books, Inc.; all rights reserved.